THE INSTITUTIONAL PRESIDENCY

Interpreting American Politics
Michael Nelson, *Series Editor*

Gerald Strom, *The Logic of Lawmaking: A Spatial Theory Approach*
John P. Burke, *The Institutional Presidency*

THE INSTITUTIONAL PRESIDENCY

...

JOHN P. BURKE

The Johns Hopkins University Press

Baltimore and London

The Johns Hopkins University Press
701 West 40th Street
Baltimore, Maryland 21211-2190
The Johns Hopkins Press Ltd., London

The paper used in this book meets the minimum requirements of the American National Standard for Information Sciences—Permanence of Paper for Printed Library Materials, ANSI Z39.48-1984.

Library of Congress Cataloging-in-Publication Data

Burke, John P., 1953–
　The institutional presidency / John P. Burke.
　　p.　　cm.—(Interpreting American politics)
　Includes bibliographical references and index.
　ISBN 0-8018-4315-4 (alk. paper).—ISBN 0-8019-4316-2 (pbk.)
　1. Presidents—United States—Staff.　2. Presidents—United States—History—20th century.　I. Title.　II. Series.　JK518.B87　1992
353.03′13—dc20　　　　　　　　　　　　　　　　　　　　　　91-36404

CONTENTS

. . .

FOREWORD

■ ■ ■

Political science, traditionally the intellectual bedfellow of history and law, has become distressingly ahistorical since World War II in its haste to imitate, in rapid succession, sociology, various branches of psychology, microeconomics, even biology. In the field of presidential studies, legal and historical ignorance has fostered an embarrassing volatility in prevailing conceptions of the presidency. New models are forged in the image of new presidents, then abandoned when they fail to explain the experiences of these presidents' immediate successors.

For example, in the aftermath of Franklin D. Roosevelt, the idea prevailed that the presidency was both a powerful office and a benign influence on the American political system. This understanding was shaken by the nation's experience under presidents Lyndon B. Johnson and Richard Nixon, who were powerful, to be sure, but from whose power flowed the Vietnam War and the Watergate crisis, two of the century's greatest political disasters. A new model of the presidency was quickly constructed by scholars: the office still was portrayed as powerful, but now presidential power was construed to be threatening. Then, virtually without pause, came Gerald R. Ford and Jimmy Carter, two relatively uninfluential presidents whose administrations sent presidential scholars back to their drawing boards, this time to emerge with a model of the presidency as far too weak—not "imperial," but "imperiled." One cannot begin to record the gyrations executed by scholars during the presidencies of Ronald Reagan and George Bush, who seemed to embody all three models at one time or another.

John P. Burke is aware of the dangers of ahistoricism in political science and has avoided them skillfully. Although he does not ignore the variety of presidential advisory systems that existed prior to Franklin Roosevelt, Burke is correct to establish the birthdate of the institutional presidency as 1937, when the Roosevelt-appointed, Louis Brownlow–chaired Committee on Administrative Management proclaimed that "the President needs help" and prescribed "salvation by staff" as the only sure remedy. Burke carries forward his account of the historical evolution of the Executive Office of the President and the more intimate White House staff through the presidencies of Harry S. Truman, Dwight D. Eisenhower, John F. Kennedy, Johnson, Nixon, Ford, and, especially, Carter, Reagan, and Bush.

Burke is also aware of another vexing problem of political analysis, this one distinctive to the study of the presidency: the tendency for scholars to confuse the person and the office, president and presidency. The person-or-office conundrum is an old one. It is apparent, for example, in the quotation by Henry Jones Ford, in his classic 1898 work *The Rise and Growth of American Government,* of Alexander Hamilton's prediction to a friend that the time "would assuredly come when every vital question of the state will be merged in the question, 'Who shall be the next President?' " Ford cited this remark to support his argument that "in the presidential office, as it has been constituted since Andrew Jackson's time, American democracy has revived the oldest political institution of the race, the elective kingship." Left unresolved, both in 1898 and nearly a century later, is the question of whether the presidency is best understood from an individual ("Who shall be the next President?") or an institutional (an "elective kingship") perspective.

"Underlying the argument of this book," writes Burke, "is the view that each of these perspectives has something to contribute to our understanding of the presidency." This view is ably implemented in *The Institutional Presidency.* Burke shows not only *that* individual "presidents can make an imprint on the office," but *how.* The same can be said for his assertion that "certain characteristics are inherent in a large-scale staff and transcend particular presidencies."

In all, Burke has aimed high in this book and hit his mark.

—Michael Nelson

ACKNOWLEDGMENTS

■ ■ ■

This study was conducted with support from the American Political Science Association, the University Committee on Research and Scholarship of the Graduate College of the University of Vermont, the Franklin and Eleanor Roosevelt Library Institute, the Harry S. Truman Institute, the LBJ Foundation, and the Gerald R. Ford Foundation. I am indebted to the Department of Government of Dartmouth College and its chair, Richard Winters, for providing a comfortable home as a Visiting Scholar during my sabbatical leave. I am appreciative of the assistance of my undergraduate research assistants at the University of Vermont, Michael Goldstein, David Lippes, Jeff Lively, and Brett Rogenski. For their various contributions to this study, I would also like to thank Fritz Gaenslen, Fred I. Greenstein, Erwin Hargrove, Harry N. Hirsch, R. Stafford Johnson, James Pacy, Terry Schutz, Henry Tom, and especially the enterprising editor of this series, "Interpreting American Politics," Michael Nelson.

INTRODUCTION

■ ■ ■

The President needs help. His immediate staff assistance is entirely inadequate. He should be given a small number of executive assistants who would be his direct aides in dealing with the managerial agencies and administrative departments of government. These assistants, probably not exceeding six in number . . . would have no power to make decisions or issue instructions in their own right. They would not be interposed between the President and the heads of his departments. They would not be assistant presidents in any sense. Their function would be . . . to assist him in obtaining quickly and without delay all pertinent information possessed by any of the executive departments so as to guide him in making responsible decisions; and then when decisions have been made, to assist him in seeing to it that every administrative department and agency affected is promptly informed. Their effectiveness in assisting the President will, we think, be directly proportional to their ability to discharge their functions with restraint. They would remain in the background, issue no orders, make no decisions, emit no public statements. Men for these positions should be carefully chosen by the President from within and without the Government. They should be men in whom the President has personal confidence and whose character and attitude is such that they would not attempt to exercise power on their own account. They should be possessed of high competence, great physical vigor, and a passion for anonymity.

These words come from the President's Committee on Administrative Management, known by the name of its chair as the Brownlow committee, in a report prepared for Franklin Roosevelt in 1937. Although the chief recommendation the Brownlow committee offered concerning the president's staff was relatively modest—the addition of six White House assistants—its effect on the nature of the presidency proved momentous. It set in motion a profound transformation that would challenge Roosevelt's successors: the transition from a presidency with few staff resources to one with a large cadre of aides to assist in carrying out the duties of the office.

The "help," to use Brownlow's word, that an enlarged presidential staff offers has proven to be a double-edged sword. Presidents have fared better and worse with staff assistance. Some have understood the challenge that a large-scale staff presents and have devised means for making what quickly became a fairly large bureaucracy work for them rather than for its own purposes. They have understood that the prescriptive vision of the Brownlow committee—"confidence," "vigor," and a "passion for anonymity" (or whatever goals they might themselves envision for their staffs)—is not automatically guaranteed. Other presidents have been less successful, failing to devise strategies and tactics of management for making the White House staff work effectively. Members of the president's staff have also varied in their understanding of their roles and responsibilities, ranging from those who have given their allegiance to the president to those who have put self-interest and personal advancement ahead of presidential priorities.

This tension between having a large White House staff and making it work effectively, as well as the experiences of presidents and members of their staffs in resolving that tension, is the theme of this book. That the presidency since Roosevelt's time has increasingly taken on the character of a large bureaucracy or that presidents must cast a wary eye on the operations of their staffs is hardly an original insight. Most observers of the modern presidency have noted that the nature of the office has changed in the twentieth century and most agree that a large staff is a principal part of that change. Most, too, see the White House staff as a challenge to effective presidential leadership. But there has been little agreement on what it is about the White House staff that may generate problems for a president, what makes the president's staff work effectively, and what presidents should or should not do to have a positive impact on the staff's operations.

In part, disagreement stems from a peculiarity in the field of presidency studies: the tendency to focus on a particular presidency and, especially, the tendency to focus on the present incumbent or the most recent occupant of the office. As a result, analysis of the presidency is often too tightly constrained to the experiences of a particular president, and, as a consequence, empirical generalizations—and often suggestions for reform—end up too narrow in scope. A simple glance at a library shelf is revealing on this score: works written during and shortly after the Eisenhower presidency depict a popular but somnolent chief executive and call for greater presidential activism, works written in the late 1960s and the 1970s decry presidential "imperialism" and call for less presidential power, works in the late 1970s raise the question of an imperilled, not an imperial, presidency, and, coming full circle in the 1980s, works once again raise the specter of a somnolent president managing the affairs of state but cast a wary eye at Reagan's skills in making popular appeals.

The problem is confounded by the different approaches that scholars take in seeking to understand the presidency, especially the organization and workings of the White House staff and the processes of presidential decision making. For some scholars, the emphasis is on the president's own style of management and the changing impact that presidential personality and management style have upon the office. Two leading academic observers, James David Barber and Richard Neustadt, who offer different assessments about what matters with respect to presidential performance in office, agree on this point. For Barber, "The Presidency exists solely in the minds of men. . . . This 'institution' is nothing more than images, habits, and intentions shared by the humans who make it up and by those who react to them."[1] Neustadt holds that "the great growth in staff since 1936 is an undoubted help to White House occupants who seek effective power for themselves . . . [but] it is not sufficient to gesture toward the 'institutionalized Presidency'. . . . A President is helped by what he gets into *his* mind."[2] So, too, with those who have observed the presidency firsthand. According to Orville Freeman, Kennedy's secretary of agriculture, "the office of the President, in my judgment, is not really an institution. I would describe it with the word 'instrument' rather than institution. It is peculiarly shaped by the man who holds it."[3] For H. R. Haldeman, Nixon's chief of staff, "you have to structure each President's staff to fit that President's method of working. You cannot institutionalize on any permanent basis the Office of the President. You must build a new Office of the President for each president, and it must evolve as that president evolves in office."[4]

For others, however, enduring characteristics of the presidency that transcend the administrations of particular incumbents can be discerned. The presidency, according to this view, resembles a bureaucratic organization with certain institutional characteristics that endure no matter who may lead it at a particular point in time. "At first blush," Hugh Heclo points out, the internal arrangements of the White House staff "are simply a matter of presidential taste." But this is misleading: a "deep structure" is present "that a president can change slowly if at all." This structure, Heclo explains, "is a web of other people's expectations and needs. On the surface, the new president seems to inherit an empty house. In fact, he enters an office already shaped and crowded by other people's desires . . . an office that is the raw, exposed ganglion of government where immense lines of force come together in ways that no single person can control. The total effect is to program the modern president."[5]

This "institutional perspective, as it might be called, also has adherents among those who have served on the White House staff. Herbert Stein, who served as chairman of the Council of Economic Advisers during the Nixon presidency, notes that "a certain organization is passed down from one administration to another; it is not organized anew every time."[6] For Robert Hartmann, White House counsellor under President Ford, "Every President, like the later Caesars, has his Praetorian Guard. And whether he can command them, or they command him, is a measure of the President's effectiveness and the confidence that will be given him by the American people."[7]

Underlying the argument of this book is the view that each of these perspectives has something to contribute to our understanding of the presidency. Studies of particular presidencies are useful in revealing the successes and failures of individual presidents, and, more important, taken together, they are helpful in crafting an approach that is comparative in scope and amenable to more generalizable empirical observations. The chapters that follow, therefore, focus in some detail on the experiences of all presidents from Franklin Roosevelt to the present. Chapter 1 will also offer some interesting comparisons of modern presidents with their predecessors in the nineteenth and early twentieth centuries.

So too with the debate over whether it is the man or the office that matters. Presidents can make an imprint on the office. Presidents can, if they choose, have a great impact in determining who serves on the White House staff, how that staff is organized, and how it operates on a day-to-day basis. This is not to suggest that all presidents have understood this power or exercised it well, but that some indeed have, for better or worse, and that it is potentially at any president's disposal.

Yet the view that certain characteristics are inherent in a large-scale staff and transcend particular presidencies is also credible. First, the presidency exists in a context in which, as Heclo rightly points out, the expectations of others have an impact on what the president can and cannot do. Second, as Hartmann's comments suggest, the behavior of those on the staff is likely to be an important constraint on what the president can do. Whether any White House staff is a Praetorian Guard, as Hartmann characterizes it, is open to question. But it is likely that patterns of behavior recur from staff to staff, as they generally do in most organizations, and that they form a powerful constraint with which the president must deal. Third, and this point is especially important for the argument of this book, the size and complex organization of the White House staff are also likely to generate certain institutional characteristics that affect how it operates. An organizational dynamic is at work within the White House staff system; it recurs across presidencies and bears common implications for how the staff operates. At the very least, it defines a range of problems with which the president must deal in order to make his staff work effectively; no president enters office with a blank slate. At the very most, it establishes certain recurring trends that may cause serious damage to a presidency if left unattended; no president leaves office with a clean slate, and many leave with far worse.

The trick then is not to choose between these competing approaches but to understand how they may be brought together, how each has some effect on the presidency, and how each is related to and reinforces the other. Thus, the argument is not that the presidency is an institution that is essentially unchanging from administration to administration—that is not the sense of "institutional" that is used here. Continuing features, of an organizational sort, exist across presidencies, but so do significant variations in both organizational structure and dynamics in each presidency and sometimes over time within a particular presidency. Conversely, the argument is not that all that matters is the style and managerial proclivities of individual presidents. Too many distinctive institutional characteristics and too many similar problems that stem from them recur across a range of presidencies. The argument is, rather, that it is necessary to discern how the institutional *presidency* is amenable to presidential management, but also to understand how the *institutional* presidency forms something of a continuing context, generating predictable problems and effects, within which that presidential management is imparted. That is the task that this work undertakes.

Chapter 1 examines the emergence of the institutional presidency during Franklin Roosevelt's administration and the changing nature of the presidency compared to that of his predecessors. Chapter 2 lays the groundwork for the substantive argument of the book. It examines the White House staff from an institutional perspective, exploring such issues as the extent to which the staff system bears characteristics that are common to bureaucratic institutions and the extent to which predictable effects of such institutions have emerged. It also examines the validity of the arguments made by some observers that the recent development of the White House staff is more appropriately understood as a process of deinstitutionalization rather than as one of institutionalization. The chapter concludes that the staff system can be profitably examined from an institutional perspective, despite significant variation from administration to administration.

Chapters 3 and 4 consider an important source of this variation and the other major thread underlying the logic of this book, namely the impact of the president's organization and management of this staff. However, both chapters attempt to combine emphases on the man and on the office, what I term the managerial and organizational perspectives, and to do so in such a way that the two are brought to bear on each other. How presidents cope with the institutional presidency might be conceptualized in two ways. The first—the theme of chapter 3—takes a top-down approach and is attentive to how presidents who fall in the two major categories of staff organization and management, the collegial and the formal, have tailored or failed to tailor their staff systems to take account of their operation within an organizational context. The second—the theme of chapter 4—takes a bottom-up approach and focuses on those features of the institutional presidency that transcend particular presidencies and the extent to which a president's organization and management of the staff system is sensitive to them. Both perspectives are key: As I try to show, taken together they advance our understanding of what makes for an effective White House staff system.

Chapters 5 through 7 examine the Carter and Reagan presidencies, and offer some preliminary observations about George Bush. In-depth examination of Carter and Reagan is especially interesting because they used very different styles of White House management—Carter a variant of the collegial model, Reagan a more formalistic system. Neither, however, was particularly successful as a manager, and both experienced similar difficulties in coping with the organizational dynamics at work in the contemporary White House staff. Finally, the conclusion raises other issues that bear upon the question of effective staff organization and management. Emphasis on the institutional factors present in today's presidency and their interaction with patterns and practices of staff management is only one cut into the complex question of what makes for an effective White House staff. However, as I attempt to argue, such an approach is likely to be of great importance.

THE INSTITUTIONAL PRESIDENCY

1

FROM PRESIDENT TO PRESIDENCY
FDR's Legacy

■ ■ ■

To many scholars of the American presidency, the tenure of Franklin Roosevelt marks a dramatic shift in the character of the office: the transition from a traditional presidency, which embraced few of the responsibilities we associate with the office today and which was largely overshadowed by Congress, to a modern conception of the office, which is proactive in the realm of domestic and foreign policy and which occupies political center stage. Roosevelt himself once told Louis Brownlow, who would play a key role in developing the institutional capacities of the modern presidency, that he personally acted on more matters every day than President McKinley saw in a month.[1]

Roosevelt's characterization of his level of activity was hardly immodest. Presidential activism marked his administration from the start. Roosevelt's hectic "hundred days" and the New Deal to which it gave birth fundamentally altered the relationship between the public and private sectors and dramatically increased the power and visibility of the presidency. As a result of Roosevelt's programs and activities, government increasingly touched the daily lives of American citizens. Most importantly, it was the president, not Congress, who took the lead in this dramatic but quiet revolution.

Roosevelt's political accomplishments cannot be downplayed. He was creative in his proposals to bring the nation out of the Depression, crafty in dealing with Congress, and reassuring in building public support. Throughout his twelve years as president, he forged new modes for exercising leadership. As the noted historian William Leuchtenburg has argued, to understand properly the presidents who have followed Franklin Roosevelt, one must comprehend how all have lived "in the shadow of FDR."[2]

For some observers of the presidency the Rooseveltian shadow is indeed long. For Fred Greenstein, it marks the end of the traditional presidency and the beginning of a modern presidency with four unique attributes, which simultaneously emerge under Roosevelt: greater formal and informal power to make self-initiated decisions; the role of chief agenda setter in federal policy making; visibility as the prime actor in the American political system; and the ability to rely on significant staff resources in carrying out official duties.[3]

Although the distinction between traditional and modern presidencies has merits, some aspects of Roosevelt's legacy may be more significant than others. Surely the particular policies and programs he fostered are important; today's politicians and political parties still battle over the political vision Roosevelt crafted. Surely FDR's ability to put the presidential mark on the nation's political agenda has set a standard that his successors are expected to follow; Jimmy Carter's inability to gain congressional assent to his ambitious laundry list of legislative proposals in 1977 and George Bush's apparent lack of effort in 1989 have all been judged—and by and large found wanting—in light of FDR's watershed "hundred days." Greater power to make decisions and greater visibility as the central actor in American politics—two other important marks of Roosevelt's presidency—have also been taken as given by his successors.

Undoubtedly all of these changes working together have produced a qualitatively different kind of presidency. But they do not include the one change in the presidency that really was unique to Roosevelt's presidency and has presented the most difficulties to his successors: the creation of a large-scale White House staff. Recognition of this development in the institutional capacity of the presidency is especially important because Greenstein's distinction between a pre-FDR traditional presidency and a post-FDR modern presidency has not gone unchallenged. Stephen Skowronek, Bert Rockman, Richard Ellis and Aaron Wildavsky, and Erwin Hargrove and Michael Nelson all argue that different cycles of presidential power can be found throughout American history and that cyclical changes may be more important than the distinction Greenstein suggests.[4] Skowronek, for example, notes that FDR may have more in common with a "regime constructor" like Andrew Jackson than with a Jimmy Carter, a modern president in Greenstein's schema but an enervated president more like Franklin Pierce in Skowronek's cyclical theory. For Hargrove and Nelson, it was Teddy not Franklin Roosevelt who distinctively redefined the presidency. For Jeffrey Tulis, on the other hand, it is the rhetorical and plebiscitary presidency of Woodrow Wilson that marks a critical stage in the evolution of the office.[5]

We need not enter this interesting debate; undoubtedly a number of events and developments have fostered changes in the character of the presidency. But it is plausible to maintain that the staff resources and advisory capacity that emerged in FDR's presidency mark a watershed event. John Hart is quite correct in his observation that "Franklin D. Roosevelt was by no means the first American president to complain about his work load, nor the first to plead for more adequate staff."[6] But Roosevelt was the first president to respond to the problem by explicitly studying his staffing needs and effectively arguing that the presidency requires a larger coterie of aides and assistants to carry out the duties of the office.

Presidents since Roosevelt have in turn been forced to contend with the institutional presidency he created. Many of the historically significant moments in subsequent presidencies have turned, for better or worse, on the decisions made by the president in consultation with his staff: Truman and Korea, Eisenhower and Indochina, Kennedy and Cuba, Lyndon Johnson and Vietnam, Nixon and Watergate, Carter and Iran, Reagan and Iran-Contra, and Bush and Iraq.

Ironically, effective use of a staff structure is one of the few aspects of FDR's leadership where he left his successors much shadow but little substance to follow. Roosevelt delegated his assistants overlapping responsibilities, often parceling out the same assignment to more than one staff aide. This managerial technique maximized the president's control over the flow of information but fostered competition, if not rivalry and jealousy, among his staff. FDR's highly personalized style could perhaps work at the onset of the institutional presidency, but it placed great demands on the president's time and failed to create coherently organized and lasting procedures. Roosevelt thus left his successors with the emerging structure of a White House staff but little they could emulate by way of managing it and making it effectively serve their ends.

The Presidency before FDR

The challenge that Roosevelt left his successors and the various ways they have dealt with the institutional presidency he began to create is treated in subsequent chapters. But in order to gain some appreciation for precisely how the presidency has changed and what challenges that change entails, it is useful to consider how the White House operated before a large-scale staff was created.

All presidents, of course, have had some staff resources at their disposal, but before FDR these were quite minimal. Thomas Jefferson served in office with only one messenger and one secretary. Sixty years later, in Ulysses S. Grant's administration, the size of the staff had grown to three. By 1900, the staff consisted of a private secretary (now called "secretary to the president"), two assistant secretaries, two executive clerks, a stenographer, three clerks, and four other office personnel. By Harding's time, the staff had grown yet larger, but most of it remained largely clerical: twenty-one clerks, two stenographers, a records clerk, an appointments clerk, a chief clerk, an executive clerk, and the secretary to the president. Herbert Hoover managed to get Congress to approve two more secretaries to the president, one of whom he assigned the task of serving as his press aide.[7]

Early presidents paid the salaries of their small staffs out of their own pockets. It was not until 1857 that Congress explicitly appropriated money, $2,500, for one presidential clerk.[8] As recently as Calvin Coolidge's presidency, the entire budget for the White House staff, including office expenses, amounted to no more than $80,000.[9] In 1992, the corresponding figures for the Executive Office of the President (EOP) amounted to more than $150 million.

From Washington's presidency through 1939, when the institutionalized presidency began to emerge, the activities of presidential aides differed from those of their successors. Yet during this period, the White House staff began to evolve in ways that anticipate its current state. There was an increasing recognition that the president needed more staff assistance, as well as a slow shift in the role of the staff from essentially personal aides to assistants with clerical and office skills and then to individuals able to provide the president with political advice and assistance in making substantive policy decisions.

In the first phase of the development of the White House staff, roughly from Washington's through Grant's administration, it was common practice for the president to hire family members and other relatives as secretaries, an indication that even though presidents had some staff resources at their disposal these persons largely functioned in the capacity of personal aides and factotums. John Quincy Adams, Andrew Jackson, John Tyler, Abraham Lincoln, Andrew Johnson, and Ulysses Grant all engaged their sons, at some point, as private secretaries.[10] Washington, Polk, and Buchanan employed their nephews. James Monroe employed his younger brother and two sons-in-law. Zachary Taylor (one must wonder how willingly) hired his brother-in-law.[11]

Presidents after Grant began to turn to what then passed for professional administrators to fill the post of secretary to the president: persons trained in the new arts of "type-writing" (Joseph Stanley Brown under James Garfield) and shorthand and stenography (George Cortelyou under William McKinley and William Loeb, Jr., under Teddy Roosevelt). Yet the position of secretary to the president remained largely clerical in nature, and many nineteenth-century presidents encountered difficulty attracting qualified applicants.

Rutherford B. Hayes had two associates turn down the position. In his diary, Hayes notes that his first choice, Judge Manning F. Force, even felt "hurt that I suggested it to him."[12] Hayes eventually persuaded an old college classmate, William Rogers, to serve as his secretary. Rogers had failed at a number of occupations before becoming secretary to the president and was no more successful serving in the White House. According to T. Harry Williams, the editor of Hayes's personal diary, Rogers "was inept at handling reporters and callers. On one occasion he turned away Mark Twain, confusing the famous author with George Train, a colorful eccentric. Much of the secretarial burden was taken on by Webb Hayes, the [president's] son."[13]

Some aides, of course, foreshadowed the modern role of presidential assistants, serving as chiefs of staff, policy advisers, liaisons with Congress, and public spokesmen. Grover Cleveland brought his long-time Albany aide, Daniel Lamont, to the White House. Lamont—dubbed the "other governor" when Cleveland was governor of New York—was as popular, effective, and powerful in Washington as he had been in Albany. In Cleveland's second term Lamont served in the cabinet as secretary of war, and following Cleveland's departure from office, Lamont accepted the position of vice president of the Northern Pacific Railroad.

McKinley's secretary, George Cortelyou, was even more notable than Lamont. Cortelyou had been a stenographer in the Cleveland White House. McKinley noticed his skills and soon appointed him his private secretary. When McKinley was shot, Cortelyou in effect served as acting president as McKinley hovered near death for eight days. After Vice President Theodore Roosevelt took the oath of office, Cortelyou guided the new president. Roosevelt kept Cortelyou on as his private secretary and was so impressed with him that he subsequently appointed him to three cabinet-level positions: secretary of the Department of Commerce and Labor (then combined in one department), postmaster general, and secretary of the treasury. In 1908, Cortelyou emerged as a leading contender for the Republican presidential nomination and at one point thought he had Roosevelt's support for the post, only to be edged out by William Howard Taft. Cortelyou then served for twenty-eight years as president of the nation's largest utility, Consolidated Gas.

None of the president's secretaries from Wilson through Hoover had the stature of Lamont or Cortelyou. With the exception of Joseph Tumulty under Woodrow Wilson, they have all been largely forgotten by history: George Christian (Harding), Bascom Slemp (Coolidge), and George Akerson, Walter Newton, and Lawrence Richey (Hoover's appointees to the three positions of secretary to the president that Congress had now budgeted). Although their administrative skills and personal qualities failed to match those of their immediate predecessors, they were increasingly used as political advisers to the president, handling relationships with Congress and the press as well as running the administrative side of the White House staff. Several held political office or were heavily involved in partisan politics before joining the president's staff: although he served under a Republican president, Christian had been active in Ohio Democratic politics; Slemp was a Virginia state legislator and had served three terms in Congress; and Newton had been a five-term Republican congressman from Minnesota. Akerson and Richey had served as top aides to Hoover when he was secretary of commerce.

Although politically skilled presidential advisers were on the ascendance during this period, it is also important to note that the number of presidential assistants still remained minuscule by contemporary standards. Presidents often did their own administrative if not clerical work. When the first telephone was installed in the White House, President Cleveland personally answered it, and Woodrow Wilson was in the habit of typing his own letters. Most presidents during this period also continued to rely on personal friends and long-time political associates who did not occupy formal staff positions for the bulk of their policy advice. Woodrow Wilson's close relationship with Colonel House and Harding's with his poker-playing cronies, for example, were more the rule than the exception.[14]

Creating the Institutional Presidency: The Brownlow Committee

All this began to change with Franklin Roosevelt. Shortly after the election of 1936, Roosevelt reflected upon his landslide victory with a group of reporters. The Republicans, the president observed, never capitalized on the chief weakness of the New Deal; he himself could have launched a more effective attack than did his opponents. "What was your chief weakness?" a reporter inquired. "Administration," FDR replied.

Roosevelt's response was telling, not only for the political acumen it revealed but also for the consequences that were shortly to issue from the diagnosis. For Roosevelt, it led to the first significant efforts to create a presidential staff that would perform a substantive role in policy decisions. For Roosevelt's successors, it left the legacy of a large-scale White House staff that has been at once a resource in enabling the president to carry out his increasingly large load of duties and an institutional bureaucracy that can sometimes thwart the president's will, hinder the achievement of his political and programmatic goals, and require him, at the very least, to be attentive to management skills in ways that were unknown to presidents before FDR.

Taking office in the midst of the Depression and with growing cries for action, Roosevelt needed administrative help that the existing White House staff could not provide. Roosevelt's ambitious legislative program clearly overwhelmed the capacities of the meager staff at his disposal. His solution was to "muddle through," borrowing staff from departments and agencies. The legislative whirlwind of Roosevelt's first "hundred days" was precisely the product of such a loosely organized group of advisers, most of whom did not have formal positions on the White House staff.

Roosevelt's disappointment with his meager staff reputedly lifted once he discovered he could dip down into the departments and "borrow" personnel for his own pet projects. He especially liked to use departmental assistant secretaries because they had no specific duties required by law.[15] Two key members of his "brains trust" had appointments of precisely this sort. Rexford Tugwell and Raymond Moley both left the faculty of Columbia University to join the new administration. But because few positions were available on the White House staff, Roosevelt made them assistant secretaries in regular cabinet-level departments—Tugwell in the Department of Agriculture, Moley at State. But they reported directly to Roosevelt, who employed their talents as he saw fit. In Roosevelt's second term, one of his closest assistants, Thomas P. Corcoran, held the unprepossessing position of counsel to the Reconstruction Finance Corporation.

Other members of Roosevelt's "brains trust" did not even join him in Washington. Judge Sam Rosenman, for example, stayed on the New York bench, almost to the end of FDR's third term.[16] What few positions Roosevelt could fill went to other long-time aides. Louis Howe was given the title of secretary to the president, with Steven Early serving as press secretary, Marvin McIntyre as appointments secretary, and "Missy" Le-Hand as the president's personal secretary.

Roosevelt's patchwork staff worked, but just barely. Aides quickly rose in prominence and then just as speedily fell from favor—Moley, then Tugwell, then Corcoran, then Harry Hopkins and Rosenman—depending on FDR's personal whims and suspicions and changing political proclivities, as well as on the pitched battles and rivalries that emerged in his inner circle. According to Arthur Schlesinger, Jr., "His favorite technique was to keep grants of authority incomplete, jurisdictions uncertain, charters overlapping. The result of this competitive theory of administration was often confusion and exasperation." But as Schlesinger also notes, there was a positive side to FDR's methods: "no other method could so reliably insure that in a large bureaucracy filled with ambitious men eager for power, the decisions and the power to make them would remain with the President."[17]

Organization of the staff shifted too. From 1933 to 1935, for example, Roosevelt went through five different organizational entities in an attempt to coordinate the various bits and pieces of the New Deal.[18] In July 1933, he created the Executive Council, an unwieldy entity composed of the full cabinet plus the heads of the newly created emergency agencies and the budget director. In November 1933, Roosevelt reduced the membership of his policy coordination group by creating the National Emergency Council, composed of the heads of the New Deal agencies plus the secretaries of commerce, labor, and agriculture. In the summer of 1934, he relied on a smaller body, the Industrial Emergency Committee, but by October he had shifted back to a revamped National Emergency Council.

Implementation of particular programs was also an organizational nightmare. Within ten days of taking over as head of the Civil Works Administration (CWA), Harry Hopkins reported to Roosevelt that he had put two million men to work. "Well they're all at work," he reputedly told the president, "but for God's sake, don't ask me what they're doing." In his autobiography, Louis Brownlow recounts another of Roosevelt's many organizational difficulties: the "five-ring-circus" FDR established to administer the Federal Emergency Relief Appropriation Act of 1933. In Brownlow's view, Roosevelt "set up a perfectly impossible plan" that "shocked every student of public administration to the marrow of his bones":

> The applications were to go to Frank Walker [head of the newly created Division of Applications and Information in the National Emergency Council]. If he approved them, a huge [twenty-three member] committee presided over by [Interior Secretary and public works administrator] Ickes [acting in the capacity of chair of the Advisory Committee on Allotments] would pass them to the President. When the President personally approved them, they would go to Harry Hopkins [federal relief administrator now acting in the capacity of head of the Works Progress Administration] to be executed, with [Treasury Secretary] Morgenthau keeping the accounts and with [Budget Director] Danny Bell doling out a nickel here and a dime there for administrative expenses. It confused nearly everybody and particularly the practitioners of orderly administration. But the confusion the experts then suffered was greatly to be compounded later on.[19]

Such "confusion" was replete in nearly all of the various agencies, boards, and commissions Roosevelt created to implement his New Deal. Roosevelt dramatically expanded the functions of federal government, yet the means he employed were usually experimental and short lived; there was little or no organizational order to his jerry-rigged and ever-changing apparatus. At best, coordination was provided by the president or by yet another newly created structure, such as the National Emergency Council. According to Frederick Mosher, "the president had no immediate machinery for directing and controlling the conduct of executive agencies."[20] Similarly, Arthur Schlesinger, Jr., notes that the president "acted as if a new agency were almost a new solution. His addiction to new organizations became a kind of nervous tic which disturbed even avid New Dealers."[21]

Roosevelt, however, was aware of the situation and responded to the administrative confusion by creating the Committee on Administrative Management, better known as the Brownlow committee, to recommend organizational changes, and it was the Brownlow committee's recommendations that were to foster the creation of an enlarged White House staff of the type we know today. In his autobiography, Brownlow observes that the organizational efforts began modestly (and surprisingly early in Roosevelt's first term). Brownlow notes a diary entry from 30 November 1933 recounting a luncheon with Charles Merriam, a prominent University of Chicago professor of political science and member of the president's National Planning Board; they discussed an appropriation by the Public Works Administration for the National Planning Board to undertake "a plan for a plan" that would attempt to solve "the top management problem" in the administration.[22]

It was not until March 1936,[23] however, that Roosevelt formally created The Committee on Administrative Management, chaired by Brownlow, then director of the Public Administration Clearing House in Chicago. The two other members were Merriam and Luther Gulick, head of the Institute of Public Administration in New York City. Brownlow, Merriam, and Gulick were assisted by a staff of twenty-seven.[24]

FDR's mandate to the Brownlow committee was typically Rooseveltian: broadly defined and unclear as to specifics. In his memoirs, Brownlow reports that, following a meeting with the president, they were "in quite close agreement" concerning the committee's aims: how to establish "simple but effective machinery which will enable [the president] to exercise managerial control appropriate to the burden of responsibility imposed upon him by the Constitution."[25] Yet Brownlow and Roosevelt meant different things by this. For Brownlow, the committee's goal was to recommend institutional reforms that would establish a presidential staff structure able to handle the day-to-day responsibilities thrust upon the president. Roosevelt had in mind a broad strategy for reorganizing the federal bureaucracy—a throwing out of the reorganizational net to see what might come in. Roosevelt apparently convinced Brownlow that the broad view would enlist the support of a Congress interested in efficiency and economy, but the president proved to be mistaken.

The Brownlow committee's report was finished by early January 1937, approved by the president without delay, and transmitted to Congress. Its recommendations were ambitious: expansion of the White House staff, strengthening of the managerial agencies of the government, extension of the merit system "upward, outward, and downward," greater presidential control over the civil service system, overhaul of the approximately one hundred independent agencies and commissions by grouping them in twelve reorganized cabinet-level departments, and a grant of broad discretionary authority to the president to carry out the mandated reorganization and any needed in the future.

The Brownlow report was particularly significant in its recognition that the task facing the president was a managerial one. Like earlier efforts at executive reorganization, which can be traced back to Theodore Roosevelt's Keep Commission and William Howard Taft's Commission on Economy and Efficiency, Brownlow sought to create an executive branch that could meet the needs of a developing administrative state. The powers invested in the president by the Constitution were insufficient to meet the political, economic, and social tasks that began to fall on the executive branch in the twentieth century. Constitutional change was politically impossible, so reorganization, within the ambit of Article II (and Congress's legislative powers in Article I), offered the only practical solution. Reorganization, in effect, offered the "energy" for the president that the framers of the Constitution recognized as necessary but that, operating under a different, more limited conception of the role of government, they had failed to embody in the president's formal powers in Article II.

But unlike earlier efforts at executive reorganization,[26] Brownlow had as its centerpiece a recognition that the task was to enhance the president's role as a manager, not just to encourage economy in government spending and organizational efficiency. Brownlow's unique contribution was to place the president front and center and to recognize, in the report's enduring phrase, that "the President needs help" in carrying out the duties of his office.[27]

The immediate consequences of the Brownlow report "were nil."[28] The report was popularly labeled the "dictator bill" and was ill fated to appear at the same time as FDR's plan to pack the Supreme Court.[29] Telegrams against the plan flooded Congress. And despite overwhelming Democratic majorities, the House and the Senate could not reach agreement on a heavily modified bill; Roosevelt's plan was dead in the water. "It was the Supreme Court fight all over again," according to James MacGregor Burns, "but perhaps even more sharp and passionate."[30]

By 1939 the climate on Capitol Hill was once again receptive to Roosevelt's leadership and Congress was able to reach agreement on a modified reorganization bill. The 1939 proposal was, however, a pale imitation of the original reorganization bill. It did not propose a dramatic overhaul of agencies and departments. The president's reorganizational authority was subject to congressional veto, and twenty-one agencies and programs were placed beyond his reach. Thus, Roosevelt's view that broad reorganization would prove more politically tantalizing to an economy-minded Congress mis-guessed Congress's vested interest in existing agencies and departments and failed to understand its mistrust of expanding executive power.

The 1939 bill, however, fulfilled Brownlow's hopes for enhancing the institutional capacities of the presidency. It authorized the president to ex-pand the White House staff by adding six assistants who, in the words of the original report, "should be possessed of high competence, great physical vigor, and a passion for anonymity."[31] Although modest, this was the open-ing wedge in the creation of a large-scale presidential staff. But as we will also see, the White House staff that has emerged since 1939 has generally been in marked departure from these prescriptions that Brownlow and his associates set out.

Following passage of the bill, FDR submitted his first reorganization plan to Congress, followed by Executive Order 8248, which specified modes of implementation. The executive order, issued on 8 September 1939, altered the organization and structure of the American presidency. It included six provisions, two of which were significant and enduring in their conse-quences.

First and foremost was the establishment of the Executive Office of the President. Roosevelt's order identified three key groupings within the presi-dent's staff. Two—the secretaries to the president and the president's cleri-cal staff—already existed. The third—six presidential assistants—was new. Executive Order 8248 also attempted to differentiate the president's secre-taries from his administrative assistants; it gave the former more substantive responsibilities and the latter, in words designed to reassure a wary Con-gress, the more circumscribed duties of "assist[ing] the President in such matters as he may direct, and at the specific request of the President, to get information and to condense and summarize it for his use."

The second provision of the executive order was the transfer of the Bu-reau of the Budget from the Treasury Department to the Executive Office of the President. Although the president had had the power to name, without Senate confirmation, the director of the Bureau of the Budget since its cre-ation in 1921, its inclusion within the EOP strengthened the president's con-trol over this key part of fiscal planning. Roosevelt's relationship with his budget director after 1939, Harold Smith, was much more significant than it had been with Smith's predecessors, and the BOB became more directly involved in administrative management and program efficiency. The guide-lines for reorganizing the budget bureau also specified an important role for it in "legislative clearance"—clearing and coordinating departmental re-quests on proposed legislation. This proposal was an attempt to channel de-partmental relations with Congress through the White House and to tailor departmental needs to the president's programmatic goals.

The staff of the BOB and its budget increased dramatically after reorganization. About thirty-five persons served in the BOB before reorganization, but by 1946 the staff had grown to more than six hundred. In 1938 the bureau's budget was $187,000, by 1940 it had grown to $645,000, and by 1946 to almost $3 million. All told, according to Allen Schick, "by 1945 the Bureau had become a different agency. It still reviewed agency estimates, but it had become the general staff for the president. The institutional presidency was in place, and the bureau's resources, skills, memory, and loyalty to the president could be passed on from one chief executive to the next."[32]

Although not all parts of Roosevelt's reorganization plan endured as central components of the institutional presidency,[33] he had succeeded in creating the basic structure of a large-scale, multifunctional White House staff. The number of staff assistants, while modest initially, was to grow dramatically under Roosevelt's immediate successors. The location of the BOB within the White House staff proved of inestimable value to FDR and his successors. And even though early entities for personnel management and national planning were short lived, they were resurrected in different forms by FDR's successors; their functions are performed today by such units as the Council of Economic Advisors, the Office of the U.S. Trade Representative, the Office of Policy Development, and the Office of Science and Technology Policy.[34]

The Institutional Presidency after FDR

The Brownlow report saw executive reorganization as a continuous process, not a "one-time shot." Its view proved to be prophetic. Although executive reorganization has not been the only impetus for the creation of a large White House staff[35]—Congress, interest groups, and presidents' own efforts to politicize and centralize their power have also played a part[36]—the years since 1939 have seen numerous attempts to enhance the institutional capacity of the presidency. Both the size and organizational complexity of the president's staff have grown accordingly.

From the handful of aides Roosevelt and his predecessors in office could appoint, the number has steadily increased (although with some variation from administration to administration). Measuring the size of the president's staff, however, has proven fraught with difficulties. Following Roosevelt's practice, presidents have often borrowed staff from other agencies and departments for service at the White House, and there is no wholly reliable measure of the number of these detailees. Presidents also have incentives to limit the officially reported size of the staff; noticeable increases in a president's staff resources can raise an outcry by Congress and the public

Table 1-1 Size of the White House
Office Staff, 1941–Present

1941	53
1945	61
1949	223
1953	248
1957	387
1961	411
1965	333
1969	344
1973	542
1977	464
1981	394
1985	367
1990	366

*Source: Statistical Abstract of the
United States,* for each year.

of an imperial presidency, and they can create the impression of a president overly reliant on his staff for carrying out the duties and expectations of his office. Thus, scholars who have attempted to measure the size of the staff at any given time have come up with very different assessments.

Despite the difficulty in measuring the size of the staff, especially the unreliability of official and unofficial statistics, "ballpark" figures show generally steady growth through most of the 1970s, although there was a slight decrease during the Reagan and Bush years (see table 1–1). By 1953, the immediate White House staff (the White House Office) included more than 250 people. Twenty years later, it had doubled to more than 500. In 1977, criticizing the size of the staff as a symptom of an "imperial presidency," Carter reduced it by 150 employees, largely through moving them to other parts of the executive branch but in many cases continuing their day-to-day service as de facto members of the White House staff. By 1980, Carter's last year in office, the staff had inched upward to about 400. It contracted somewhat to about 360 under Reagan and Bush. When all the administrative units under executive control (the entire Executive Office of the President) are included—such as the Office of Management and Budget, the National Security Council, and the Council of Economic Advisers— the numbers swell to more than fifteen hundred appointees and a 1992 budget well above $150 million. Physically, the entire Executive Office of the President (EOP) has spilled out from the east and west wings of the White House to occupy the Old Executive Office building (once large enough to house the Departments of State, War, and Navy) next door to the White House and now encompassing a New Executive Office Building on the north side of Pennsylvania Avenue and other smaller buildings in the vicinity.

Although, as discussed in chapter 2, the process of institutionalization of the White House staff has sometimes been uneven—many organizational entities of the EOP proved short lived (see Appendix)—the organizational structure of the staff and the different functions it performs have grown in complexity.

As of the early 1990s, eleven major units compose the EOP (or what might be generally termed the "White House staff"): (1) the White House Office, (2) the National Security Council, (3) the Office of Policy Development, (4) the Office of Management and Budget, (5) the Council of Economic Advisors, (6) the Office of Science and Technology Policy, (7) the Council on Environmental Quality, (8) the Office of the U.S. Trade Representative, (9) the Office of Administration, (10) the Office of National Drug Control Policy, and (11) the Office of the Vice-President.[37]

The White House Office

At the core of the EOP is the White House Office. Members of the White House Office serve at the pleasure of the president; their positions carry no tenure and few statutory constraints. The organization of the various units within the White House staff varies from administration to administration; presidents define the job descriptions of their aides and assistants as they wish, shift responsibilities from one unit on the staff to another, and even abolish units as they see fit. It is thus difficult to compare the organization and working of the White House Office among administrations. In general, however, a number of units persist, although particular titles, responsibilities, and organizational groupings may vary considerably.

Under Presidents Roosevelt and Truman, members of the White House Office were by and large generalists. With the exception of the president's personal secretary, military aides, press secretary, and legal counsel, members of the staff were generally not housed within functionally demarcated staff units, nor were they generally assigned functionally specific duties. Furthermore, aides with responsibilities in a particular area did not have large staffs at their disposal—as they do today—and in some instances, most notably the legal counsel during the Truman presidency, performed duties that were not limited to those suggested by their titles.

This generalist perspective changed greatly under Eisenhower, whose "assistant to the president" was intended to be a chief of staff with responsibility for coordinating the day-to-day workings of the staff system. Eisenhower also established functionally defined staff positions, each with a separate staff to handle cabinet affairs, legislative liaison with Congress,[38] and liaison with the Republican party.[39] Although Kennedy and Johnson chose not to designate formally an aide as chief of staff,[40] the specialized staff units that existed during the Eisenhower era continued to exist. Under Nixon, a White House communications office was created, separate from the press secretary and his staff, to handle broader aspects of the president's relationship with the media, especially more general efforts to manage the presentation of the president's image and message to the news media and the public. Nixon also established an intergovernmental affairs staff to act as liaison with state and local levels of government.[41] During the Ford and Carter presidencies, the office of public liaison was established to provide a conduit between the White House and various interest groups and organizations.[42] Under Ronald Reagan, the White House personnel office emerged as an important staff unit in screening potential presidential appointees and making sure that committed Reaganites held key appointed positions throughout the executive branch. Since the 1940s, then, the White House Office has grown in size, organizational complexity, and specificity, especially with discrete units falling into clearly demarcated functional categories: policy advice and staff management; communications management; liaison activities; and management of the president's daily activities.

The Office of Management and Budget

The other components of the EOP generally replicate this pattern of increasing size, complexity, and specificity. The Office of Management and Budget (OMB), and its predecessor, the Bureau of the Budget (BOB), has been one of the more institutionalized components of the president's staff. Created in 1921 and housed in the Treasury Department, the BOB was one of the first units established as part of the EOP as a result of the Brownlow recommendations. Its most important function has traditionally been to prepare the president's annual budget request to Congress. The BOB/OMB also has had a long history of involvement in legislative clearance and program coordination and development, thus giving it not only a strong role in determining agency and department spending but also how and what goods and services are delivered by the federal government. Since the reorganization of the BOB into the OMB in 1970, the OMB has also taken on a management role by advising the president on the efficiency and effectiveness of various federal programs. As a result of these increasing responsibilities, the OMB has become a political as well as professional resource for the president.

Today the OMB is a prominent and influential part of the EOP with a budget in 1990 of more than $42 million and approximately 550 full-time personnel slots, a far cry from the thirty-five staffers FDR could rely on in the old BOB. As table 1–2 indicates, the size of the OMB/BOB staff

Table 1-2 Size of the OMB/BOB
Staff, 1941–Present

1941	305
1945	565
1949	509
1953	457
1957	442
1961	485
1965	524
1969	582
1973	637
1977	709
1981	616
1985	566
1990	552

Source: Statistical Abstract of the
United States, for each year.

has been relatively large, with especially large staffs during the Truman administration—the so-called golden era of the BOB—and the Nixon-Ford years, when the OMB was a central component of Nixon's "administrative presidency."[43]

The National Security Council

The National Security Council (NSC) was created by the National Security Act of 1947 to coordinate foreign policy advice to the president and assist him in arriving at coherent and cohesive foreign policy judgments. In 1949, the NSC and its staff were formally incorporated within the EOP and since then have proven to be one of the most important components of the president's staff structure. Since its creation, the NSC has assumed the following duties: providing to the president information and policy recommendations pertinent to the nation's national security interests, aiding the president in national security crisis management, coordinating agency and departmental activities bearing on national security, and monitoring implementation of national security policy.

From its inception, the NSC system did not have the impact on defense policy that Congress had anticipated in creating it. As I. M. Destler points out, Congress's aim in creating the NSC "was to constrain both the permanent agencies and the government by linking them to one another, through the persons of the Cabinet members who would sit on the council as the president's senior advisers. Policy would thus be both stabilized and integrated." However, Truman's efforts and those of his first NSC executive secretary, Admiral Sidney Souers, to link the NSC integrally to the White

House caused the council to have less than its planned impact on foreign policy decision making and presaged the increasing influence of the NSC secretary and his staff. According to Destler, the reform intended in the 1947 legislation gradually "was turned on its head. The National Security Council became in practice not the powerful, senior advisory forum that was envisioned, but the staff instituted under the council's name. Presidents employed this staff, not just as a link to the permanent government but also as an alternative to it."[44]

When Eisenhower took office in 1953, the NSC system was extensively reorganized. Weekly meetings of the council were scheduled, and the number of invitees was expanded. Most important, Eisenhower greatly expanded the size and functions of the NSC staff, creating an NSC Planning Board and an Operations Coordinating Board. He also redefined the position of executive secretary as the *president's* "special assistant for national security affairs," thereby making the role clearly subservient to the Oval Office.

Although some presidents since Eisenhower have chosen to organize their national security policy processes differently—Kennedy and Johnson, for example, preferred smaller, less formally structured processes—and their NSC special assistants have been more (rarely less) active as policy advocates, the NSC staff has retained an important if not primary role in providing the president with foreign and defense policy advice. The exact size of the NSC staff is difficult to determine, especially in view of its number (increasing in the Reagan years) of military detailees. Under special assistant McGeorge Bundy (1961–66) the NSC had approximately twelve professional policy advisers, midcareer level and up. Under Walt Rostow (1966–69) the number rose to eighteen, then dramatically shot up to fifty under Henry Kissinger (1969–75). Under Brent Scowcroft (1975–77) the number subsided to about forty. It dropped to approximately thirty under his successor Zbigniew Brzezinski (1977–81).[45] By 1985, the Reagan NSC staff had grown to its pre-Carter levels, increasing by 25 percent. Under Bush, the NSC, surpassing its size in the Kissinger era, numbers about 70 policy professionals and 101 support staff; approximately 114 of the 171 total personnel are detailees from other agencies and departments.

These calculations of the size of the NSC staff, while probably reliable, differ from other estimates. The *Statistical Abstract of the United States,* which compiles figures each year from official sources, shows much smaller numbers. But from any source, the growth of the staff is apparent (see table 1–3). Perhaps the most important characteristic of the development of the NSC staff system was summarized by the authors of Jimmy Carter's 1977 reorganization report: "Each President since 1947 has confronted problems in deciding how to use the national security process inherited from his

Table 1-3 Size of the
NSC Staff, 1947–1985

1947	17
1949	17
1953	24
1957	26
1961	56
1965	38
1969	46
1973	82
1977	73
1981	67
1985	62
1990	N/A

*Source: Statistical Abstract of the
United States,* for each year.

predecessor. Under each administration the NSC has proven sufficiently adaptable in meeting Presidential styles and needs. Since 1968, the NSC has expanded considerably both in size and scope of operations, becoming in essence a Presidential foreign policy staff."[46]

The Office of Policy Development

The Office of Policy Development (OPD) is the domestic counterpart to the NSC. Its general functions are to provide policy analysis and advice to the president in the area of domestic policy, to implement and monitor presidential decisions on domestic policy, and to provide the OMB with advice on budget issues involving domestic policy.

For presidents from Roosevelt through Lyndon Johnson, domestic policy advice came from aides, by and large generalists, on the White House staff (for example, Benjamin Cohen and Thomas Corcoran in FDR's second term, Harry Hopkins in his third term, and Clark Clifford in Truman's presidency) and whatever other sources of advice they might choose to consult. Under Kennedy and Johnson, the nucleus of a domestic policy staff began to emerge within the White House Office. Johnson, in particular, delegated much of the work of designing his Great Society legislation to aides such as Bill Moyers and Joe Califano, at times distrusting his cabinet officers to give him the kind of bold policy initiatives he desired.

The Nixon White House attempted to create a powerful Domestic Council patterned after the NSC. Emerging at the time of Watergate and fears of an imperial presidency, the Domestic Council did not achieve a strong, centralized status. Cabinet-level councils, which had been specified as the means of formulating the administration's domestic proposals, rarely met, and the White House was too preoccupied with Watergate to offer new policy initiatives. The resignation of John Ehrlichman, who headed the Domestic Council, also weakened its development. According to Peri Arnold, "Far from becoming a mechanism for policy formulation, the Domestic Council became a large staff for presidential errands, admittedly increasing presidential reach, but providing little analytic or formulative impact over policy."[47]

President Carter reorganized the Domestic Council into a Domestic Policy Staff (DPS) more closely linked to the White House Office. Carter initially favored a small, streamlined domestic staff. He mistrusted Nixon's attempts to bypass departments and agencies and hoped to decentralize policy development by relying on his cabinet. But Carter soon learned that cabinet government has its drawbacks, and the Domestic Policy Staff increasingly played a major role in his domestic policy initiatives. He attempted to strike a balance between centralizing policy development in the White House and maintaining an open and collegial policy process in which agencies and departments had an entrée to policy decisions as they were being formulated.

In the Reagan years, the staff was again renamed; it became the Office of Policy Development (OPD). And its responsibilities were greatly lessened. Reagan and his top aides reduced the staff roughly by half. More important, the OPD was overshadowed by the OMB in orchestrating the budget and tax reductions that marked the centerpiece of Reagan's policy agenda. The ill-fated attempt to use cabinet councils as sources of policy advice to the president also weakened the OPD's role; instead of having a direct relationship to the president in formulating policy, the OPD provided staff assistance to the cabinet officers grouped in each of seven councils. Although Chief of Staff Donald Regan virtually eliminated the cabinet council system in Reagan's second term—reducing their number from seven to two—the OPD failed to reemerge as the central source of domestic advice. It had been eclipsed by a powerful chief of staff.

Under George Bush, the OPD has again emerged as an important provider of policy advice. But Bush's decision not to develop many new domestic policy initiatives and his preoccupation with foreign policy, especially the war in the Persian Gulf, has not led the OPD to occupy political center stage, as its predecessor did in the Carter years.

The Council of Economic Advisers

Established in 1946, the Council of Economic Advisers (CEA) was designed to provide the president with expert advice on economic matters. At its core is a three-member council, generally composed of leading academic economists, with one member serving as chair. The CEA is assisted in its efforts by a staff of approximately thirty-five short-term appointees, both senior and junior economists.

The CEA's impact on economic policy has varied from administration to administration, often depending on the rapport between the president and the three members of the council. Presidents from Truman through Johnson all had, by and large, close personal ties to members of the CEA, who were the "only game in town" capable of providing the administration with accurate and timely economic advice.

According to a senior member of the Carter administration, however, the preeminence of the CEA has been steadily eroding as other agencies and departments have developed their own capacities for economic analysis: "Every agency has an economic policy and planning group and it is not easy to tear their argument apart. CEA cannot blow people out of the water with the depth of its analysis like it could in the 1960s."[48]

The decline of the CEA was especially pronounced during the Reagan presidency, with several chairs of the CEA failing to enjoy close relationships with the White House. Under George Bush, the CEA has reestablished its role as an important source of economic advice to the president, especially during the economic downturn of 1991 and 1992. In general, although the CEA staff is small compared to other EOP units, "it's a very strategic location," according to former CEA chair Murray Weidenbaum. "You're one of the few people both at Cabinet meetings and at senior staff meetings every morning in the White House."[49]

The Council on Environmental Quality

The Council on Environmental Quality (CEQ) was established in 1970. It flourished through the Carter administration. Its formal duties are to assist the president in developing and recommending environmental policies and to advise the president on national environmental issues, report annually to Congress on the state of the environment, review the environmental impact of federal programs, guide and evaluate the performance of federal agencies in fulfilling their responsibilities under the National Environmental Policy Act of 1969, and analyze long-run trends in environmental quality.

The chair of the CEQ serves as director of the Office of Environmental Quality (OEQ), whose staff assists the CEQ. The CEQ shares responsibility for environmental policy with the Environmental Protection Agency (EPA, an independent regulatory agency in the executive branch). The CEQ generally focuses on broader issues of environmental policy, while the EPA sets and enforces specific environmental regulations, especially pollution control policies and standards.

Although the CEQ started out propitiously under the Nixon administration, its involvement in policy matters declined. Because its mandate is broad but vague, its analyses are subject to presidential directive and interest, which has varied from administration to administration. In 1972, the staff had reached a peak of some fifty-seven positions, but it declined to forty by the end of the Ford administration. The CEQ recovered a bit under Carter, attaining a staff of forty-nine and a budget of almost $3.7 million. Under President Reagan, its budget was cut to only $700,000 annually and its staff reduced from forty-nine to thirteen.

The Office of Science and Technology Policy

Established by Congress in 1976, the Office of Science and Technology Policy (OSTP) aims to create within the White House staff an organized entity to replace the informal scientific and technical advice that had been provided by the president's science adviser, a post dating back to the Eisenhower administration, and the informal pattern of consultation with the nation's leading scientists, which dated from Roosevelt's reliance on Vannevar Bush during World War II. In 1962, President Kennedy moved the President's Science Advisory Committee from the White House Office to the EOP, where it was renamed the Office of Science and Technology (OST). Neither Lyndon Johnson nor Richard Nixon enjoyed warm relationships with their science advisers, who were prone to offer "objective" criticism of the presidents' policies. Nixon finally abolished the OST, after it opposed a number of his pet projects, such as the supersonic transport aircraft.

In 1975, Gerald Ford proposed legislation to create a new OST, which would include greater emphasis on technology, not just science, and in 1976, Congress enacted the proposal. Although its statutory functions are vague—to provide scientific and technical advice to the president—the new OSTP has provided presidents with timely advice on health care, herbicides, and population growth. In the Reagan years, the OSTP increasingly provided advice on military matters, especially on Reagan's Strategic Defense Initiative. During the late 1980s, the OSTP professional staff numbered approximately thirty, and its budget in 1990 was approximately $2 million.

The Office of the U.S. Trade Representative

Established in 1963 (as a result of the Trade Expansion Act of 1962) as the Office of the Special Representative for Trade Negotiations, the current Office of the U.S. Trade Representative (USTR) advises the president on important matters of trade, conducts international trade negotiations, and coordinates U.S. trade policy. Its staff of approximately 120 has been headed by highly visible Washington figures: Christian Herter under Kennedy, Robert Strauss under Carter, Bill Brock and Clayton Yeutter under Reagan, and Carla Hills under Bush. The head of the USTR in recent administrations has had cabinet-level status and the rank of ambassador.

The USTR generally serves as the chief source of advice on trade policy and coordinates its implementation. The most important role of the trade representative is to serve as the president's chief representative and negotiator at trade talks, such as the General Agreement on Tariffs and Trade (GATT) rounds, sessions of the United Nations Conference on Trade and Development (UNCTAD), and meetings of the Organization for Economic Cooperation (OECD). The trade representative also serves as the president's negotiator in bilateral trade talks, such as those with Japan and the European community. The representative chairs the cabinet-level Trade Policy Review Group, the Trade Negotiations Committee, and the Trade Policy Staff Committee. This person is also a member of the board of directors of the Export-Import Bank and the Overseas Private Investment Corporation and serves on the National Advisory Committee for International Monetary and Fiscal Policy.

The Office of Administration

Established in 1977, the Office of Administration manages the day-to-day administrative details of the EOP and provides support services to its other units. Assigning offices, arranging for secretarial support, and determining who is assigned what parking spaces and other perks of service fall within the domain of this office. The Office of Administration also handles the White House payroll, purchasing and other accounting functions, data processing, record keeping, printing and duplication, and mail handling and messenger services. During the Carter years, the Office of Administration was headed by Carter's cousin Hugh Carter. Presently the office has approximately 170 full-time positions and 35 temporary and part-time employees; these are divided into five sections—personnel, financial, library and information services, automated services, and administrative operations.

The Office of National Drug Control Policy

Established by Congress in 1989, the Office of National Drug Control Policy is the latest organizational entity of the EOP. It serves as the new institutional home for several EOP units charged with formulating a national antidrug strategy and directing the war on drugs; it is also the coordinating unit for the efforts of more than sixty federal agencies involved in drug control. Bush's selection of William Bennett, Reagan's highly visible secretary of education, as the first director of the office indicates its importance to the president. In 1989, Bennett's office had a staff of seventy and a budget of $2.6 million; by 1990, the budget had grown to $12 million. In late 1990, Bennett resigned and was replaced by former Florida governor Bob Martinez.

The Office of the Vice-President

The Office of the Vice-President is the last major component of the EOP. Until Lyndon Johnson took office in 1961, the vice-president had only several aides at his disposal and operated out of his offices on Capitol Hill. Kennedy found quarters for Johnson in the old Executive Office Building, and since that time both the size of the vice-president's staff and its role as part of the institutional presidency have increased.

Currently, a budget of over $3.5 million dollars and some sixty staff positions[50] are at the vice-president's disposal. The vice-president's staff replicates many of the key positions on the president's staff: chief of staff, press secretary, national security adviser and staff, domestic policy adviser and staff, legal counsel, scheduling and advance office, press apparatus, and assistants for congressional relations.

The institutionalization of the vice-presidency was especially marked under the Carter, Reagan, and Bush presidencies. Walter Mondale, (Vice-President) George Bush, and Dan Quayle enjoyed large offices in both the Executive Office Building, where their staffs were located, and in the West Wing of the White House, in closer proximity to the president. Mondale, Bush, and Quayle were also intimately involved in the policy-making processes of their respective administrations. Each was a close adviser of the president and sometimes the administration's crisis manager and political troubleshooter.

2

THE WHITE HOUSE STAFF AS AN INSTITUTION?

■ ■ ■

A marked change in the character of the presidency has occurred in the years since the Brownlow report. As this chapter will attempt to establish, it is by recognizing that the American presidency bears some of the markings of being an institution, a presidency not merely a president, that we can begin to better understand the office, how it operates, what kinds of challenges it raises for presidents, and, more broadly, how it affects our politics.

The importance of the White House staff and the president's working relationship with his staff has been widely noted by journalists, scholars, and politicians, especially those who have served in the White House. Since the Kennedy administration, presidents have received, solicited and unsolicited, a range of advice on organizing their White House staffs.[1] Journalists have become increasingly attentive to the role of staff members in the politics and operations of the presidency, lavishing attention on staff assistants in lengthy and detailed feature articles that were once saved for high-level cabinet officers or the occasional Harry Hopkins or Sherman Adams. Presidential memoirs also are replete with references to and discussions of the White House staff, often including emphatic assertions that the president did make the policy decisions during his tenure in office, although sometimes blaming poor performance on various staff failures. Memoirs of former members of the White House staff, often written immediately after their service, not only have proliferated in recent years, but they have highlighted, often with juicy tales, the personalities and proclivities of staff members as an important key to understanding the workings of a particular presidency.

Scholars too have focused on the White House staff, offering detailed dissections of particular decisions made by the president and his advisors (studies of the Bay of Pigs invasion, the Cuban missile crisis, and American intervention in Vietnam have become veritable cottage industries), extensive histories of particular units of the White House staff (such as the NSC or the BOB/OMB), and historical accounts of the evolution of the presidential staff system.

Although there is general consensus that the emergence of an institutional presidency has profoundly affected the office of president, there is little agreement on *how* it has done so. Two general arguments seem prevalent in the literature.

The first approach to understanding the institutional presidency, far from downplaying the impact of personal and noninstitutional factors, tends to emphasize how the president's personality and managerial style affect staff operations. This approach is dominant in the literature on the White House staff. It essentially treats the staff as a dependent variable strongly affected by the president's interpersonal style, managerial skills, and work ways. As Fred Greenstein summarizes, there is "virtually unanimous agreement that White House operation is a reflection of the personal qualities and needs of the president."[2]

Scholars in this camp differ over the degree to which the president exercises control over the White House staff and the degree to which the staff affects its own operations. According to one survey of the literature, the typical conclusion is that "expert assistants are only significant to the extent that presidents come to depend on them for advice." Studies of presidential advising "are dominated by a concern with the politics and processes of getting the president's ear."[3] A more complex relationship between the man and the institutional office emerges from the literature on presidential "managerial style" (for example, works by Richard Neustadt, Richard Tanner Johnson, Alexander George, and Roger Porter), which generally involves comparison across several administrations and detects striking variation in how presidents organize their White House staffs.[4] Those organizational differences, in turn, are thought to bear consequences for how the staff system operates and what advice and information the president receives.

The other approach claims just the reverse: the staff is an independent variable with marked continuity in organization and performance that transcends the managerial proclivities of individual presidents. As Hugh Heclo notes, the internal arrangements of the president's staff are a matter of presidential taste only "in most unimportant respects." "In terms of its deep structure, the office is largely a given that a president can change only slowly if at all."[5] According to Joseph Pika, relatively few studies have explored the dynamics of the White House staff by emphasizing organizational variables, but such an approach is likely to prove profitable: "As an organization, the modern presidency *is* . . . a complex structure marked by collective rather than personal properties and action," and the "emergence of a large, articulated structure . . . [has] resulted in the differentiation of the presidency into multiple actors whose interests, attitudes, and goals may differ from those of the elected chief."[6]

The argument of this book is that both approaches contribute important insights to our understanding of the institutional presidency. Both the management style and practices of the president and the day-to-day operations and organizational dynamics of the staff can strongly affect performance and outcome; both thus can act as independent variables. Presidents can powerfully influence their staffs depending on the kind of persons they choose to serve them, the way they organize staff operations, and their day-to-day management of the staff system. But it is also true that the president's staff can be an entity unto itself, filtering if not modifying the force of the president's managerial demands in accord with its own organizational realities, pursuing its own rather than the president's interests, and exhibiting many characteristics of large-scale organizations. But both, too, are dependent in some sense: the pattern of management the president pursues over time is usually modified or tailored according to his past experiences with his staff, and the extent to which organizational factors assert themselves may depend on the strengths and weaknesses of the president's skill as a manager.

This dual role of president and staff as both determining and determined, independent and dependent, is useful not only in suggesting that each approach is in some way "right" in its insights, but that taken together both have something of merit to contribute to our understanding of the institutional presidency. By combining both perspectives we can gain better insight into how the institutional presidency has developed over time and how it contributes to or detracts from effective presidential performance. This is the approach that is pursued in the remaining chapters. I first examine the institutional features of the staff system that seem to persist across administrations and then consider the impact of various presidents' staff organization and management practices in coping with that staff system.

By proceeding in this order, the discrete characteristics of the institutional presidency are acknowledged first and presidential management is considered second. As I attempt to show, this makes sense descriptively: the impact of the president's managerial style and practices is best seen against the backdrop of the organizational dynamics of the institutional president. But it also makes sense prescriptively in that it acknowledges that the staff system is a resource *for* the president—and, hence, ultimately subject to his managerial control and discretion.

Table 2-1 The White House Office, 1939

Secretary to the president	Stephen Early
Secretary to the president	Brig. Gen. Edwin M. Watson
Secretary to the president	Marvin H. McIntyre
Administrative assistant	William H. McReynolds
Administrative assistant	James H. Rowe, Jr.
Administrative assistant	Lauchlin Currie
Personal secretary	Marguerite A. LeHand
Executive clerk	Rudolph Forster

Source: United States Government Manual, 1939 (Washington, D.C.: U.S. Government Printing Office, 1939).

The Case for the Presidency as an Institution

If the presidency is best understood as an institution bearing certain properties that transcend particular presidencies, then clearly it should embody certain characteristics of an institution. But what do we mean by terms like *institution, institutional,* or *institutionalization?* Our concern here is for understanding the impact of the organizational character of the presidency—its growth in size, the complexity of its workways, and the general way in which it resembles a large, well-organized bureaucracy.[7] Although there is no agreed upon definition of *institution,* three features are generally included. First, an institution is organizationally complex both in terms of what it does (its functions) and how it operates (its structure). Second, an institution is generally universalistic and routine in its decision-making and operating procedures: precedent, impersonal codes, and merit govern, not fiat, personal preferences, and favoritism. Finally, an institution is well bounded and differentiated from the larger environment in which it is situated.[8] Does the White House staff meet these conditions?

Complex Organization

Institutions are complex: they are relatively large in size; subunits tend to proliferate, with each generally performing a specialized function; and some form of central authority coordinates the parts' various contributions to the work of the institution. Each of these aspects of complexity to some degree characterizes the White House staff.

The large size of the institutional presidency can be seen by comparing the White House staff available to President Roosevelt in 1939, before Brownlow, with the staff at work in the Bush White House.

The eight individuals that the 1939 *Government Manual* lists as members of the White House staff (table 2-1) are clearly dwarfed by the long list of staff members serving under President Bush (table 2-2). Moreover, as we saw in chapter 1, the staff positions listed in table 2-2 are only the top layer of the five to six hundred aides and assistants at Bush's disposal in the White House Office and the approximately fifteen hundred persons serving in the Executive Office of the President (EOP) as a whole.

Comparison of tables 2-1 and 2-2 also illustrates the second aspect of organizational complexity: increasing specialization of function. Roosevelt's aides were by and large generalists; they were simply called secretary to the president or administrative assistant. In the Bush presidency, by contrast, we find titles such as assistant to the president for communications, deputy assistant to the president for legislative affairs (Senate), special assistant to the president for agricultural trade and food assistance, deputy assistant to the president for public liaison, associate counsel to the president, and so on. These titles reveal significant differences in the rank of staff members and the emergence of functional specialization in their titles, a practice that began in the Johnson administration.

Furthermore, not only do staff members perform limited functions, but also various subunits of the staff operate within functionally defined, specialized areas. This is especially true of the units, not listed in table 2-2, that compose the other components of the EOP, such as the National Security Council staff and the Office of Management and Budget. All told, the once relatively simple tasks of the president's staff—writing speeches, handling correspondence, and orchestrating his daily schedule—have evolved into substantive duties that affect the policies the president proposes, how he disposes of them and, more generally, how he deals with the steadily increasing demands placed upon his office.

In addition to functional specialization, the organizational structure of the White House staff has become more complex. Again, the proliferation of subunits in the EOP is telling: the very simplified structure in FDR's 1939 EOP has grown to eleven large-scale staff units. More strikingly, the structural complexity within each unit has increased. For example, under Roosevelt and Truman the organizational hierarchy of the White House Office was relatively flat. Roosevelt's aides held several titles—secretary to the president and administrative assistant, for example—but these bore little relation to their status within the organization or to their access to the president. Under Truman, the size of the staff increased markedly, but with only a slight increase in the degree of organizational hierarchy. According to Pika, "while all were technically equal, the Special Counsel, Clark Clifford and later Charles Murphy, was aided by the Administrative Assistants. There were also several noncommissioned assistants . . . and John Steelman enjoyed the title *the* Assistant to the President." At most, Pika

Table 2-2. The White House Office, 1990

John H. Sununu, *Chief of Staff to the President*

Andrew H. Card, Jr., *Assistant to the President and Deputy to the Chief of Staff*

James W. Cicconi, *Assistant to the President and Deputy to the Chief of Staff*

David Q. Bates, Jr., *Assistant to the President and Secretary to the Cabinet*

Richard C. Breeden, *Assistant to the President for Issues Analysis*

David F. Demarest, Jr., *Assistant to the President for Issues Analysis*

Max Marlin Fitzwater, *Assistant to the President and Press Secretary*

C. Boyden Gray, *Counsel to the President*

Frederick D. McClure, *Assistant to the President for Legislative Affairs*

J. Bonnie Newman, *Assistant to the President for Management and Administration*

Roger B. Porter, *Assistant to the President for Economic and Domestic Policy*

Gen. Brent Scowcroft, USAF (Ret.), *Assistant to the President for National Security Affairs*

Stephen M. Studdert, *Assistant to the President for Special Activities and Initiatives*

Charles G. Untermeyer, *Assistant to the President and Director of Presidential Personnel*

Debra Anderson, *Deputy Assistant to the President and Director of the Office of Intergovernmental Affairs*

Paul W. Bateman, *Deputy Assistant to the President for Management and Director, Office of Administration*

Phillip D. Brady, *Deputy Assistant to the President and Director, Office of Cabinet Affairs*

Nicholas E. Calio, *Deputy Assistant to the President for Legislative Affairs (House)*

B. Jay Cooper, *Deputy Assistant to the President and Deputy Press Secretary*

Robert M. Gates, *Deputy Assistant to the President for National Security Affairs*

Joseph W. Hagin, II, *Deputy Assistant to the President for Appointments and Scheduling*

E. Boyd Holingsworth, Jr., *Deputy Assistant to the President for Legislative Affairs (Senate)*

Ronald C. Kaufman, *Deputy Assistant to the President for Presidential Personnel*

John G. Keller, Jr., *Deputy Assistant to the President and Director of Presidential Advance*

Barbara G. Kilberg, *Deputy Assistant to the President for Public Liaison*

C. Gregg Petersmeyer, *Deputy Assistant to the President and Director, Office of National Service*

James P. Pinkerton, *Deputy Assistant to the President for Policy Planning*

Roman Popadiuk, *Deputy Assistant to the President*

Patricia Presock, *Deputy Assistant to the President*

Table 2-2. *continued*

Edward M. Rogers, Jr., *Deputy Assistant to the President and Executive Assistant to the Chief of Staff*

William L. Roper, *Deputy Assistant to the President for Domestic Policy and Director, Office of Policy Development*

Susan Porter Rose, *Deputy Assistant to the President for Domestic Policy and Chief of Staff to the First Lady*

John P. Schmitz, *Deputy Counsel to the President*

Sichan Siv, *Deputy Assistant to the President for Public Liaison*

Roscoe B. Starek III, *Deputy Assistant to the President and Deputy Director of Presidential Personnel*

Chriss Winston, *Deputy Assistant to the President for Communications*

James Wray, *Deputy Assistant to the President and Director, Office of Political Affairs*

Gary J. Andres, *Special Assistant to the President for Legislative Affairs (House)*

Robert D. Blackwell, *Special Assistant to the President for National Security Affairs*

Everett E. Briggs, *Special Assistant to the President for National Security Affairs*

William Canary, *Special Assistant to the President for Intergovernmental Affairs*

David M. Carney, *Special Assistant to the President and Deputy Director for Political Affairs*

Paul Collins, Jr., *Special Assistant to the President for National Service*

Nancy P. Dorn, *Special Assistant to the President for Legislative Affairs (House)*

Juanita Duggan, *Special Assistant to the President for Cabinet Affairs*

Robert A. Estrada, *Special Assistant to the President and Associate Director of Presidential Personnel*

Cooper Evans, *Special Assistant to the President for Agricultural Trade and Food Assistance*

John S. Gardner, *Special Assistant to the President and Assistant Staff Secretary*

Alixe R. Glen, *Special Assistant to the President and Deputy Press Secretary*

Martha H. Goodwin, *Special Assistant to the President and Associate Director of Presidential Personnel*

Shirley M. Green, *Special Assistant to the President for Presidential Messages and Correspondence*

George O. Griffith, Jr., *Special Assistant to the President for Intergovernmental Affairs*

Anne B. Gwaltney, *Special Assistant to the President and Associate Director of Presidential Personnel*

Richard N. Haass, *Special Assistant to the President for National Security Affairs*

Stephen T. Hart, *Special Assistant to the President and Deputy Press Secretary*

Table 2-2. *continued*

Deane E. Hoffman, *Special Assistant to the President for National Security Affairs*

John W. Howard, *Special Assistant to the President for Legislative Affairs (House)*

G. Philip Hughes, *Executive Secretary of the National Security Council*

Hector F. Irastorza, Jr., *Special Assistant to the President and Deputy Director of the Office of Administration*

Karl D. Jackson, *Special Assistant to the President for National Security Affairs*

Arnold Kanter, *Special Assistant to the President for National Security Affairs*

Thomas F. Kranz, *Special Assistant to the President and Associate Director of Presidential Personnel*

Virginia A. Lampley, *Special Assistant to the President for National Security Affairs*

Burton Lee III, *Physician to the President*

Lehmann Li, *Special Assistant to the President and Executive Secretary, Economic Policy Counsel*

Antonio Lopez, *Special Assistant to the President and Director of the White House Military Office*

Nelson Lund, *Associate Counsel to the President*

Timothy J. McBride, *Special Assistant to the President*

Mary A. McClure, *Special Assistant to the President for Intergovernmental Affairs*

David C. Miller, Jr., *Special Assistant to the President for National Security Affairs*

Nancy F. Miller, *Special Assistant to the President and Associate Director of Presidential Personnel*

Jeannette L. Naylor, *Special Assistant to the President and Associate Director of Presidential Personnel*

Robert J. Portman, *Associate Counsel to the President*

Peter W. Rodman, *Special Assistant to the President for National Security Affairs*

Charles Nicholas Rostow, *Special Assistant to the President for National Security Affairs*

Amy L. Schwartz, *Associate Counsel to the President*

David P. Sloane, *Special Assistant to the President for Legislative Affairs (Senate)*

Brian K. Waidmann, *Special Assistant to the President for Legislative Affairs (Senate)*

R. Douglas Wead, *Special Assistant to the President for Public Liaison*

Gordon B. Wheeler, *Special Assistant to the President for Legislative Affairs and Director of Congressional Affairs*

William W. Working, *Special Assistant to the President for National Security Affairs*

Source: United States Government Manual, 1989–1990 (Washington, D.C.: U.S. Government Printing Office, 1989).

concludes, there were two or three structural levels. Beginning with the Eisenhower administration, organizational complexity markedly increased, with at least five levels dividing the staff. Subsequent administrations have similar structural divisions and "considerably finer distinction in salary structure."[9]

The final characteristic of institutional complexity is the presence of some central authority that coordinates the contributions of the institution's functional parts. For the presidency, such authority nominally resides in the president himself. But in recent administrations, coordinating authority has been especially manifest in the increasing importance of a White House chief of staff.

It was Eisenhower who established the formal role of a chief of staff. On taking office, Eisenhower complained, "Do I have to be my own sergeant major?" His perception of the organizational needs of the White House, plus his military experience, led him to appoint Sherman Adams as the first real presidential chief of staff (Adams's title, however, was never "chief of staff" but "assistant to the president"). Although Adams's duties and powers appear in retrospect to have been less significant than was assumed during the Eisenhower years, his role does mark a significant change in the character of the presidency: the transition from an informal network of advisers surrounding a presidentially dominated staff to a more formally organized institutional presidency with the chief of staff at its apex.

During the Kennedy and Johnson presidencies, more informal patterns of staff organization again prevailed, although in both staff systems, one or two key aides emerged as first among equals: Theodore Sorensen in the Kennedy White House and Bill Moyers and Harry McPherson in the Johnson White House.[10] In the administrations that followed, the chief of staff position has become a regular feature of the institutional presidency: H. R. Haldeman and Alexander Haig under Nixon; Donald Rumsfeld and Richard Cheney under Ford; Hamilton Jordan and Jack Watson under Carter; James Baker, Donald Regan, Howard Baker, and Kenneth Duberstein under Reagan; and John Sununu and Samuel Skinner under Bush. Each played substantive roles in policy making and in most cases possessed day-to-day operational authority over the workings of the White House staff.

The centralization of power within the White House staff in the role of chief of staff seems unavoidable, regardless of the president's own initial wishes. For example, Carter, at the start of his administration, publicly announced that he wanted no chief of staff of the sort H. R. Haldeman had been under Nixon. However, by the end of Carter's second year in office Hamilton Jordan functioned as de facto chief of staff, and by Carter's third year the appointment was official. So, too, with the Reagan White House.

Reagan took office with a unique configuration for managing his staff and organizing his decision making: a troika of top aides (Edwin Meese, Michael Deaver, and James Baker) with the responsibilities of previous chiefs of staff parcelled out among them. But by 1982, Baker had emerged as the most important of the three, and in Reagan's second term, former Treasury Secretary Donald Regan became the most powerful chief of staff yet witnessed.

Recruitment Criteria

Comparison of the Roosevelt staff with that of recent presidents also indicates the second trend toward institutionalization of the presidency: the increasing reliance upon universalistic criteria, especially educational credentials and other job-related experience and skills, for recruitment to the president's staff. For Roosevelt and presidents before him, White House aides were largely drawn from political cronies and other longtime associates. Howe first went to work for then New York State Senator Franklin Roosevelt in 1912. Most of the other Roosevelt aides listed in table 2-1—Early, McIntyre, and LeHand—first served Roosevelt during his unsuccessful vice-presidential campaign in 1920.

Today, the résumés of key presidential aides look a bit different. Longtime associates of a president—for example, Ed Meese and Michael Deaver under Reagan—still make their way onto the president's staff. But once they are transplanted to the hothouse of Washington politics, they often find themselves pushed from positions of real power by persons with experience in national government, expertise in substantive policy areas, and adeptness at Washington politics. Again the Reagan presidency is revealing: although James Baker's tasks seemed the most difficult and his authority weakest, his political skills and well-honed Washington expertise enabled him to displace his two rivals, whose political experience (save for serving in Reagan's quest for national office) had been limited to the environs of Oakland and Sacramento, as the real center of power in the Reagan White House. Not only had Baker been under secretary of commerce in the Ford administration, but he was national chairman of Ford's 1976 election bid and had managed Bush's campaign in the 1980 presidential race—both times against then candidate Reagan.

Even when a Meese or Deaver is visible at the top, the lower levels of the White House are staffed with relatively young, skilled, and well-educated individuals. Richard Neustadt has estimated that approximately half of the five hundred or so aides in the Carter (180) and Ford (250) White House Offices can be considered "professional-level" personnel.[11] Comparable data is not available for the Reagan and Bush administrations, but some evidence supports the notion that staffers are increasingly drawn from those with professional expertise. For example, among the initial appointees to Reagan's Office of Policy Development, the unit that helps to frame domestic policy proposals, 31 percent held M.B.A.'s and other management-related degrees, 31 percent were lawyers, 16 percent had Ph.D.'s, and only 23 percent held no advanced degree. The office was headed by Martin Anderson, an economics professor from Stanford.[12] Under George Bush, according to one estimate, twenty-four of twenty-nine top-level White House staff appointees had prior experience in the White House.[13]

Differentiation from Environment

Increasing complexity and growing reliance on expert skill and advice have given the presidency its own unique place in the policy process, differentiating it from its political environment. One way this has occurred is through increased White House control over new policy initiatives. Presidents now routinely try to shape the nation's political agenda, and the staff resources they have at their disposal enhance their ability to do so. Kennedy, Johnson, and especially Nixon, with the creation of the Domestic Council, all emphasized White House control of policy proposals, deemphasizing involvement of the cabinet and the bureaucracy. Carter and Reagan both began office with calls for more presidential reliance upon the cabinet but quickly found that goal to be unworkable in practice and turned inward to the White House staff for policy advice.

Those outside the White House—Congress, the bureaucracy, the news media, and the public—have responded to presidential direction by expecting more of it. Political lobbying and influence seeking, especially by those directly involved in national politics, are increasingly centered on the president. American politics remains highly decentralized, incremental, and with multiple points of access. But persons and groups seeking an impact upon national politics try to cultivate those who have most to do with policy proposals: the White House staff.

A second aspect of the presidency that differentiates it from the surrounding political environment is the way parts of the staff are organized explicitly to manage external relations. The press secretary and his staff coordinate and in many cases even control the presidential news passed on to the media.[14] Since 1953, specific staff assistants have been assigned solely to lobby Congress on the president's behalf. Today, White House lobbying efforts are formally organized within the large, well-staffed Office of Congressional Relations.

To manage relationships with the political environment presidents increasingly have established special channels of influence for important constituent groups. This began in the Truman administration, when David

Niles became the first staff aide explicitly assigned the task of serving as a liaison to Jewish groups. Eisenhower hired the first black presidential assistant, E. Frederic Morrow, and added a special representative from the scientific community as well. In 1970, President Nixon created the Office of Public Liaison as the organizational home within the White House staff for the increasing numbers of aides who served as conduits to particular groups. By the time Jimmy Carter left office, there were special staff members specifically assigned to such diverse groups as consumers, women, the elderly, Jews, Hispanics, white ethnic Catholics, Vietnam veterans, and gays, as well as such traditional constituencies as blacks, labor, and the business community.[15] The increasing differentiation of the presidency as a discrete entity thus complements its increasing complexity and reliance upon expertise as evidence of its status as an institution.

Effects of an Institutional Presidency: Three Traits

Even if the presidency bears the marks of an institution, do its distinctly institutional characteristics matter, as opposed to the individual styles, practices, and idiosyncracies of each president? Despite the tremendous growth in the president's staff, perhaps it remains mainly a cluster of aides and supporting personnel, whose tasks, organization, and tenure vary greatly from administration to administration, and even within the term of a particular president. After all, both scholarly analysts and journalistic observers of the presidency have noted enormous differences between the Kennedy and the Eisenhower White Houses, between Johnson and Nixon, Carter and Reagan, and even Reagan and Bush. It is the personality, character, and individual behavior of each president that has generally attracted the attention of press and public.

Some of these observations are undoubtedly true. But numerous traits discernible across presidencies stem from institutional sources. Three of these traits, or "institutional effects," stand out: (1) centralization of control over the policy-making process by the White House staff, (2) centralization of power *within* the staff in one or two key aides, and (3) emergence of behavior and routines that are typical of bureaucratic organizations.

As we will see, not only have each of these three institutional traits been manifest in very different presidencies, they have each had significant effect on the operations of the White House staff system. And as we shall explore in chapters 3 and 4, they establish an organizational context that presidents must deal with in order to make their staff systems work effectively.

External Centralization: Staff Control over Policy Making

The creation of a large presidential staff has centralized much policy-making power within the presidency. Most presidents have found that they cannot rely solely on the regular line agencies and departments to provide the kind of advice they need or to carry out initiatives that reflect uniquely on their performance in office—liaison with Congress, press relations, crisis management, and setting new directions in foreign and domestic policy.

The Washington political climate, especially within the federal bureaucracy, is not naturally receptive to the president's political initiatives. In some instances, new programs and policies compete for programmatic authority and budget allocations with older programs that generally are well established in agencies and departments, have strong allies on Capitol Hill, and enjoy a supportive clientele of special interest groups. Even when departments are receptive to the president's initiatives, they may subordinate them to their own policy agenda.

Reliance on his own staff, by contrast, may provide the president with aides and assistants who, loyal largely only to him, are also more able to guard his interests. At least compared to others on the Washington scene, they are more inclined to make the system—the president's system—work to achieve his policy goals.

Centralization has both positive and negative aspects. On the positive side, presidents have found that it can protect programs they wish to foster. In creating the Office of Economic Opportunity (OEO), Lyndon Johnson, a president whose legislative skills were matched only by his political wariness, recognized this advantage. The OEO was designed to be a central component of Johnson's War on Poverty. As Congress was considering the legislation to create the OEO, the Departments of Commerce, Labor, and Health, Education, and Welfare all lobbied to have it administratively housed within their bailiwicks. Johnson, fearing subordination of the OEO to whatever other goals a department might pursue, lobbied Congress to have the OEO report directly to the president. He was especially swayed by the views of Harvard economist John Kenneth Galbraith, who warned: "Do not bury the program in the departments. Put it in the Executive offices, where people will know what you are doing, where it can have a new staff and a fresh man as director."[16] Locating a new policy initiative within the institutional presidency gives the president a freer hand: greater control over expenditures, personnel, organizational structure, and achievement of the policy's mission. As Bradley Patterson concludes, "if wholesale relandscaping of the federal turf is in prospect, only the White House can put the federal bulldozer in gear."[17]

Centralization of power in the president's staff has not, however, always redounded to presidential advantage. Power breeds contempt. As Frederick Mosher explains, "presidential aides afflicted with hubris, from at least the Johnson administration on, have given orders to Cabinet departments, sometimes contradictory orders from different assistants. Often they have given orders directly to subordinate officials in the departments, bypassing the [Cabinet] secretaries."[18]

Increasing White House staff control of the policy process, especially in foreign policy, has at times diminished and even excluded other sources of policy advice. Since the creation of the National Security Council in 1947, presidents increasingly have relied for policy recommendations on its staff, especially the president's special assistant for national security. Ironically, Congress's intent in creating the NSC was to check the foreign policy power of the president by creating a deliberative body whose members (set by law) would provide the president an alternative yet timely source of advice.

Except during Eisenhower's presidency, the NSC has not generally functioned as an effective deliberative body. What has developed is a large, White House–centered NSC staff headed by a highly visible special assistant, which has dominated the foreign policy–making process. The reasons why the NSC staff and special assistant have come to dominate the process are plain: proximity to the Oval Office, readily available staff resources, and a series of presidents whose views about decision-making processes differed from those held by Eisenhower. Beginning with McGeorge Bundy under Kennedy, and continuing with Walt W. Rostow under Johnson, Henry Kissinger under Nixon, and Zbigniew Brzezinski under Carter, national security assistants not only have advocated their own policy views, but also have eclipsed other sources of foreign policy advice, especially the secretary of state and his department.

In Nixon's administration, for example, Secretary of State William Rogers repeatedly battled with NSC adviser Kissinger to exert at least some measure of influence over American foreign policy. The feud between Rogers and Kissinger was open to full view. One senator remarked that Rogers had become a joke in Washington, with Kissinger "secretary of state in everything but title." According to another senator, "They let Rogers handle Norway and Malagasy, and Kissinger would handle Russia and China and everything else he was interested in."[19]

In his memoirs, Kissinger's tone in discussing his relationship with Rogers is revealing. He reports that "few secretaries of state have been selected because of their president's confidence in their ignorance of foreign policy." Rogers, Kissinger notes, "must have considered me an egotistical nitpicker who ruined his relations with the President; I tended to view him as an insensitive neophyte who threatened the careful design of our foreign policy." By 1970, Rogers was being excluded from foreign policy decisions on all issues except the Middle East, with Nixon and Kissinger deliberately making major decisions while Rogers was out of the country. Kissinger concludes that his relations with Rogers deteriorated to the point where they "exacerbated our policy differences and endangered coherent policy. . . . I believed that Rogers had no grasp of the geopolitical stakes."[20]

Further testimony to the problems created by centralized control over foreign policy by the NSC staff can be found in the memoirs of two recent secretaries of state. Cyrus Vance, who served under Carter, repeatedly battled NSC assistant Zbigniew Brzezinski. Vance's resignation was precipitated by the ill-fated decision—from which Vance and the State Department were effectively excluded—to try to rescue the American hostages in Iran. Vance had earlier opposed the mission as poorly conceived and difficult to execute, yet while Vance was on a weekend vacation in Florida, Carter hastily called a meeting of his top foreign policy advisers. The meeting was dominated by members of Brzezinski's staff and the military, who favored the rescue attempt. The State Department, which favored a more cautious, diplomatic solution to the hostage crisis, was represented only by Vance's under secretary, Warren Christopher. Christopher reported that he was isolated in his dissent: "Everyone else at the meeting supported the rescue attempt." When Vance returned to Washington on Monday morning, he was "stunned and angry that such a momentous decision had been made in my absence." After several days of "deep personal anguish," he decided to resign.[21]

Alexander Haig, Reagan's first secretary of state, encountered similar problems with the NSC and the White House staff. Although Reagan had promised Haig that he would be his chief "vicar" of foreign policy, Haig soon found that he did not enjoy direct access to the president but had to go through Ed Meese. In his memoirs, Haig lists numerous incidents that are revealing about his exclusion from the administration's inner circles: memoranda sent to the White House would somehow become lost; he sometimes learned about the administration's foreign policy only from news reports, on one occasion reading in the Sunday *Washington Post* that Vice-President George Bush had been appointed crisis manager in foreign policy; and Haig's opponents on the White House staff often made unflattering comments and reports about Haig to the news media. Haig even had difficulty getting appropriate aircraft for his trips abroad; during his shuttle diplomacy between Britain and Argentina at the time of the Falkland Islands crisis, he was forced to use a windowless converted KC-135 cargo plane that lacked adequate working space and communications equipment, even though more comfortable aircraft were available. Shortly after Haig's return from his negotiations, he learned from a close friend "who was in a position to know the truth" of a meeting at the White House in which James Baker was quoted as saying, "Haig is going to go and go quickly and we are going to make it happen."[22] Shortly afterward, Haig resigned.

Haig's claim in his memoirs that he had only secondhand knowledge of many of President Reagan's decisions is especially revealing of the tensions between the State Department and the White House staff and their effect on the administration's policies. In a chapter tellingly entitled "Mr. President, I Want You to Know What's Going on around You," Haig reports:

> William Clark, in his capacity as National Security Adviser to the President, seemed to be conducting a second foreign policy, using separate channels of communications . . . bypassing the State Department altogether. Such a system was bound to produce confusion, and it soon did. There were conflicts over votes in the United Nations, differences over communications to heads of state, mixed signals to the combatants in Lebanon. Some of these, in my judgment, represented a danger to the nation."[23]

Haig's successor as secretary of state, George Shultz, also found himself cut out of a number of important policy decisions by the NSC. The most notable was the Reagan administration's secret negotiations with Iran to exchange arms for American hostages in Lebanon and its use of the profits generated by the arms sales to fund the Contras in Nicaragua covertly. The arms deal violated standing administration policy against negotiating for hostages, and the disclosure of the secret Contra funds undermined congressional support for Reagan's policies in Central America. Testimony before the Congress's Iran-Contra hearings revealed not only strain but open hostility between the State Department and the NSC staff. The two NSC special assistants at the time, Robert McFarlane and John Poindexter, kept the department in the dark about their secret travels abroad, with Poindexter at one point putting the State Department on a special list of those who "don't need to know" about Iran-Contra activities. In Shultz's testimony before the hearings, he noted his own sense of estrangement and not being in "good odor" with the White House.[24] The Iran-Contra affair not only intensified Shultz's conflicts with the NSC but was politically damaging to President Reagan, weakening his credibility both at home and abroad.

Two exceptions to this general pattern of conflict within the president's foreign policy community have occurred, one during the Ford administration and the other apparently in the Bush presidency. In both cases input from the State Department and the NSC was balanced. But both cases also reveal conditions under which presidents have avoided excessive centralization. In both presidencies Brent Scowcroft served as NSC adviser, deliberately crafting his role as "honest broker" of the foreign policy–making process rather than as policy advocate and rival source of advice. Furthermore, in both administrations the secretaries of state had extensive White House staff experience. Kissinger had served under Nixon as NSC special assistant, and for part of his service under Nixon and Ford, as both NSC special assistant and secretary of state. Bush's secretary of state, James Baker, had served as White House chief of staff and secretary of the treasury under Reagan.

Internal Centralization: Hierarchy, Gatekeeping, and Presidential Isolation

The general centralization of policy-making power by the White House staff has been accompanied by centralization of power *within* the staff by one or two chief aides. This internal centralization of authority is further evidence of the institutional character of the presidency; although the degree of hierarchy varies among administrations, all exhibit some degree of it. Like other institutional characteristics, it can affect the way the president's staff system operates, providing both opportunities and risks for a president.

On the positive side, centralization of authority within a well-organized staff system can provide clear lines of responsibility, well-demarcated duties, and orderly ways of working. Some chiefs of staff and NSC special assistants have kept business in the White House running smoothly, making sure that the president has all the information he needs for making a decision and organizing the president's contacts with persons he may wish to consult both within and outside the staff system. When presidents lack a centralized, organized staff system, the policy-making process suffers.

In addition to making the staff more effective, a system in which one member serves as chief or at least is *primus inter pares* (first among equals) has proven advantageous for other reasons. Chiefs of staff often handle some of the difficult tasks that presidents have sought to avoid, especially hiring and firing aides and evaluating their performance. As H. R. Haldeman, Nixon's longtime chief of staff, once noted, "every president needs his son-of-a-bitch" to do the dirty work.[25] One major piece of dirty work fell to Haldeman after Nixon's landslide 1972 reelection. Nixon assembled his staff and thanked them profusely for their good work over the previous four years. He then turned the meeting over to Haldeman, who informed the assembled staff that all were required to turn in letters of resignation immediately; only later would they be informed whether they would keep their jobs during Nixon's second term. Nixon had ordered the housecleaning, but Haldeman took the blame and carried it out.

Powerful aides have also used their authority to protect the president. "Some in the White House, so committed," Frederick Mosher notes, "have even deterred an impulsive president by appealing from Philip drunk to Philip sober."[26] Haldeman was repeatedly put in the position of carrying out impossible Nixon commands. "This president had to be protected from himself," Haldeman recounts in his memoirs:

> Time and time again I would receive petty vindictive orders. "Hugh Sidey is to be kept off Air Force One." (Sidey was *Time*'s man.) Or even, once or twice, "*All* the press is barred from Air Force One." (Pool representatives of the press accompanied the President on every trip.) Or, after a Senator made an anti-Vietnam War speech: "Put a 24-hour surveillance on that bastard." And on and on. If I took no action, I would pay for it. He'd be on the intercom buzzing me ten minutes after such an order. "What have you done about Sidey?" I'd say, "I'm working on it," and delay and delay until Nixon would one day comment, with a sort of half-smile on his face, "I guess you never took action on that, did you?" "No." "Well, I guess it was the best thing."[27]

On one occasion, Nixon, piqued about repeated foreign policy leaks in his administration, ordered Haldeman to direct the CIA to undertake immediate lie detector tests of all State Department employees, *worldwide*, to discover who the leakers were. Haldeman realized that the order would not only prove politically embarrassing to Nixon once it got out but was physically impossible to accomplish.[28]

High-level presidential assistants have often been especially useful in protecting the president's political standing and reputation. A highly visible staff member with significant authority within the White House can act as a kind of lightning rod, handling politically tough assignments and deflecting controversy away from the president and toward himself.

Perhaps the best example of this useful division of labor comes from the Eisenhower presidency. Part of Eisenhower's success as president derives from a leadership style in which he projected himself as a chief of state who was above the political fray, while allowing his assistants, especially his chief of staff, Sherman Adams, to seem in charge of day-to-day decisions. Although in reality it was Eisenhower who made the decisions, Adams's reputation as the "abominable 'No!' man" helped "preserve Eisenhower's image as a benevolent national and international leader."[29]

But a well-organized, centralized staff has also on occasion worked against presidents' interests: highly visible staff assistants with large amounts of authority have sometimes acted as gatekeepers, controlling and filtering the flow of information to and from the president.

In the Nixon administration, Chief of Staff H. R. Haldeman was frequently accused of erecting a Berlin Wall around Nixon. Although the lack of access many in Washington felt was as much Nixon's doing as Haldeman's (Nixon disliked meetings and preferred long periods of solitude in which he would contemplate the nation's problems and make policy decisions), Haldeman agreeably structured the president's schedule to Nixon's preferences. As a result, cabinet members complained that they never saw the president.

Similarly, both Hamilton Jordan under Carter and Donald Regan under Reagan were criticized for limiting access to the president and selectively screening the information and advice their presidents received. Joseph Califano, Jr., Carter's secretary of health, education, and welfare, had repeated run-ins with Jordan. For example, while lobbying Congressman Dan Rostenkowski, the influential chairman of the Health Subcommittee of the House Ways and Means Committee, on a hospital cost containment bill, Califano found that Rostenkowski resented the treatment he was receiving from Jordan. "He never returns a phone call, Joe," Rostenkowski complained. "Don't feel slighted," Califano replied. "He treats you exactly as he treats most of the Cabinet."[30] In July 1979, Carter fired Califano and promoted Jordan.

Donald Regan, who succeeded James Baker as Reagan's chief of staff when they switched positions in 1985, acquired tremendous power over domestic policy, played a major role in important presidential appointments, and even was touted in the media as Reagan's "prime minister." Immediately upon taking office, Regan flexed his political muscle by revamping the cumbersome cabinet council system, substituting instead two streamlined bodies: an Economic Policy Council and a Domestic Policy Council. Regan retained control of the two councils' agendas. According to White House aide Becky Dunlop, "Don Regan more than anyone else has the authority to say [an] issue has to be dealt with by the Cabinet council. And he does that on a regular basis." Subsequent council reports to President Reagan also flowed through Regan: "The simplified system strengthened Regan's direct control over policy, establishing him as a choke point for issues going to the President."[31]

Centralized authority of the type Haldeman, Jordan, or Regan practiced is clearly preferable to organizational anarchy. But as hierarchy and centralization develop within the White House staff, presidents have sometimes found themselves increasingly isolated, relying on a small core group of advisers. If that occurs, what information the president gets may already have been selectively filtered and interpreted. What deliberations occur may take place within an inner circle of like-minded advisers. Neither is beneficial to the quality of presidential decision making nor to the overall goal of effective presidential performance.

Bureaucratization

As the top levels of the White House staff have increased in authority and political visibility, the rest of the staff has often taken on the character of a bureaucratic organization. This development is in marked contrast with the role of the presidential staff that the Brownlow committee originally envisioned. The Brownlow committee's hopeful rhetoric calling for aides who would be presidential loyalists with a "passion for anonymity" and its organizational goal of a staff of neutral facilitators who would aid the president in his duties but not interpose themselves between the president and the cabinet or make policy outright failed to predict the normal consequences of bureaucracy, even a presidential one.

Brownlow and his associates envisioned a small presidential staff, numbering no more than six to ten. Such a staff would enjoy close proximity to the president and have intimate knowledge of his policy wishes and the roles in which he would have them serve. With some measure of presidential control, such a small staff could be reined in if it began to usurp the operational responsibilities of agencies or departments, deviated from presidential intentions, or became too conspicuous; its limited size made it an easy candidate for successful presidential watchfulness. Today, as we have seen, the staff is a large-scale organization with many bureaucratic characteristics: complexity, fragmentation, competition, and self-serving advocacy.

One such characteristic is the emergence of complex work routines, which often stifle originality, generate intrastaff controversy, and reduce differences on policy to their lowest common denominator. According to Paul Light, "The Carter decision loop covered well over a dozen separate offices within the White House; the process could take several weeks to complete, and it often generated considerable conflict."[32] Drawing on his experience in the Carter White House, Greg Schneiders complains that if one feeds "advice through the system . . . what may have begun as a bold initiative comes out the other end as unrecognizable mush. The system frustrates and alienates the staff and cheats the President and the country."[33] Schneiders also notes that the frustrations of staffers do not end with the paper flow: "There are also the meetings. The incredible, interminable, boring, ever-multiplying meetings. There are staff meetings and task force meetings, trip meetings and general schedule meetings, meetings to make decisions and unmake them and to plan future meetings, where even more decisions will be made."

"All of this might be more tolerable," Schneiders suggests, "if the staff could derive satisfaction vicariously from personal association with the President." But few aides have any direct contact with the president: "Even many of those at the highest levels—assistants, deputy assistants, special assistants—don't see the President once a week or speak to him in any substantive way once a month." In her memoirs, Reagan speechwriter Peggy Noonan recalls that more than four months passed after she started work on the Reagan staff before she met the president. Colleagues of

Noonan felt no pity: some grumbled that they had not seen the president in more than a year. The lack of contact with the president was especially problematic in the Reagan White House, Noonan argues, because "speechwriting was where the philosophical, ideological, and political tensions of the administration got worked out. Speechwriting was where the administration got invented every day."[34]

The absence of personal proximity to the president, in turn, can encourage attitudes and behavior that detract from allegiance to broader presidential goals and purposes. According to George Reedy, who served under Lyndon Johnson, "The White House does not provide an atmosphere in which idealism and devotion can flourish. Below the president is a mass of intrigue, posturing, strutting, cringing."[35] Reedy's comments are a bit harsh, to paint the staff with such a broad and negative brush is a bit unfair. But certain patterns of behavior do deflect the staff from the mission of devotion and idealism Reedy embraces and can lead to the intrigue, posturing, and other deleterious actions on his list.

"Bureaucratic politics" can develop. The maxim "where one stands depends on where one sits" is applicable to the White House staff just as to any bureaucratic organization. The individual staff member's particular place within the presidential bureaucracy can lead to a narrow view of priorities and goals, sometimes reflecting the self-serving interests of a particular subunit of the staff rather than its presidentially set purposes.

Kissinger's relations with Secretary of State William Rogers are again revealing. In his memoirs, Kissinger notes that one result of their competition for influence over foreign affairs was a "bureaucratic stalemate in which White House and State Department representatives dealt with each other as competing sovereign entities, not members of the same team." Symptomatic of their bureaucratic infighting was their battle over the president's annual report to Congress and the public on the state of foreign affairs. For three years, the State Department published its own volume rather than cooperate, as it had done before and has done since, on a common draft with the NSC staff. "This rivalry was not always on the plane of high policy," Kissinger reports. The State Department and the White House battled over which report would be issued first; Kissinger notes that he always prevailed. Kissinger also writes that his report always gave some credit to the secretary of state, while the State Department's report rarely mentioned Kissinger and his staff. In 1972, the landmark year of Kissinger's secret trip to China, secret negotiations with the North Vietnamese, and a breakthrough in the SALT talks, "the State Department's report referred to the President 172 times, to Rogers 96 times, and to me once—in reprinting the text of the announcement of the President's trip to China, from which I could not be deleted. It included four photographs of the President, eight of Rogers, and none of me. . . . I don't know which was more petty, State's snub or my noticing it."[36]

The attempts by the Bureau of the Budget to guard its own prerogatives against presidential reorganization of the White House staff and the bureau provide another classic example of bureaucratic politics in the EOP, one stretching over several presidencies. According to Larry Berman, the history of presidential reform of the White House staff reflects "to a remarkable degree the Budget Bureau's resourceful struggle to preserve its venerable post-1939 status as 'first among equals' in the EOP." Three presidential reorganization commissions battled with the bureau. In 1957, Percival Brundage, Eisenhower's budget director, "vehemently opposed," according to Berman, the recommendation of Eisenhower's reorganization advisers (the President's Advisory Committee on Government Operations, PACGO) that an office of administration with broad responsibilities be created as part of the White House staff; Brundage felt that the "director of administration would create an added layer between the budget director and the president." Eisenhower sided with the bureau. PACGO's fallback position called for an assistant for management within the White House Office who would coordinate the work of the BOB and other units in the EOP. Again the bureau resisted interposition of a White House staffer between the president and it. "The Budget Bureau's response to PACGO's proposals is a textbook illustration," according to Berman, of the law "where you stand depends on where you sit": "From the chair of the BOB director, PACGO's recommendations were viewed as a downgrading of the BOB's Office of Management and Organization and another potential barrier between the budget director and the president. From where PACGO was seated, the recommendations were seen as restructuring the existing management processes to reduce the president's workload."[37]

In 1966, Lyndon Johnson commissioned the Heineman task force on administration and management. It recommended the creation of an Office of Program Coordination as an independent staff unit of the EOP as well as reorganization of the BOB. Although Johnson ultimately decided not to act on the Heineman task force's recommendations, the bureau was not slack in its efforts to fend off further reorganization efforts. Budget Director Charles Schultze undertook his own study of the BOB as the Heineman group was first shaping its recommendations. According to one Heineman task force member, "Schultze saw where the Heineman group was moving in its critique of the Bureau and he decided to implement his own study to see what was wrong." Once Johnson shelved the Heineman task force's report, "Schultze seized the opportunity to reorganize the Bureau in accord with the self-study recommendations."[38]

Nixon's reorganization efforts, crafted by the Ash council, met with more success but again faced budget bureau opposition, especially to the proposal to create an Office of Executive Management to which the bureau would be subordinate. Even though Nixon had appointed Robert Mayo as budget director with the understanding that Mayo and the bureau might become subordinate to the new OEM, the bureau fought hard to retain its organizational autonomy and proximity to the president. In a conversation with Mayo, Roy Ash, the council's head, told the budget director that he knew the "BOB has many ways at its disposal to kill the plan and asked Mayo's assurance that neither he nor his people would sabotage the plan through extra-legal channels."[39] Mayo complied with Ash's request; he did not publicly oppose the Ash council's recommendations, refusing to heed the entreaties of staff members who thought he should do so. He did, however, argue against reorganization that would change the character of any White House staff entity.

Although Mayo technically kept his promise not to thwart the Ash council's recommendations, members of his staff did not follow suit. The bureau used a number of different stratagems. One tactic involved the Ash council's request for an additional million dollars to complete its work. According to Berman, "the BOB had very little desire to see the Council continue. They simply 'misplaced' the Council's budget request until it was too late to incorporate it into the President's Special Fund Budget. This had gone to the printers a week earlier. The BOB was thus forcing the Council to make a special line-item request to the congressional committee. Such a request was subject to congressional veto."[40]

Some bureau staff members also covertly lobbied Congress to oppose the council's recommendations. This initially succeeded when the House subcommittee of the Committee on Government Operations reported negatively on the critical centerpiece of the council's recommendations, Reorganization Plan No. 2. The bureau also succeeded in thwarting the plan to create an all-encompassing Office of Executive Management. But the bureau's victories were not to last. In July 1970, the bureau was reorganized as the Office of Management and Budget. Reflecting on the politics of his reorganization efforts, Roy Ash specifically singled out the bureau's opposition as his biggest stumbling block: "One of the biggest problems in trying to convert the Bureau of the Budget to the Office of Management and Budget was that the pocket of greatest resistance, of political resistance, was the Bureau of the Budget. Some of those guys went up to the Hill to sabotage that thing, and to really turn the screws up on some of them. That was the biggest resistance block right there."[41]

Frustration with the working of a bureaucratic organization and with bureaucratic politics is complemented by the kind of interpersonal competition that arises from "court politics." Not only can bureaucratic priorities displace broader goals, but furtherance of personal priorities and career gain can affect attitudes and behavior. White House staff members often compete for assignments and authority that serve as a measure of their standing and prestige on the staff and ultimately with the president. Sometimes these turf battles are physical in character, with staff members competing for more office space and closer proximity to central figures in the administration, especially to the president and his Oval Office in the West Wing. At the start of each presidential term, for example, there is intense journalistic speculation about the size of staff offices and the location of offices in relation to the president; the Washington political community takes these as signs of relative power and influence.

Staff perquisites is another area of court politics among the staff. Who can dine at the White House mess, who is included in the list of first and second seatings for lunch, and who sits at certain tables are all taken as signs of prestige on the staff and are thus the object of much competition. During Nixon's presidency, Henry Kissinger coveted the private bathroom (the only one adjacent to an office besides that of the president) that was part of Communication Director Herb Klein's office suite. While Klein was away from the White House on an extended trip, Kissinger reportedly ordered workmen to wall up Klein's door to the bathroom and cut a new entrance to Kissinger's office next door. There is no record of what Klein did when he returned, but the bathroom remained Kissinger's.

Robert Hartmann, who was a longtime associate of Gerald Ford, Ford's chief of staff as vice president, and counsellor to the president with cabinet rank when Ford assumed the presidency, describes another incident, small in import but revealing about court politics in the White House, in this instance a battle between Ford loyalists and holdovers from the Nixon White House, whom Hartmann dubs the "praetorian guard."

The incident involved what portraits of former presidents would grace the Cabinet Room. Presidents traditionally pick a favorite predecessor or two, whom the press regard as clues to his conception of the presidency. Eisenhower hung Lincoln's portrait, Kennedy put up Jefferson, Johnson replaced him with Roosevelt, and Nixon installed Teddy Roosevelt and Woodrow Wilson. Ford decided on Lincoln and Harry Truman. Shortly after Ford took office, Hartmann left Alexander Haig, Ford's chief of staff held over from the Nixon staff, a note informing him of the president's wish to switch portraits and have it done in time for Ford's first cabinet meeting the next day. Nothing happened. At Ford's first meeting in the Cabinet Room "the faces around it were all the same: Nixon's Cabinet and the heroes on the walls were the same; they were Nixon's heroes. The praetorian guard had encountered insurmountable difficulties in locating a portrait of Mr. Truman."[42] A week passed and Nixon's portraits stayed in place. Hartmann spoke to Haig, who asked him, "What's the big rush?" According to Hartmann, Haig knew exactly what the big rush was, "but his purpose was to show that there was no change, that the Nixon-Ford White House was carrying on without Nixon." Hartmann advised Ford to intervene and directly order Haig to change the portraits, which Ford did. A portrait of Truman was finally located in the National Portrait Gallery, but several more days passed and the portrait still was not hung. Hartmann wrote another memo to Haig that the portrait had better be hanging by the time the president returned from a trip to Chicago. Finally, after nearly two weeks of delay, Truman's picture went up.[43]

Court politics in the Ford White House also erupted when Ford decided to make Nelson Rockefeller the chair of the Domestic Council. Ford loyalists on the president's staff balked at the idea. The staff began to protest that "such was not the way to run the establishment."[44] The arrangement never worked, and Rockefeller eventually backed off from his attempt to exert influence over domestic policy. Some members of the Ford staff lobbied Ford to dump Rockefeller as his running mate in 1976.

Occasionally something as insignificant as a *the* can make the world of difference to a staff assistant. In 1946, President Truman appointed John Steelman as "assistant to the president." When Steelman's charter of operations was being drawn up by the Bureau of Budget, he cleverly inserted "the" before his title, telling Elmer Staats of the BOB, "My understanding is that I am supposed to be the chief of staff of the White House."[45] The article stayed and was printed at the top of Steelman's stationery, thereby enhancing his status in dealing with other staff members, as well as outside the administration. Truman continued to call him assistant to the president, while other staff members grumbled over Steelman's self-assumed importance.[46]

As the Steelman example suggests, not only are staff members concerned about their standing within the staff; they are attentive to how they are perceived outside the staff. Staff members often develop allies on the outside—members of the press, members of Congress, lobbyists, and other political influentials—who can aid the programs and political causes of particular parts of the institutional presidency or the personal careers of staffers. Conversely, they also can create hostility and enmity among those outside the staff who compete for presidential attention. Perhaps the classic example of this is the "us versus them" attitude that develops in foreign policy making between the NSC staff (inside the White House) and the State Department (outside) or between the Office of Policy Development (inside) and regular departments (outside) in domestic policy. In part, such attitudes may stem from different orientations and perspectives. "Political appointees seem to want to accomplish goals quickly while careerists opt to accomplish things carefully."[47] But they also may arise from simple bureaucratic politics generated by the competition of powerful bureaucracies or from the court politics of influential advisers vying for the president's ear and attempting to enhance their own status and policy turf.

A Process of Deinstitutionalization?

Although a plausible case can be made that the institutional presidency bears many characteristics of a bureaucratic organization and embodies certain effects—positive and negative—common to bureaucratic institutions, the White House staff also has been subject to much change and variation of a sort not often seen in bureaucracies. The Appendix lists all the major units of the EOP, some forty in all. The "organizational lives" of some of these units are quite brief, perhaps indicative not of the development of an institutional presidency but of a process of deinstitutionalization. Approximately 75 percent (thirty out of forty) of these units are no longer in existence, with thirteen of the thirty (43 percent) not surviving more than one administration. Several units have been dissolved by a president, only to be established again by a successor. The post of telecommunications adviser, created by Truman but abolished in 1953, was revived by Nixon as the Office of Telecommunications Policy. The Office of Science and Technology was created by Kennedy in 1962 but dissolved by Nixon in 1973, only to be revived by Ford in 1976. The Special Action Office for Drug Abuse Prevention, created in 1971 lasted until 1975; an Office of Drug Abuse Policy existed from 1977 until 1978, when drug policy was absorbed into the functions of the White House Office; but then in 1989 an Office of National Drug Control Policy was created.

Although these changes in the EOP could be taken to indicate a strong presidential influence over the structure and organization of the staff system rather than a continual process of institutional development, this interpretation may be misleading. Some of these units, for instance, have been absorbed by other units, a process of consolidation that may support the thesis that the White House staff is becoming increasingly institutionalized. For example, the functions of the Office of Emergency Management were absorbed into the other war agencies of Roosevelt's EOP. As the end of the war loomed, the Office of War Mobilization was reorganized into the Office of War Mobilization and Reconversion. As the Cold War developed, the National Security Resources Board was created but then folded into the Office of Defense Mobilization, which in turn became the Office of Civil and Defense Mobilization. In each instance changes in particular units of the staff may reflect shifts in the nature of the policy environment—in this instance, changes in the policy focus of national security in war and peacetime—and the organizations needed to carry them out. What may appear, then, to reflect weakness in the institutional status of a particular staff entity may only be a reflection of developments in the political environment that necessitate organizational change and evolution: an adaptive process characteristic of a viable organization, rather than simple failure to meet the conditions for survival as an institution. Excessive change in response to the demands issuing from the environment, of course, may call into question the institution's ability to differentiate itself from its environment, thus weakening one of its claims to institutional status.

Apart from changes in the organizational structure of the EOP, the role that particular staff units perform within the EOP also bears on the question of institutionalization. In particular, to the extent that the role of a staff unit changes from administration to administration or even within a particular administration, its claim to institutional status may weaken. Although the precise formal, and especially informal, functions performed by staff units are difficult to determine precisely, there are some indications of significant variations over time in the role of various EOP units.

Margaret Wyszomirski, for example, has argued that the domestic policy units in the EOP have performed very different roles from administration to administration.[48] According to Wyszomirski, three types of role relationships, drawn from legal doctrines on agency, are possible: principal and agent; master and servant; and advisee and advisor. An agent is commissioned to transact business in the name of his principal, performing loyally and competently and exercising whatever skills and discretion may be necessary; a servant assists his master but exercises little discretionary judgment; and an advisor offers advice based on expertise or skill but bears no responsibility for execution. Each of these roles can be found in the domestic policy staffs of recent presidents. Nixon's Domestic Council (in its pre-Watergate phase under the direction of John Ehrlichman) is close to the first pattern, agent, with the president as principal. Under Ford, the Domestic Council waned in influence, performing essentially the tightly constricted role of servant. Under Carter, the Domestic Council was revitalized and reorganized as the Domestic Policy Staff, performing the role of key policy advisor to the president. Reagan's Office of Policy Development started out on a promising note, but its succession of directors and its subordinate role to the OMB led to its regression to something like the servant and master role it had under Ford. Each role relationship suggests greater (principal and agent, advisee and advisor) or lesser (master and servant) institutionalization, with the variation across time indicating strong presidential rather than institutionally determined influence upon the staff's role in the policy process.

John Kessel's study of the Carter and Reagan White Houses depicts a staff that at times confirms the presence of differences of the sort Wyszomir-ski has found but that also suggests strong institutional characteristics. One of Kessel's findings suggests a high level of turnover in personnel, which organizational theorists generally take as a sign of a weak organization. In studying the Reagan White House, Kessel undertook two sets of interviews. Of the thirty staff members he initially interviewed, just one year later only sixteen remained in service at the White House and ten had left the administration altogether.[49]

More substantively, Kessel found significant differences between the Carter and Reagan administrations in staff members' attitudes regarding "desirable public policy" (which Kessel terms "issue structure") and their perceptions about which staff members had significant power ("influence structure"). In the Carter White House, although staffers were by and large moderately liberal in general attitude, there was little agreement on policy issues. In contrast, in the Reagan White House not only were attitudes generally conservative, but there was significant consensus about specific issues. According to Kessel, "not a single pair of persons on the Carter staff had a high enough rate of agreement to begin forming an issue group. On the Reagan staff, a single issue group was formed that included over 80 percent of the staff members."[50]

With respect to influence structure, Kessel found that the organizational units of the two staffs fell approximately in the same order in each adminis-tration, although the heads of each unit were perceived to wield somewhat different amounts of power in the two administrations. Thus, while attitudes about issues may reflect individual-level determinants (i.e., the policy preferences of individuals or the skill or willingness of the president and his personnel officers in selecting like-minded staff members), the influence of the staff units as a whole reflects both individual and organizational-level determinants.

In examining a third dimension, the pattern of communication among the staff (communication structure), Kessel found remarkable similarities in the two White Houses. Although the OMB received more communica-tions from other staff units in the Reagan White House than it did in the Carter White House, the domestic policy staffs of both presidents were centrally located in the communications network, with the NSC staff in both administrations showing similar degrees of isolation.

The power and influence wielded by a particular staff unit can also vary within a presidency according to the importance of persons holding key positions, rather than the importance of the president or the organization. In Eisenhower's administration, for example, the duties of the chief of staff changed somewhat following Sherman Adams's departure. His successor, Wilton Persons, was not the practitioner of centralized management that

Adams had been, and observers noted less hierarchy and more openness in the post-Adams staff system.

Significant variation in hierarchical organization also was noticeable in the Reagan staff system. The troika of Meese, Deaver, and Baker encouraged some fluidity in the early days of the Reagan presidency; more centralization followed under Baker as the president's single chief of staff; a high degree of hierarchy and centralization of power and control emerged under Donald Regan; then under Howard Baker and Ken Duberstein there was again more openness.

The influence of particular units in the Reagan White House also waxed and waned. The Council of Economic Advisers, the Council on Environmental Quality, and the Office of Science and Technology Policy all enjoyed less influence on the policy process than had been the case under Carter, and each progressively enjoyed less influence as the Reagan years went on. The NSC staff was not given direct access to the president in the first year of the administration, but following Richard Allen's departure as NSC special assistant and his replacement by trusted Reagan aide William Clark, the NSC's access began to increase (although it was still dampened somewhat by Clark's relative lack of experience and expertise in foreign policy). Under Clark's successors, Robert McFarlane and John Poindexter, the importance of the NSC markedly rose—extending both to the formulation of national security policy and its implementation—but after the Iran-Contra debacle, its role was once again reduced.

Other general trends in some of the staff units of the EOP also call into question their degree of institutionalization. Based on an extensive study of the BOB/OMB, the CEA, the Domestic Council, and the NSC staff, Wyszomirski concludes that the organizational life of each has by and large come increasingly to be dependent on its identification with the president. This has produced fewer, not more, "vital life patterns" for each. In sum, she suggests, "the tendency is away from, not toward institutionalization."[51]

The debate about the institutional character of the White House staff is important and not easily resolvable; evidence can be marshaled on both sides. But that there is such a debate is probably testimony to the presence of at least some measure of institutionalization. That presidents increasingly seek to control the staff, change its organizational structure, and alter its impact on the policy-making process may be indicative of its institutional immaturity. But it also may be a sign of responsiveness to the effects of an institutional staff system—centralization, hierarchy, and bureaucratization—which presidents have sought to remedy. As we will see in the next two chapters, both perspectives—seeing the staff system as a discrete institution or set of institutions and viewing it as an instrument subject to presidential management and control—may be illuminating.

3

THE INSTITUTIONAL PRESIDENCY
Through a Managerial Lens

■ ■ ■

The institutional presidency that has emerged during the last fifty years undoubtedly offers the president important resources to meet the complex policy tasks and expectations of his office. But those same resources can work against the president; as we have seen, the effects of an institutional presidency—centralization of policy making by the president's staff, centralization of power within the staff, and bureaucratization—can hinder, as well as serve, a president's policy goals.

Presidents are not, however, simply at the mercy of their staffs. The White House staff has certain institutional characteristics, but it is not an institution that has escaped the hand of presidential leadership, if indeed any institution can elude some measure of managerial control. Presidents have changed features of its organization and operation to suit their particular needs, reaping its benefits while deflecting institutional forces that can detract from their goals. By the same token, effective management has sometimes eluded a president's grasp. As General Andrew Goodpaster, who served as President Eisenhower's staff secretary, observes, "The president's desk is where everything comes together, or where it comes apart."[1] In a similar vein, George Reedy, who served in Lyndon Johnson's White House, states that "presidents glory in telling people that they are prisoners of a system and of circumstances beyond their control. . . . The fact is that a president makes his decisions as he wishes to make them, under conditions which he himself has established, and at times of his own determination."[2]

Patterns of Presidential Management

Reedy's observations invite us to consider the organizational choices that confront presidents and, in contrast to the theme of the last chapter, to focus on the man, particularly the differing managerial practices of presidents, not just the dynamics of the office.

There are some limits on what the president can and cannot do, of course. Legal constraints limit the size and structure of some entities, especially the units of the Executive Office of the President. Statutes specify the size of the Council of Economic Advisers and the National Security Council, for example, and define some of their responsibilities, although generally only in broad terms. Congress can also have some effect on the president's staff through its control of annual budgetary appropriations.

But these constraints notwithstanding, presidents have great discretion over how most units of the EOP are organized and especially what role they play in the day-to-day workings of the presidency. Even when statutory constraints are present, as with the NSC, presidents can choose whether to convene a particular group of advisers or to what extent to heed their advice.

As the institutional presidency developed, scholars began to note general patterns in how presidents organized their White House staffs. In *Presidential Power*, first published in 1960, Richard Neustadt set forth an influential account of what was known at the time about how the first three modern presidents (FDR, Truman, and Eisenhower) organized their White House staffs. Although Neustadt's emphasis was on the general leadership style of each president rather than an explicit analysis of organizational variations, his descriptions of each presidential style bore clear implications about organizational differences.

Neustadt argues that Roosevelt favored an approach that blended reliance on an ever-changing pattern of organization (he quotes Arthur Schlesinger, "His favorite technique was to keep grants of authority incomplete, jurisdictions uncertain")[3] with personal competition among his aides for his ear. According to Neustadt, "Competing personalities mixed with competing jurisdictions was Roosevelt's formula for putting pressure on himself, for making his subordinates push up to him the choices they could not take for themselves."[4]

Truman, Neustadt concludes, was not as well informed as FDR, because he spurned his predecessor's practice of making advisers compete for his ear. But Truman's informal openness to his advisers did help him approximate Roosevelt's rich fare of information and advice. Eisenhower, Neustadt argues, had a management style that was particularly ill suited to well-informed and well-advised presidential leadership. Echoing a common

1950s view of Eisenhower as a figurehead president, Neustadt presents an account of a management style that, by relying extensively on delegation, rendered the president ill equipped to formulate creative policies and advance them effectively. Eisenhower, Neustadt observes, did impact "more superficial symmetry and order to his flow of information and of choices than was ever done before." But, Neustadt concludes, "he became typically the last man in his office to know tangible details and the last to come to grips with acts of choice."[5]

In 1974, Professor Richard Tanner Johnson of Stanford University Business School offered an influential classification of the presidential management styles that had emerged from Roosevelt through Nixon. Johnson concluded that three general patterns of White House organization were identifiable, each with distinctive strengths and weaknesses.

Roosevelt, Johnson asserts, had a *competitive* advisory system, one in which advisers' responsibilities overlapped and the president fostered rivalries among them. Like Neustadt, Johnson notes that such an arrangement puts the president in the center of the flow of information, generates "creative ideas," and "is more open to ideas from the outside."[6] Johnson also suggests that a competitive system tends to favor policy options that are politically feasible and bureaucratically "do-able" rather than analytically optimal. But, unlike Neustadt, whose account of Roosevelt's style is largely favorable, Johnson also argues that a competitive style can bear costs for the president: it places large demands on his time and requires his vigilant attention; it may expose him to partial or biased information because it relies on a limited number of channels of advice; it may sacrifice optimality to do-ability; it tends to aggravate competition if not jealousy and hostility among the staff and lead members to pursue their own interests to the detriment of the president's interests; and it may lead to high attrition in personnel.

The Eisenhower and Nixon White Houses, in Johnson's view, exemplified a *formalistic* system, a pattern of management involving much delegation of authority to the president's top advisers and a system in which the information and advice that reaches the president is funneled through a hierarchical structure of clearly designated organizational channels. Formalistic arrangements conserve the president's time and encourage an orderly analysis of policy issues. But in screening advice and information through a complex staff hierarchy, they may distort what the president receives. Formalistic arrangements also tend to undervalue political pressures and public sentiments in their search for the optimal policy choice, and they tend to respond slowly or inappropriately in crises.

The third pattern, a *collegial* system of White House organization, involves "building a team of colleagues who work together to staff out problems and generate solutions, which, ideally, fuse the strongest elements of divergent points of view."[7] Whereas the formalistic model of management might be likened to a hierarchical pyramid, the collegial model resembles a wheel: the president serves as the hub and his advisers as spokes directly connected to him and to each other. A collegial system, Johnson holds, seeks to achieve both optimality and do-ability, and by involving the decision maker directly in the information network it can ease the demands on him by emphasizing teamwork rather than competition. Collegial systems, however, put great demands on the decision maker's time and require him to be skilled in dealing with his associates, especially in maintaining a collective ethos that is conducive to effective decision making.

Johnson unequivocally identifies Kennedy's management of the White House as collegial, noting the many accounts of Kennedy's close personal involvement in deliberations, the fluidity of his consulting practices, and the camaraderie of his White House group. He finds Lyndon Johnson hard to classify, arguing that LBJ preferred formal procedures but that his personality tended to undermine them.[8]

Recognizing that presidential personality tempers, modifies, and otherwise alters the effects of advising arrangements, Johnson nevertheless argues that the types he proposes are analytically distinguishable and have predictable costs and benefits. He treats the collegial approach as the golden mean between the extremes of formalism and competition. Unlike formalism, it does not insulate the president. Unlike competition, it does not subordinate the advice and information that reaches the president to his aides' skill at bureaucratic and court politics.

Most modern presidencies plausibly fall in one of the three categories Johnson distinguishes. Presidential staffs, by and large, tend to be collegial (e.g., Kennedy and Johnson) or formal (Eisenhower and Nixon) in their basic organization, with some recent staff systems (Carter, Reagan, and Bush) exhibiting elements of both styles. No presidency, it should be noted, has replicated Roosevelt's competitive arrangement, however.

The difficulties with Professor Johnson's typology come in the way the patterns are characterized and the effects predicted to issue from them. These problems are endemic to all typologies because variations develop and effects differ; most typologies, Johnson's included, set out something on the order of ideal types that real cases more or less meet. But Johnson's schema shows more fundamental divergence between the ideal and the real, and it does not differentiate clearly between systems in the same category. For example, the chief characteristic of the collegial system—cooperation—does not characterize Lyndon Johnson's system as much as it does

Kennedy's. Johnson's relationships with his advisers and their relationships with each other were often not cooperative. Furthermore, whereas Kennedy encouraged dissent and debate among his advisers, Johnson sometimes bullied or otherwise pressured his subordinates to conform to his own policy preferences.[9]

With respect to formal staff systems, Richard Tanner Johnson's basic observation that some White House staffs rely more strongly on formal procedures and organizational structures is correct as far as it goes. But it fails to distinguish, as we will see in more detail, Eisenhower's more open and fluid staff system from the one that prevailed in the Nixon White House.

It is also not clear that particular patterns of management have the effects Johnson predicts for them. Nixon's experience with a formal staff system led to many of the problems Johnson analytically identifies, but Eisenhower's did not. Kennedy's reliance on a collegial approach is especially vexing: it cannot alone explain the marked differences a number of scholars (including Johnson) have noted between how his advisory arrangement worked before the Bay of Pigs fiasco and how it functioned afterward. That Kennedy used the collegial mode of organizing his staff is clear, but its effectiveness appeared to improve after the Bay of Pigs although the hub and spokes remained the same.

Comparison of Richard Tanner Johnson's and Roger Porter's respective typologies reveals disagreement over what constitutes the distinguishing characteristics and the predicted effects of different management styles. Although Porter's concerns are a bit broader—policy making within the whole executive branch—both analysts identify roughly similar patterns of staff organization: Porter's tripartite schema of centralized management, "adhocracy," and multiple advocacy essentially replicates Johnson's formalistic, competitive, and collegial classification.[10] Porter's analysis of the consequences of each pattern, however, differs from Johnson's. Porter seems more optimistic about the benefits of centralized management, noting that it leads to careful review of policy options: Johnson regards formalistic systems as searching for the "best" policy alternative at the price of the most "do-able" solution. For Porter the problem with centralized management is that it values policy formulation at the price of policy implementation, whereas for Johnson, formalistic arrangements screen and distort information, creating a problem largely for policy formulation. Porter and Johnson also diverge on the characteristics and value of competitive management styles. Porter's view of "adhocracy" is that it generally produces low quality, noncomprehensive reviews of policy options and may actually be less politically responsive than more formal arrangements if the president fails to consult widely. Although Johnson concedes that a competitive style may lead to a less developed range of policy options, he concludes that it is usually marked by creativity and is particularly sensitive to political feasibility and responsiveness.

To be fair to Johnson, he does note that the intent of his schema "is not to confine complex behavior to single boxes" with predictable costs and benefits, and he acknowledges that most presidents follow "mixed models" in which one pattern is usually "dominant."[11] But more significant differences than Johnson's schema readily admits seem to exist in the staffing arrangements of presidents who fall within each category and in the extent to which they reap the benefits and bear the costs associated with it. There are also significant differences over time in the experiences of one president using basically the same staff system throughout his administration.

Managerial Style and the Institutional Presidency

The various problems with the typologies that Johnson, Porter, and others have offered do not diminish, however, the importance of the theoretical concerns that produce an impulse to classify differences in president's managerial styles and to predict the effects of those differences. How the president and his advisers interact is of great importance for the functioning of the White House staff. But to understand how patterns of staff management affect the institutional presidency, a broader perspective must be taken.

First, as we saw in the previous chapter, features of the institutional presidency that transcend particular administrations should be taken into account. As Pika notes, "the tendency has been to cast the staff in a wholly subordinate role—they *amplify* presidential views and mannerisms, serve as *agents* of presidential directives, or *muffle* his real preferences."[12] This perspective in the literature is too narrow; organizational characteristics can, as we have seen, exercise an independent effect upon the White House staff.

Furthermore, organizational characteristics can themselves affect patterns of staff organization and management. The costs and benefits that Johnson, Porter, and others have linked to particular managerial styles and arrangements may stem in part from the effects of their application within an institutional context rather than from characteristics that are inherent to a particular structural arrangement. The differences between presidents who use similar patterns of staff organization may thus result from features of the presidents' modes of staff organization and managerial practices that are or are not attentive to the organizational context in which they are applied (for example, on the positive side, Eisenhower's blend of formal and informal procedures or the changes in Kennedy's style in the aftermath of the Bay of Pigs fiasco; on the negative, Lyndon Johnson's disorganized procedures and his mode of interaction with his advisers, which often tended to discourage open discussion). That some presidents may be attentive to the nature of the staff organization with which they interact may be a particularly important ingredient in the success of their management; conversely, their inattention may bode failure.

There is then a need to combine the organizational and managerial perspectives, to look at both man and office, *and* to do so in such a way that the two approaches are brought to bear on each other. This perspective suggests that how presidents cope with the institutional presidency might be conceptualized in two ways. The first takes a top-down approach and seeks to enrich our understanding of the personal, presidential dimension of the institutional presidency by paying particular attention to how presidents who fall in the two major categories of staff organization—the collegial and the formal—have tailored or failed to tailor their staff organization and management practices to their application within an institutional context. The second takes a bottom-up approach and focuses on features of the institutional presidency that transcend particular presidencies and the extent to which staff organization and management practices are cognizant of them. These views are obviously related: each considers personal and organizational factors. But by looking at the institutional presidency through the lens of managerial style and then through the lens of its organizational dynamics, we can bring to bear the claims of both schools of thought— the personal and the organizational—on the institutional presidency *and* identify and take into account the interrelationship between them.

Through a Managerial Lens: Patterns of Formalistic Management

In examining how patterns of staff organization and management fare within the context of the institutional presidency, let us first consider the experiences of two presidents who are largely thought to have relied on highly formal staff systems: Dwight D. Eisenhower and Richard Nixon.

Eisenhower

The elaborate Eisenhower staff system for establishing national security policy offers an especially interesting window for examining the operations of formal staff structures and procedures because it has been regarded, at least until recently, as the archetype of formal systems and has been thought to illustrate the dangers inherent in them. According to Richard Tanner Johnson, Eisenhower used his NSC machinery as a "shield" that would provide him with "recommendations to ratify." NSC meetings, Johnson notes, lacked "thorough-going deliberations" and were occasions when

Eisenhower "usually remained silent."[13] In Richard Neustadt's view, the system produced "the lowest common denominators of agreement" and did not allow "quarrels—and issues and details—[to be] pushed up to" the president.[14] Former Secretary of State Dean Acheson characterized the Eisenhower NSC procedures as "agreement by exhaustion" and beset by excessive willingness to compromise and a "plastering over" of differences.[15] Other observers characterized participants as reticent about expressing their views in front of the president and operating like a congressional committee in which votes were taken that Eisenhower was expected to follow.[16] Indeed, the problems perceived to affect Eisenhower's national security procedures sparked a congressional inquiry toward the end of his presidency. The inquiry was led by Senator Henry Jackson, a Democrat from Washington, and the conclusions of the Jackson subcommittee— largely critical in tone—were one of the factors that led Kennedy to dismantle the bulk of Eisenhower's formal machinery upon taking office in 1961.[17]

Eisenhower and his aides, however, took particular pride in the NSC staff system they devised. Managed by a special assistant who was part of the White House staff rather than a staff secretary who reported to the NSC (as had been the case under Truman), the system and its procedures were designed to sharpen NSC discussion and make it more effective. The NSC process, described by Eisenhower's first NSC assistant Robert Cutler (1953–55, 1957–58)[18] as the "policy hill," was deliberately designed to identify policy disagreements so that they could be resolved at higher levels and to monitor implementation of policy decisions.

One side of the hill was the Planning Board, which prepared drafts of the policy papers to be considered by the NSC. Composed largely of second-level officials of departments dealing with foreign affairs and chaired by the NSC special assistant, who was tied to no department, the Planning Board met approximately three times a week during Eisenhower's first term and twice weekly thereafter, often for three or four hours per session. Cutler reports that during his tenure as chair of the Planning Board, he conducted 504 meetings in three and three-quarters years. The deliberations of the Board, Cutler notes, were exceptionally productive: "This hard, intellectual, driving work taught the Board members always to seek for a better word, a more explicit phrase, a sharper set of alternatives, a more distinct expression of views and to bring out every inflection and side of an issue."[19] The operating rules of the board were democratic. According to S. Everett Gleason, who served on both the Truman and Eisenhower NSC staffs, "Any Planning Board member [is] free to speak to any issue which may arise whether or not this issue is within the precise sphere of his department's official responsibility or is presumed to be his area of expertise." Ralph Reid, the Bureau of the Budget's representative for a time on the board, recalls that, "according to the ground rules under which we operated, any member of the board was entitled to suggest an alternative, a turn of phrase, an alternative recommendation, an alternative conclusion." As a result, Reid notes, "essentially every NSC paper which came before the Council had in it a variety of alternatives, which represented imagination, innovation, and . . . occasionally, just sheer disbelief."[20] Disagreements among board members were generally presented in the final papers to the NSC, their "policy splits" often laid out in parallel columns.

The Planning Board was assisted in its work by the NSC support staff, headed by an executive secretary and composed of a cadre of foreign and national security policy experts. The NSC staff also identified gaps in national security policy and issues that were not receiving sufficient attention and brought these to the NSC's attention. As Phillip Henderson notes, the NSC staff during the Eisenhower era emulated the "neutral competence" that had been characteristic of the Bureau of the Budget: it provided professional expertise and "institutional memory."[21]

At the apex of the policy hill was the regular (generally weekly) meeting of the NSC. Eisenhower presided over an expanded council that included not only the statutory members (the president, the vice-president, secretaries of defense and state, and the director of the Office of Defense Mobilization) and the statutory advisers (chair of the Joint Chiefs of Staff, and the director of the CIA), but also the NSC special assistant, the NSC executive secretary and his deputy, the secretary of the treasury, the attorney general, the director of the budget bureau, the director of foreign aid, and other ad hoc participants that the president often chose to invite. "Those who sat at the Council table had a right to speak; none was denied a chance," Cutler recollects. "As long as the managing hand was mine, people whose responsibilities entitled them to be heard by the Council were to be heard. . . . Nothing was to be swept under the rug or compromised or glossed over." Cutler also notes that the NSC meetings were lively: "The President liked a good debate. . . . He wished to hear frank assertions of differing views, if they existed; for from such interchanges might emerge a resolution which reasonable men could support."[22]

Following discussion by the NSC and whatever presidential decisions were required, the Operations Coordinating Board (OCB) formed the other side of the policy hill. Generally, as Cutler points out, the mission of the OCB was "to coordinate, 'ride herd on,' and report to the Council on the performance by the departments and agencies charged with responsibility to carry out national security policies approved by the President."[23]

The operations of the Eisenhower "policy hill" belie the formalistic characterization Richard Tanner Johnson ascribed to them and the negative effects upon national security policy that contemporaries, such as Senator

Jackson and his subcommittee, believed they generated. The OCB was set up with the specific aim of assisting the NSC in planning proper implementation, which Johnson suggests formalistic systems tend to undervalue. Furthermore, both the NSC Planning Board and the OCB were composed of second-level department officials, but there is no evidence that covert bargaining of the sort Johnson predicts took place.

Recently declassified information about decision making in the Eisenhower White House—which was not available to Richard Tanner Johnson in 1974—also reveals meetings of the cabinet and, especially, the NSC in which there is lively give-and-take among the participants rather than, as Tanner Johnson holds, a discouragement of discussion and a reticence to voice conflicting views. Eisenhower, in particular, was an active member of NSC deliberations, not a passive participant as Tanner Johnson and others have suggested: he felt free to air his own views, sometimes vehemently, and his subordinates felt comfortable challenging the president. Participants also felt free to raise points not covered in the formal papers and presentations. Thus, although meetings of the NSC were preceded by extensive staff work, there is little evidence that the participants confined their discussion to options that had been outlined beforehand, nor is there evidence that extensive staff work had screened or otherwise distorted information. In December 1960, Eisenhower met with President-elect Kennedy as part of the transition to a new administration. Eisenhower especially stressed to Kennedy, he recalled, that:

> the National Security Council had become the most important weekly meeting of the government; that we normally worked from an agenda, but that any member could present his frank opinion on any subject, even on those that were not on the formal agenda. I made clear to him that conferences in the White House are not conducted as Committee meetings in the Legislative Branch. There is no voting by members and each group has only one purpose—to advise the president and to make him such recommendations as each member may deem applicable. I described to him how "splits" in Planning Board papers were handled.[24]

The expectations that Eisenhower put upon the roles and responsibilities of his advisers, especially those who held critical positions in his staff system, is another facet of his managerial style that enabled his formal procedures to work to his benefit. One of the explicit duties of the NSC special assistant during the Eisenhower years, for example, was to act as an "honest broker" (or managerial custodian, as it is also sometimes termed) to make sure that members of the NSC were alerted to substantive differences in the options under discussion and to the differing positions of the various parties involved in the staff work. Eisenhower's NSC assistants were also expected to make efforts in meetings of the NSC to ensure that relevant points of discussion and divergent views were fairly and fully aired and to keep the discussion on track.

Thus, although Eisenhower created a highly formal national security policy–making system, its particular features were intentionally engineered to alleviate the negative effects that formal staff systems are thought to engender: the president encouraged a generalist rather than a parochial perspective, the dual Planning Board and OCB structures emphasized a concern for policy implementation not just formulation, high-level departmental representation on each committee fostered communication about both sides of the policy process, differences in policy options were emphasized, and lively debate was usually the order of the day. Eisenhower was not a passive participant who entered into the process only to render the final decision, nor was he a prisoner of a staff system that papered over differences and narrowed his options.

Eisenhower was acutely aware of the strengths and weaknesses of the deliberative forums to which he turned for counsel. At one point in his memoirs, he reflected on the interpersonal dynamics among his top advisers, noting both the diversity of strong opinion he normally encountered as well as his realization of what could lurk behind seeming agreement:

> Such a thing as unanimity in a meeting of men of strong convictions working on complex problems is often an impossibility. Could anyone imagine George Humphrey, Foster Dulles, Ezra Taft Benson, Harold Stassen, Arthur Summerfield, Herbert Brownell, Lewis Strauss, C. D. Jackson, and James Mitchell reaching a unanimous conclusion. . . . They would not. I never asked or expected them to do so; in fact, had they presented a unanimous conclusion I would have suspected that some important part of the subject was being overlooked, or that my subordinate had failed to study the subject.[25]

Eisenhower's reflections especially indicate an awareness of the dangers of groups of advisers who are too willing to come to consensus. Yet this did not come to pass: given the caliber of persons he had appointed, disagreement rather than hasty agreement was the planned order of the day, and Eisenhower himself was on guard, as he clearly indicates in the last lines, against premature closure during policy deliberations.

Eisenhower was flexible in his organizational practices and procedures. As Joseph Pika observes, "Eisenhower was not so rigid as to believe there was 'one best way' for the presidency to operate. His record is one of continual adjustment and a surprising tolerance for features that might have been considered irrational by someone committed to designing the perfect system." Eisenhower often made changes in his staff system in light of his experience and the particular strengths and weaknesses of those charged with particular tasks. Following Cutler's departure as NSC assistant, for example, the Planning Board and OCB were placed under increasing control of the NSC assistant, with changes occurring as late as 1960. Furthermore, according to Pika, "the president proved surprisingly tolerant of practices that emerged from staff interaction rather than rational design." He also kept the staff and cabinet secretariats as separate organizational entities (even though their consolidation had been considered), "quite possibly due to Eisenhower's assessment of the staff's personal capabilities, an explanation suggested for why Sherman Adams had not been appointed staff coordinator in the first place," Pika notes.[26] Differences between the operations of the national security process and those of domestic policy were also notable. In foreign affairs, Eisenhower took an active role in determining the NSC's agenda, while in domestic policy, Adams was the key player in determining what fell on the cabinet's agenda. Nor did Eisenhower feel the need to establish, on the domestic side, the formal interdepartmental groups of the Planning Board and OCB, preferring instead the more ad hoc arrangements with departments that the cabinet secretariat would periodically create, depending on the policy issues at hand.

Overarching the way Eisenhower crafted particular systems and procedures, such as his NSC, was a general recognition of both the strengths and weaknesses that organization presents to a decision maker. In an oft-quoted passage from his memoirs, Eisenhower observes that

> organization cannot make a genius out of an incompetent; even less can it, of itself, make the decisions which are required to trigger the necessary action. On the other hand, disorganization can scarcely fail to result in inefficiency and can easily lead to disaster. Organization makes more efficient the gathering and analysis of facts, and the arranging of the findings of experts in logical fashion. Therefore organization helps the responsible individual make the necessary decision, and helps assure that it is satisfactorily carried out.[27]

In this passage, Eisenhower not only acknowledges that organization alone cannot guarantee genius, but in the last sentence he indicates that its chief purpose is to "help" the "responsible" decision maker to fulfill his tasks. For Eisenhower, this meant that in practice it was he, as president, who ultimately decided, not the NSC or Cutler or other White House aides. The importance of the relationship of White House organization to Eisenhower's actions as president cannot be underestimated. Formal procedures and bodies were established to aid the president in making and carrying out policy decisions, not to serve as a substitute for his own active and ultimately determinative participation. Eisenhower was careful to reserve final judgment for himself, often waiting to announce his decisions until NSC or cabinet meetings had ended. In direct response to critics who charged that the NSC determined policy by casting votes and that Eisenhower insisted on unanimous approval of the NSC before acting, Eisenhower emphatically stated that

I have never in my life, except on a court martial, seen a vote to decide a question. Some people have alleged that my way of making decisions—and this was actually quoted—was to insist on unanimity, and if there was a divided or minority opinion, I'd send all of them back and say "Get it unanimous." Then I'd adopt it. Well, I could not think of anything more ridiculous and more wide of the mark than this. All of my life is a refutation of such a theory, and why someone dreamed it up, I don't know.[28]

Eisenhower also did not rely exclusively on the formal systems and procedures he established. As noted earlier in this chapter, the characterization of his policy-making process as "formalistic" fails to recognize the informal channels of information and advice he also employed. As Andrew Goodpaster recollects, Eisenhower not only "controlled the flow of information," but "he had his outside sources, beyond the organized process, providing information to him."[29] These included a range of persons within his administration whose responsibilities might not bring them in direct contact with the policy discussion at hand but whose views Eisenhower solicited and appreciated, such as U.N. Ambassador Henry Cabot Lodge and NATO Commander General Alfred Greunther. Eisenhower maintained especially close contact with persons outside government, such as prominent media and corporate leaders and his former military associates, many of whom were regularly invited to the White House for monthly "stag dinners" and many of whom maintained extensive correspondence with the president. His brother Milton Eisenhower was an especially close and candid source of informal advice, and Milton arranged to spend several days a week at the White House while serving as president of Penn State and later the Johns Hopkins University.

Eisenhower also frequently convened ad hoc groups of consultants from both inside and outside his administration. The reforms he made in his national security procedures upon taking office, for example, were based in part on advice solicited from General George C. Marshall and a study committee headed by NSC adviser Cutler and including Harvard professor W. Y. Elliott, Paul Nitze, and Allen Dulles. Within a month of his inauguration, Eisenhower also called together a group of "wise men," who would act as consultants to the NSC. These included the president of Cornell University, the head of Pacific Gas and Electric, and a prominent scientist who had worked on the Manhattan Project. In 1955, Nelson Rockefeller headed an advisory group called the Quantico Panel, which was charged with developing recommendations for the upcoming Geneva summit conference. In 1957, Rowan Gaither of the Ford Foundation and the Rand Corporation headed a panel of outside advisers to take stock of the administration's strategic defense capabilities. According to Phillip Henderson, Eisenhower created these and other advisory groups "in order to provide a fresh perspective, untainted by bureaucratic perspectives," and they epitomized his "efforts to go beyond established governmental channels by deliberately seeking the opinions and expertise of prominent individuals outside the government setting.[30]

Finally, Eisenhower used the information and deliberations to which he was exposed, from whatever source, effectively. A number of observers have noted Eisenhower's well-developed cognitive abilities. Robert Bowie, for example, who served in the State Department and on the NSC staff during the Eisenhower years, has emphasized Eisenhower's inclination to render, as he phrases it, "net judgments," that is, an ability to pull diverse strands of argument together or to cut through them and get at the heart of the issue.[31] Andrew Goodpaster, Eisenhower's staff secretary, recalls that he "had a great ability to shift gears mentally and move from one subject to another."[32] In our study of Eisenhower's decision making in Indochina in 1954, Fred Greenstein and I found evidence of other cognitive attributes, such as a highly analytic cognitive style (explicit reasoning about means and ends), thinking in terms of the trade-offs presented by policy alternatives, an ability to consider long-term as well as short-run consequences, a propensity to weigh both political and military implications of the policy problems he faced, and an ability to perceive issues and phenomena as part of more comprehensive patterns.[33]

Nixon

Unlike Eisenhower's deliberate attempts to offset the weaknesses of a formal staff system, Richard Nixon's White House staff organization is almost a textbook case of a formalistic system that went awry. John Ehrlichman warns that it is risky to make generalizations about Nixon's staff system: "Anybody who takes a cross section of the Nixon administration White House and says it is this kind of creature will be right [but only] for a certain moment in time."[34] But certain trends are discernible. Nixon's White House staff bore the characteristics of a formal staff system without the compensatory mechanisms that Eisenhower had created. It generated many of the negative effects thought common to such an arrangement, and it seems particularly to have suffered from the characteristics of the institutional presidency that detract from effective use of the White House staff.

Nixon's eventual difficulties, however, could not have been readily predicted as his presidency commenced. He had, as vice-president, participated firsthand in the Eisenhower decision-making process, becoming the first vice president in history to be closely involved in the day-to-day workings of the presidency. Nixon's views on how he wanted his administration to operate, which began to emerge shortly after his election in 1968, also were in marked contrast to the kind of staff system that would soon develop. Two general themes emerged from reports from his aides assembled at the Pierre Hotel in New York City.[35] The first was that Nixon wanted to rely on his cabinet as a source of policy advice. The second concerned the White House staff. Nixon, the reports indicated, wanted to be surrounded by a small coterie of assistants, of equal rank, who would have direct access to him. Neither a strong cabinet nor a more collegial White House staff materialized for very long.

They did not come to fruition as Nixon planned because of the same problems he would encounter once a more formal staff system developed. Neither a strong role for the cabinet nor a small group of coequal staff assistants meshed with Nixon's personal style as a decision maker or his daily work habits. With respect to the cabinet, John Ehrlichman recollects that "we began to get these long soliloquies about how tough it was to be President surrounded by idiots. . . . He began taking back all of those delegations of absolute authority that had been rather frivolously handed out in transition time." Nixon evidently felt ill at ease in lengthy cabinet meetings and did not believe that prolonged discussion by his cabinet officers, often of matters outside their jurisdiction or expertise, was useful. Also, according to Ehrlichman, Nixon "didn't want meetings around the Cabinet table with passionate advocates pounding away at each other and at him and he cross-examining them. He was not comfortable with face to face contact."[36]

So, too, with the White House staff: Nixon disdained collegial deliberations, especially their tendency to generate lively if not adversarial modes of interaction. In domestic affairs, his initial impulse to turn to two very different-minded advisers—Daniel Patrick Moynihan, a liberal, and Arthur Burns, a conservative—proved especially at odds with his propensity to avoid being at the center of controversy in the physical presence of his advisers. According to John Ehrlichman, "Nixon quickly became disenchanted because both were pounding on him all the time." "Henry [Kissinger] never bothers me like this," Nixon told Ehrlichman. Henry always brings me nice neat papers on national security problems and I can check the boxes. Nobody badgers me and picks on me. But these two wild men on the domestic side are beating me up all the time."[37]

Nixon's response was to develop a Domestic Council that would replicate the operations at Kissinger's NSC. The council provided a formal system for defining and refining options for the president. A working group, composed of White House staffers, a member of the OMB, and representatives of relevant cabinet departments, would be constituted and chaired by one of Ehrlichman's deputies. Once a position paper was developed, it would be sent to cabinet members and the White House staff. Then,

Ehrlichman recounts, "I would hand it to the President for his weekend reading. He might carry two or three of these away on a weekend, fairly thick documents with a covering memo of anywhere from half a page to ten pages. The covering memo ended with a summary of what we thought his options were."[38]

The options the staff provided Nixon were rarely discussed in a collective setting, however. Instead, Nixon liked to work through these materials privately, retiring to his hide-away office in the Executive Office Building. Once there, he would lean back, according to Bryce Harlow, "on a kind of lounge and, half-supine, would read, study, make notes and prepare an outline of it all on his pad."[39] Although Nixon has not been the only president to do extensive reading and engage in solitary contemplation—both Kennedy and Carter did likewise—he was unique in that he did not like to complement this preferred work mode with other, more deliberative decision-making practices. Thus, while his mode of making decisions fit his personal needs, it did not ensure that the policy choices with which he was presented were exhaustive, well researched, and fairly presented or that his insights and judgments were well founded. There was no mechanism for the president to "walk around the problem" as he was mulling over his options, nor was there any forum where he justified and defended his views, both of which were present in the Eisenhower staff system.

Nixon at times deliberately sought to exclude staff members who he thought might disagree with his views from bringing their concerns to his attention. In a June 1969 memorandum, Nixon informed Ehrlichman that he intended in his press conferences to start "calling on those press men who are not anti rather than constantly calling on those who are trying to give us the hook." Nixon then instructed Ehrlichman that his two chief press aides, Herb Klein and Ron Ziegler, "will disagree with this. I don't want you to consult with them. This is my decision and I intend to follow it up."[40] On 2 March 1970, Nixon informed Haldeman that he wanted "to initiate a program [of White House recognition] for teachers, judges, policemen, and others who have taken a strong stand against demonstrators and other militants." "I do not want you to tell Garment or any of our liberal groups of this matter," Nixon added. "I know that Garment et al. would strenuously object. . . . I intend to follow through regardless of the consequences."[41]

At times, Nixon seemed to reach out for advice, on occasion to individuals outside his official family. On 24 November 1969, he informed Henry Kissinger that he would "like to have George Kennan come in for a talk. I have never met Kennan except casually and while I have often disagreed with him I do think it would be useful . . . when it could be fitted into the schedule." But Nixon's interest in meeting with Kennan seems not to have been motivated just by the need to hear out the foreign policy views of someone with whom he disagreed, but also for the public relations value of a White House visit by such a distinguished foreign policy expert: "I am sure," Nixon added, "that he would get it around in the proper circles that we were talking to people, other than those in the bureaucracy."[42] In a similar vein, on 30 November 1970, Nixon instructed Haldeman, "Before Moynihan leaves would you try to get him pinned down on that list of intellectuals he believes we should be talking to." But again Nixon emphasized the public relations value of such activity: "As a matter of fact, once he is gone he can cultivate a few of these people."[43] "Cultivation" of public figures must have been on Nixon's mind. That same day he also instructed Haldeman to make sure that "our celebrity list" for the upcoming election included old Hollywood stars as well as new ones: "When we look at some of those who might go with us now, it is a pretty imposing list: Ruby Keeler, Gloria Swanson, Joan Crawford, Ginger Rogers, Bette Davis. Consequently, let's be sure . . . that we get some of them lined up as well as the new ones."[44]

Nixon's heavy reliance on written memoranda rather than verbal deliberation or some mix of both also may have worked to his disadvantage. As Ehrlichman recalls, Kissinger once told him that memoranda to Nixon could be structured in such a way as to bias the outcome. Nixon usually selected option two among the three options Kissinger would outline for him: "You people are very foolish to give him more than three options. You must always arrange it so that the one you favor is the second one," Kissinger reportedly told Ehrlichman.[45]

Although Kissinger's assertion that Nixon regularly favored option two cannot be definitively determined, it is clear that Nixon desired a system in which policy options were outlined for him and in which he could simply check off the box next to the option he preferred: memoranda abound in the Nixon archives that follow such a format, often with a simple checkmark next to Nixon's preference and no further comment. Furthermore, for Nixon a checkmark might signal the end of his need to attend to a policy matter. After receiving a memorandum from Ken Cole listing a range of actions requiring presidential attention, Nixon sent the memo back with a scrawled order that with regard to lists of "presidential action requests" from White House staff members, "1. Where I have checked [checkmark in original] no further report to me is needed; 2. Where I have ?—I want a report."[46]

Nixon's reliance on written memoranda may also have led him to approve unwittingly policy positions he disagreed with. In a 28 December 1972 memorandum to John Ehrlichman and Ken Cole, Nixon complained that a recent policy paper on welfare reform contained, in his words, "the tired old reference to subsidizing the 'working poor.' " Nixon then instructed his aides that "in the future . . . I want to be sure that where such papers are sent in to me items like this are heavily flagged so that when I read them hurriedly I will not scan over them and all of a sudden find that I am approving something with which I have expressed total disagreement in the past."[47]

Ironically, Nixon's attempts to fit his staff structure to his personal needs led to the creation of a powerful staff system that would reduce his control over White House policy making, contributing no doubt to the Watergate debacle. The vacuum that was created in his initial attempt to have a system of five coequal staff assistants led to the emergence of H. R. Haldeman as a powerful chief of staff. Haldeman was a tough taskmaster, but there is little evidence that he fostered his own political agenda. In that sense, his relative lack of political experience on the Washington scene worked to Nixon's advantage (although his lack of substantive policy expertise may have prevented him from recognizing problems in the information and advice the staff gave Nixon). Haldeman also acted as a brake on Nixon's rasher actions and his not infrequent attempts to lash out at his opponents. As Leonard Garment, another top Nixon aide, recalls, "When the President began to have an excessive reaction to something or to propose doing things that shouldn't be done, it was Haldeman's job, which he performed with diligence, to find ways to say no, to let the paper slide, or to make sure it didn't happen."[48]

The problem that arose in Nixon's relationship with Haldeman, and also with his successor Alexander Haig, was that Nixon was able to use his well-oiled staff machinery to isolate himself from contact. According to Ehrlichman, "We've got the reputation—some terrible books have been written about this—of building a wall around the President." But as Ehrlichman notes, this was less a function of the staff seeking to maintain exclusive access to Nixon than of Nixon using Haldeman and Ehrlichman to keep others away: "The fact is that *he* was down there under his desk saying 'I don't want to see those fellows,' and we were trying to pull him out." Similarly, Haldeman recalls that "there was screening of who saw the President, but the President himself did the screening. I just carried it out. It worked out well because I took the blame for those decisions, and this was better than the President taking the blame."[49]

Nixon was also isolated from members of his staff. As former Nixon staff aide and under secretary of the army Kenneth BeLieu concludes, Nixon "had great abilities but didn't always seem to know how to bridge a gap between his own staff and the agencies, which were the horses that had to pull the wagon. That was one of his fundamental weaknesses. He couldn't or didn't want to talk to a staff member, so the message often didn't get through." Ehrlichman, for example, was required to act as a buffer between the president and those he sought to avoid. During the early days of the administration, as the tension between Moynihan and Burns increased, Nixon delegated Ehrlichman the task of mediating between them and resolving their differences before they reached the president. Nixon also disliked his budget director, Robert Mayo; but rather than firing Mayo, Nixon had him report through Ehrlichman, rather than directly to the president.[50]

Nixon sometimes thought out loud about policy issues before a passive audience of one staff member. Ehrlichman describes it as "chewing the cud": "Richard Nixon was like a cow. He would chew his cud over and over on a subject and turn it over and chew some more, and turn it over and chew it some more. So if you could enlist some junior staff man for that process, it was a whole lot better than to have your whole day soaked up with those long monologues." During the period in Nixon's first term as the courts considered the merits of busing as a mode of desegregation, Ehrlichman designated one of his aides, Ed Morgan, to deal with the president on the administration's policy and later reported, "I was delighted to have someone like Ed designated because if Nixon didn't chew on him he was going to chew on me." "It was the way his mind worked," Ehrlichman observes. It was "a unilateral [exchange]. Probably you'd grunt at the right times or make some comment or other."[51]

Nixon's conception of what policy areas required close presidential attention and what could be delegated to his staff or others in the executive branch not only contributed to the importance—as policy makers, not just process managers or honest brokers—of Ehrlichman in domestic affairs and Kissinger in foreign affairs but compounded Nixon's isolation from his staff. In March 1970, in a lengthy, single-spaced memorandum to Haldeman, Ehrlichman, and Kissinger, Nixon clearly set out what he felt he should attend to and what should be delegated to his assistants. In foreign affairs, he instructed Kissinger that the only policy areas he wanted brought to his attention were East-West relations, policy toward the Soviet Union and China, policy toward Eastern Europe but only where it significantly affected East-West relations, and policy toward Western Europe but only where NATO and major countries were involved. As for the rest of the world, Kissinger was told to "farm out as much of the decision-making" as possible. In domestic affairs, Nixon listed only three areas: crime, school integration, and economic matters, the latter only where recession or inflation were involved. "I do not want to be bothered with international monetary matters," he told Ehrlichman. "Problems should be farmed out." On environmental policy, Nixon recognized its importance, but "I don't want to be bothered with details. Just see that the job is done." On Nixon's New Federalism initiative: "Our team is adequate to carry out our policies and

I am going to count on them to do so without submitting to me the day-to-day decisions. . . . I am only interested when we make a major breakthrough or have a major failure. Otherwise don't bother me." In the fields of education, housing, health, transportation, post office affairs, agriculture and labor, "I want lead men, either within the Administration or within the Department, to assume responsibility. . . . They are not the kind of matters which should require my attention."[52]

Nixon recognized, arguably correctly, that presidents cannot have their hands in all affairs that pass through the executive branch or even the White House. But his simple and at times wholesale delegation of decision-making authority to Ehrlichman and Kissinger, or to those they deemed appropriate for the job, created a powerful staff with which Nixon chose to have little contact; "farm it out" and "don't bother me" were his watchwords. No mechanisms of presidential oversight were part of Nixon's concerns, no procedures were established to ensure that those entrusted with authority came to the right decisions, nor was Nixon concerned with establishing informal means to encourage teamwork and other strategies, such as those that had preoccupied Eisenhower, that aimed to make the staff work effectively.

Nixon's practice of delegation may have exacerbated the isolation his ways of working encouraged. In the memorandum, not only did Nixon reserve only the most important policy areas for presidential attention, but he expected Ehrlichman and Kissinger to follow his lead. "While this applies primarily to my time," Nixon wrote, "I want Ehrlichman and Kissinger to apply the same rules in allocating their time." And in those areas of foreign policy that Nixon felt were unimportant, he explicitly told Kissinger that "he should farm that subject out to a member of his staff, but he himself should not bother with it. I want him to concentrate just as hard as I will be concentrating on these . . . major policy issues." Nixon thus not only did not want to be bothered by his staff on some issues but also felt that Ehrlichman and Kissinger should likewise not be burdened.

Nixon's views on delegation directly validate the criticisms made of formalistic staff systems. At the end of the memo, Nixon states, "A recommendation should be made and responsibility given at other levels and I will then act without getting involved at lower levels of the discussion," a practice that accords with the criticism that decision makers at the top of formal systems are not exposed to the controversies at the bottom and simply passively ratify decisions. Richard Tanner Johnson's view that Eisenhower used his staff system as a "shield" that would provide him with "recommendations to ratify"[53] and Neustadt's view that Eisenhower's system did not allow "quarrels—and issues and details—[to be] pushed up to him"[54] seem apt characterizations not of Eisenhower's practices but of the kind of staff system Nixon set out in his memorandum.

At times Nixon recognized that his staff system was not performing effectively and attempted to exercise control over it. But Nixon's practice was simply to issue orders, often in one- or two-sentence memoranda written as he perused staff papers during the evening or in his solitary hours during the day in his hideaway office. These memos have almost a military quality: the general, alone in his quarters and away from the battlefield, issuing orders to his lieutenants in the field. For example, in a memorandum to John Ehrlichman dated 23 September 1969, Nixon was concerned that "with regard to our staff activities on consumerism and the environment . . . we are not grasping and maintaining the initiative as well as we might." Nixon's solution was to direct Ehrlichman to find "a Moynihan type, not at the top of the heap, but somewhere in each group, who will constantly needle and come up with new ideas." "As a matter of fact," Nixon continued, "using Moynihan in environmental problems from time to time is worth considering."[55] Nixon's approach to the problem he perceived is revealing. He recognized the need for initiative and the type of person he thought capable of carrying out the task. But there is little beyond that: no reflection on why the staff was not performing effectively, just a belief that putting Moynihan or a Moynihan surrogate in place would resolve the problem. It is also interesting to note that Nixon's attempts at remedy take the form of a short, one-paragraph memo dictated to Ehrlichman, with no further analysis or evidence of follow-up. Again the military analogy may be apt: the commander perceives a weakness along the battle line, and his solution is to deploy a new field officer. Yet military problems are not resolved by simply putting a new lieutenant in place, and resolving policy problems is more complex than responding to military weakness.

This pattern of responding to a problem by issuing a simple order to a top aide without extensive reflection or further attention pervades Nixon's memoranda. For example in a memo to John Ehrlichman on 17 June 1969, Nixon was dissatisfied with the information he was receiving on homicide statistics in the District of Columbia. In a one sentence memo to Ehrlichman Nixon emphatically told his assistant, "We *must* have some good statistics on crime by Dec. 31, keep on top of this and see that the bureaucrats don't dodge the issue."[56] The memo also reveals a related facet of Nixon's attempts to assert managerial control: his distrust of the bureaucracy and his attempts to circumvent it by relying on orders to his top assistants.

On 17 June 1969, Nixon responded to a policy paper from Tom Huston that Arthur Burns had forwarded to him. The paper concerned IRS audits of "left-wing" organizations. Nixon's response was: "Arthur: 1. Good

2. But I want *action* have Huston follow up *hard* on this." Nixon's short response to what might be a questionable if not illegal activity reveals the dangers of relying on abbreviated orders to staff members, based on decisions made during solitary reflection. In the memo, Nixon does add, in parenthesis and almost as an afterthought, that "you [Burns] of course should supervise it."[57]

What actions Nixon's top aides took in response to his "orders" is unclear. In June 1969, Nixon sent a memo to Haldeman in which he complained, "I have an uneasy feeling that many of the items that I send out for action are disregarded when any staff member just reaches a conclusion that it is unreasonable or unattainable. . . . I want to know when that kind of decision is made." Nixon then ordered Haldeman "to keep a check list of everything I order and I want you to indicate what action has been taken (and I want no long memoranda indicating why it can't be taken) and particularly I want to know when the action that I have ordered has *not* been taken."[58] For the remainder of 1969 and into 1970, John Brown of Haldeman's staff issued weekly action reports, often short, that made their way back to Nixon. At some point in 1970, Haldeman himself took on this task, issuing individual action reports in response to Nixon's commands. But many of Nixon's requests simply fell through the cracks. As Haldeman admitted at a 1986 conference of former chiefs of staff, it was his practice simply to ignore or otherwise stonewall some of Nixon's more extreme orders.[59]

It is also interesting to note that Nixon's procedures for insuring implementation of his orders and decisions, a matter that clearly caught his concern, seem crude by comparison with Eisenhower's Operations Coordinating Board or Cabinet Secretariat. In a 10 March 1970 memorandum to Haldeman marked "High Priority," Nixon instructed Haldeman, "I do not want to see reports of action on various orders that I may send. I do, however, want to see reports where orders are not carried out for one reason or another, or are delayed unreasonably." Even then, Nixon added, "I want these memorandums covering such items to come to me weekly, and to be quite precise and limited."[60] Beyond this, there is little attention on Nixon's part to establishing procedures to assure the carrying out of what at least to him were important presidential directives, and the procedures that were in place were surprisingly informal, depending on the predilections of Brown or, later, Haldeman. It is also not clear what actions were taken or procedures put in place for monitoring the president's directives to John Ehrlichman or other staff members besides Haldeman who received Nixon's written dicta. Indeed, there is some evidence that Nixon never even read the memoranda that were sent to his lieutenants; generally his practice was to dictate into a recording machine, from which his secretaries would then transcribe.[61]

Through a Managerial Lens: Patterns of Collegial Management

Kennedy

John F. Kennedy's experience with his staff system offers useful lessons for presidents who choose to operate in a more informal, collegial setting. Unlike the weekly meetings of the cabinet that were a regular feature of the Eisenhower presidency, Kennedy convened his cabinet usually only once a month and was reputed to be bored by their lengthy proceedings (he regarded them as "pretense en masse" according to Fred Dutton, his liaison to the cabinet). Agendas, usually short, were prepared by a staff member and forwarded to Kennedy for approval, but no records of action were kept. Large staff meetings were also avoided; as one staff aide recalls: "He never had a staff meeting all the time I was in the White House. I'm told he never had one all the time he was President. . . . He just didn't believe in them. . . . There was something about *large* group meetings that bothered Kennedy."[62] Kennedy preferred individual contact—sometimes small groups were convened—with his staff aides or, on occasion, departmental representatives, and would parcel out assignments and receive reports. In such a setting Kennedy was at his best:

> Every day there were at least three or four. . . . In these he'd come to the point; he'd quite informally (with a sentence or two at most) ask whoever was the principal participant to say what the problem was, what were they [prepared] to do. . . . By the end of the presentation he had sized up pretty well what he wanted. He might ask shotgun questions; he might not. At the end he'd give instructions, and that was about it. It was in and out very fast.[63]

Kennedy prodigiously consumed enormous amounts of information provided by his staff or by cabinet officials.[64] Upon taking office, Kennedy requested that each cabinet member provide him with a brief synopsis of his or her activities and anything else that might merit presidential attention. After receiving the first batch, a pile of some sixty or seventy pages according to Fred Dutton, his liaison to the cabinet, he had them summarized down "to five or six pages." Kennedy then read these and would scrawl instructions (not unlike Nixon) in the margin: "I want more information from Goldberg" or "Tell him I don't want that." According to Dutton "it was very crisp, to the point, no nonsense stuff." But unlike Nixon, on more important matters, Dutton recalls, "he'd obviously get on the phone or [convene] a face to face meeting."[65] Kennedy also maintained an extensive network of contacts with persons who were outside his official circle of top advisers. As Bundy once told Sorensen, "The President relies heavily on others for all sorts of follow-up intercommunication, and preparation and recommendation. . . . But he is still probably the most personal President of modern times—doing more himself. You know the millions of examples."[66]

In foreign and national security policy, the differences from his predecessor were even more striking. Shortly after taking office, Kennedy dismantled most of the national security staff that had existed under Eisenhower. His abandonment of formal procedures may have been unwise, but his experience with the collegial Ex-Com (his executive committee of top foreign policy advisers) offers lessons about how presidents can work effectively with informal patterns of advice seeking and giving.

Kennedy got off to a rocky start. His penchant for more fluid procedures led him initially to favor ad hoc task forces for dealing with international problems and crises. Some of these efforts were productive—task forces on NATO (led by former Secretary of State Dean Acheson) and Latin America (led by Adolf Berle). But as McGeorge Bundy pointed out in a 4 April 1961 memo to Kennedy, "Over and over since January 20th we have talked of getting 'task forces with individual responsible leaders' here in Washington for crisis situations." But what we got for Laos, the Congo, and Cuba were "working groups with nobody in particular in charge. . . . we did not get clearly focused responsibility." The result, according to Bundy, was that "it has repeatedly been necessary to bring even small problems to you and still smaller ones to the White House staff, while more than once the ball has been dropped simply because no one person felt a continuing clear responsibility."[67]

The issue came to a head almost immediately. That same month, April 1961, Kennedy's advisers performed poorly, leading him into an ill-conceived, poorly planned, hastily decided, and badly executed invasion of Cuba by Cuban exiles supported by the United States—the Bay of Pigs disaster. Although a number of factors undoubtedly affected the performance of Kennedy and his advisers—the inexperience of a new team in the first months of Kennedy's presidency, too much attention to the political consequences of appearing weak on Cuba, and excessive secrecy—Kennedy's collegial decision-making process was an undoubtedly important, if not primary, cause of failure. In Theodore Sorensen's view, Kennedy's national security process was at fault. The formally organized procedures of the Eisenhower administration were largely gone, but Kennedy had yet to replace them with an effective alternative: "The new administration had not yet fully organized itself for crisis planning." In particular, Sorensen argues, Kennedy "had not yet geared the decision-making process to fulfill his own needs, to isolate the points of no return, to make certain he was fully informed before they passed, and to prevent preshaped alternatives from being presented to him too late to start anew."[68]

Part of Kennedy's difficulties stemmed from the absence of adequate procedures for review and discussion of the proposed operation. According to Maxwell Taylor, meetings "were held without a prepared agenda." "No record was kept of meetings," Taylor also noted. "Hence there was always doubt in the minds of participants in the planning as to where the plan stood at any given moment."[69] In meetings with the president, Sorensen recalls, "only the CIA and the Joint Chiefs had an opportunity to study and ponder the details of the plan. . . . Memoranda of operation were distributed at the beginning of each session and collected at the end, making virtually impossible any systematic criticism or alternatives."[70]

Kennedy's team was also beset by inadequate definitions by the participants of their respective roles and contributions to the deliberative process. For Taylor, "the leaders of this operation were very anxious to carry it through and to obtain approval; [they] accepted restrictions on their operations without explaining their implications clearly to the President and the senior officials."[71] In his testimony to Taylor's committee, McGeorge Bundy concluded that "military planners . . . became advocates rather than impartial evaluators of the problem." "Moreover," Bundy continued, "many people were reticent in their representations to the President."[72]

As Bundy's last comments indicate, one of the most important factors contributing to the failure of the decision process was the dynamics among Kennedy's small decision-making group. This accords with Irving Janis's conclusion that the Bay of Pigs debacle was a "perfect failure." The episode, according to Janis, exemplifies the anomaly that in a number of cases where important policy decisions were made by participants who were otherwise highly intelligent, experienced, and politically sophisticated, actions were taken that should have been known to be self-defeating.[73] Janis attributes this failure to a process he calls "groupthink," a largely unconscious "concurrence-seeking" tendency on the part of members of a cohesive group to engage in uncritical thinking, thus reaching premature and overly optimistic closure on policies.

Even more than Kennedy's Bay of Pigs experience reveals the tendency of collegial groups to degenerate into groupthink, it shows how Kennedy, in the aftermath, sought to remedy the defects in his decision making. Kennedy was shaken by the experience. But rather than punish or blame those who had served him poorly, he took a more constructive course: he commissioned a study group, led by Maxwell Taylor, to find out what had gone wrong. According to Taylor, Kennedy "emphasized that he was not angry at anyone, that he did not have in mind punishing anyone, but he did feel it was essential to know the causes of failure."[74]

Kennedy gave Taylor and his group a free hand, and on the basis of their findings and his own assessment of what had gone wrong, he reorganized his decision-making procedures and explored the faults in his own leadership style. In particular, Kennedy realized that, although he valued the small-group decision-making structure, changes in its dynamics were necessary. He brought persons whose views he trusted and who had served with him for many years (especially Theodore Sorensen and his brother Robert Kennedy) more directly into his decision making; their personal ties to Kennedy made them less susceptible to groupthink. Kennedy put his own people in charge of intelligence and the military; shortly after the Bay of Pigs, Allen Dulles and Richard Bissell were replaced in the CIA, and General Maxwell Taylor became Kennedy's personal military adviser and then chairman of the Joint Chiefs of Staff. Kennedy also made his most trusted advisers— Sorensen, Robert Kennedy, and McGeorge Bundy—watchdogs over the process, much along the lines of McGeorge Bundy's assessment that the president needed "impartial evaluators," not just policy advocates.

The changes proved beneficial while enabling Kennedy to retain a collegial decision-making system. By the time of the Cuban missile crisis in October 1962, Kennedy and his advisers had become an effective decision-making group. Information was readily at hand, the assumptions and implications of policy options were probed, pressures that could lead to a false group consensus were avoided, and Kennedy deliberately did not disclose his own policy preferences—sometimes even absenting himself from meetings—in order to facilitate candid discussion and head off a premature decision.

Kennedy and his advisers also scrutinized the staff procedures that encompass particular decisions, whether momentous, such as the Bay of Pigs episode or the Cuban missile crisis, or mundane. In the early months of his presidency, Kennedy was beset by the predictable consequences of informal, collegial procedures: a heavy burden on his time and attention, disorganization in staff work, and ineffective use of his advisers. Kennedy's own memoranda to members of his staff during this period show a president essentially acting as his own chief of staff, at times "micro-managing" the White House paper flow and parceling out assignments to his aides. Kennedy generally dictated his instructions to Mrs. Lincoln, his secretary, who would send them out as memoranda from the president. The following set of instructions from 5 July 1961 is typical and illustrates Kennedy's close personal involvement in the policy process and politics of his administration:

1. Remind me to congratulate [Senator] Frank Church for his speech.

2. Check on what we are doing on the Moroccan air bases.

3. Arrange for other speeches like Church's to be given on various elements of the Democratic party's program and then circulate them, especially Latin America.

4. Prepare a memorandum for the Members of Congress and Democrats every place [sic] on the budget allocations and expenditures of money. [Treasury Secretary] Doug Dillon has some figures. The job should be entrusted to [Budget Director] Dave Bell, showing Eisenhower deficit in 1960.

5. Write a letter to Adlai Stevenson thanking him for his report to me. Also Ambassador Elias Briggs. Have Dick Goodwin read the report. Also Ambassador Woodward when he comes back. Tell Dick Goodwin to arrange for Berle to present his report this week before Woodward goes up to the Senate for confirmation.

6. Have Ralph Dungan tell me what has happened to McKinney's nomination for Switzerland. Has it been approved by the Senate yet?

7. Speak to Bobby about Senator Kerr's judgeship.

8. Have Max Taylor look over the June 30th memorandum from Walt Rostow on the present situation on Southeast Asia. Would like to have his reaction.

9. Remind me when I see the Secretary of State to discuss the exchange.

10. Check with [Under Secretary of State] Bowles and [United States Information Agency Director] Murrow on the proposed Adlai's speech [sic] and Bundy on the test bans here in Washington.

11. Remind me to speak to Dick Goodwin about Montevideo report which is in my files. Want him to go to work on it.

12. In response to the Secretary's message on the Guinea program, is there any chance we could finance the dam in Guinea if we omitted all the other elements of our aid program?[75]

These instructions and other memos and notes to staff members show Kennedy clearly on top of the situation—issuing instructions, calling for relevant information, and demanding timely briefings. Yet Kennedy also operated within a staff network that made it incumbent on him to monitor closely the policy-making process of his White House and involve himself in details of the policy process that other presidents normally delegate to a chief of staff. It is difficult to determine what aspects of this role Kennedy failed to perform effectively: evidence of problems in the policy process occur within a context of presidential awareness and response, not omission or neglect.[76] But Kennedy's memos at times show his concerns about weaknesses in his policy processes and procedures, especially failures to inform him fully about matters requiring his attention. For example, in a memo to Bundy on the question of differences in how aid was provided to India and Pakistan, Kennedy wrote, "As I understand it some of the economic aid we give to India is used to purchase military equipment while we give the military equipment directly to Pakistan," and added, "Perhaps someone who is informed about all of this could talk with me sometime."[77] On the question of mainland China's admission to the United Nations, then under consideration, Kennedy asked Bundy to get an up-to-date report on the issue. He then placed before Bundy a number of queries and comments: "What is the latest word from Stevenson? Do we have a strategy? Is it going to be successful? We can't permit ourselves to get beaten. If we are not going to be able to win it on this basis we better think of another one. Would you speak to me about this?"[78]

Kennedy's missives to Bundy also show his attempts to make sure that matters he wished to decide were brought before him for resolution. In a 4 February 1961 memo, Kennedy told Bundy that "it is my understanding that there is a sharp difference of opinion between the defense [department and] CIA on what we should do about Cuba and Berle. Can you find out if the differences of view have been settled, or if they continue. I believe we should have an opportunity to have them placed before me and have them argued out again. Would you let me know right away on this?"[79] The next day, Kennedy again raised the matter of policy toward Cuba with Bundy: "Has the policy for Cuba been coordinated between Defense, CIA (Bissell) and Man[n] and Berle? Have we determined what we are going to do about Cuba? What approaches are we going to make to Latin American governments on the matter? If there is a difference of opinion between the agencies I think they should be brought to my attention."[80]

Kennedy also exhibited pique if not frustration at his staff's performance. For example, on 14 April 1961, he sent the following memo to Bundy:

1. I believe that you, General Taylor and Walt Rostow were all dissatisfied with our organizational set up on Southeast Asia.

2. An example of this is a military mission going to Southeast [Asia], the purpose of which is rather vague in our minds.

3. Should we not propose to the Secretary of State a more precise organizational set up with specific missions to do the kind of job that was done by Dean Acheson?

4. Who should we get to do it?[81]

On some occasions Kennedy voiced his concerns sharply: "I want a report from the State Department. I asked Secretary Rusk about this on [sic] whose idea it was for me to send letters to the Middle Eastern Arab leaders. The reaction has been so sour I would like to know whose idea it was, what they hoped to accomplish and what they think we have now accomplished."[82]

Kennedy was not the only member of his official family to perceive difficulties in the informal procedures that had developed in the early months of his administration. On 16 May 1961, McGeorge Bundy in a memo frankly told the president, "We need some help from you so that we can serve you better." Although Bundy conceded that the White House had become "a center of energy," "we do have a problem of management; centrally it is [a] problem of your use of time and your use of staff. You have revived the government, which is an enormous gain, but in the process you have over-strained your own calendar, limited your chances for thought, and used your staff incompletely. You are altogether too valuable to go [on] in this way; with a very modest change in your methods you can double your own effec-tiveness and cut the strain in half."

Bundy then proposed three correctives, each of which sought to bring more order if not formality to Kennedy's procedures. First, Kennedy needed a "real and regular time each day for national security discussion and ac-tion." For the past several weeks, Bundy noted, "I have succeeded in catch-ing you on three mornings, for a total of 8 minutes. . . . Moreover, 6 of the 8 minutes were given not to what I had for you but for what you had for me from [journalists] Marguerite Higgins, David Lawrence, Scotty Reston, and others." "You must not stop reading the papers," Bundy added, but regularly scheduled opportunities for more substantive discussion of foreign affairs were needed: "After lunch? Tea? You name it. But you have to mean it, and it really has to be every day." In Bundy's view, a more fixed schedule of meetings

> can save you a lot of time . . . [and] can give your staff a coordinated sense of what you want and it can give everyone who needs it a time of day when they can reach you through an easy channel. It also gives you a way of keeping track of your own tremendous flow of ideas. Right now it is so hard to get to you with anything not urgent and immediate that about half of the papers and reports that you personally ask for are never shown to you. . . . If we put a little staff work on these and keep in close touch, we can be sure that *all* your questions are answered.

Second, Bundy told Kennedy that he must stick to his schedule. And third, "there is staffwork. . . . We need to be sure we are doing what you want." Better briefings on those with whom Kennedy had appointments were needed, but most of all: "You are entitled to feel confident that (a) there is no part of government in the national security area that is not watched over closely by someone from your own staff, and (b) there is no major problem of policy that is not out where you can see it and give a proper stimulus to those who should be attacking it." "With your stimulus and lead-ership," Bundy concluded, "we'll do the job."[83]

Kennedy's procedures began to change. Bundy met more frequently with the president, and he convened morning staff meetings of top foreign policy advisers.[84] In a 22 June 1961 memorandum to the president, Bundy noted some of these changes and their positive contribution to national security procedures. More were suggested: some, such as the appointment of a senior military adviser (a post that Maxwell Taylor would soon occupy[85]), Kennedy accepted; others, such as more frequent meetings of the NSC, he chose not to adopt. Bundy also advised the president that better staff work should precede meetings of the NSC. Although he did not advocate a return to the Planning Board system of the Eisenhower years, a more formal system of staff analysis was needed: "Against its schedules there should be a more clearly defined pattern for preparation for new policy papers, and reporting on crisis areas. . . . Much could be ordered that is now somewhat haphazard." Interdepartmental coordination on the other side of the "policy hill" should be "carefully, but sparingly, increased." Eisenhower's OCB went too far, in Bundy's view, "but in the first few months we have probably gone too far the other way." Although the White House should not replace departments or specially constituted task forces as "the agency of daily action," "I am proposing . . . weekly meetings to ensure that somewhat more formal processes are followed."[86]

Although Bundy had not abandoned Kennedy's emphasis on collegial procedures, he clearly saw the need to add formal mechanisms to bolster their effectiveness. This fine-tuning of the national security system continued throughout Kennedy's presidency. Kennedy's creation of an Executive Committee of the National Security Council [Ex-Com] to counsel him during the Cuban missile crisis is the best known of these efforts. Although both Kennedy and Bundy had acknowledged the need for more meetings of the NSC to be held on a regular basis so that proper staff work could be obtained, it was not until the missile crisis and the creation of the Ex-Com that Kennedy devised a deliberative forum in which he felt comfortable.[87] Kennedy held only twelve meetings of the NSC in all of 1962[88] and only five in 1963,[89] but forty-two meetings of the Ex-Com were convened from 23 October 1962 through 29 March 1963, a five-month period. Subcommittees of the Ex-Com were also established to deal with particular policy problems that developed after the resolution of the Cuban crisis and to handle advanced planning and coordination.[90]

Other changes were made as well. One of the most interesting developments came to fruition in 1963: a Standing Committee of the NSC. Bundy's concerns in his 22 June 1961 memo for more interdepartmental coordination had led to the creation in January 1962 of a standing group of largely second-level White House and departmental officials, whose functions would be to "organize and monitor the work of the National Security Council and to take up such other matters as may be presented to the Group by the members [of the NSC]."[91] But it was not until the aftermath of the Cuban missile crisis in October 1962, when Kennedy realized the advantages of some type of modified National Security Council apparatus and developed a national security advisory mechanism that he felt was workable, that concerted attention was paid to the development of policy planning and coordination below the level of the major members of the NSC and as a backdrop to the administration's national security deliberations.

In a 2 April 1963 memorandum, Bundy told Kennedy, "As you know, there has been considerable discussion in recent months of the need for strengthening interdepartmental planning and coordination on major national security issues." A first step had been taken during the Cuban missile crisis with the creation of the Ex-Com, which, in Bundy's view, was "a good instrument for major interdepartmental decision" but "not so good for lesser matters of coordination." Bundy noted that "it has not proved effective at all, except during the extraordinary week of October 16–22, in the process of forward planning."

Bundy's solution was to propose a "plans and operations" committee. The committee would be parallel in membership to the NSC and at a senior level, but without the president and vice president and the two major cabinet officers with responsibilities in the area of foreign and national security policy: the secretaries of state and defense (their deputies would attend in their place). Bundy had in mind a committee that would combine the functions of the Eisenhower Planning Board and OCB, but without an extensive staff of its own.[92] In his memo, Bundy especially emphasized characteristics of the proposed group that were crucial to its effective operation and that, for our purposes, illustrate an understanding of some of the weaknesses to which small groups are prone. He advised against including the two cabinet-level members because "neither . . . can speak in committee without engaging the whole weight of a great advisory department." As to the other members of the group, Bundy advised that they "should attend as individuals and not as representatives of agencies." "If a man cannot come," Bundy added, "no one automatically comes in his place."[93] On 15 April 1963, Kennedy approved the creation of what was now the Standing Committee of the NSC, and its first meeting was held the next day.[94]

Although the remaining months of Kennedy's presidency provide too little time to assess the effectiveness of the national security procedures that had been put in place, it is clear that by the time of his death, on 22 November 1963, Kennedy and his staff had developed, albeit slowly and piecemeal, policy-making procedures that (1) were designed to avoid some of the pitfalls of informal, collegial mechanisms that they had initially experienced, (2) introduced some measure of formal structure and routine, but (3) retained Kennedy's desire to avoid an overly formalized system. Whether a more formal staff system might have served Kennedy better cannot be determined, but within the parameters he set, concerns were raised and procedures established to make a collegial staff system work more effectively. The "organizational learning" that took place during his brief tenure as president was in marked contrast to the experience and track record of his successor.

Johnson

Lyndon Johnson's organization and management of the White House staff system paralleled Kennedy's, but without attention to remedying the problems that routinely crop up in collegial settings. Johnson's decisions about American policy in Vietnam during 1965 illustrate the Johnson process in operation and reveal some of its shortcomings. In January 1965, there were approximately 23,000 American military advisory personnel in South Vietnam. By the end of July 1965 Johnson had authorized deployment of some 200,000 troops to Vietnam, leaving open the possibility that more might come: "I have asked the Commanding General, William Westmoreland, what more he needs to meet this mounting aggression. He has told me. He will meet his needs."[95] However, the sequence of successive commitments—retaliatory bombing, sustained bombing, and the use of ground troops—that led up to Johnson's announcement of an open-ended American commitment in Vietnam was marked by numerous problems in the operation of the president's White House and advisory systems.

The changes in national security policy making that Kennedy had made on taking office in 1961 hampered his foreign policy making, and continued to do so under Johnson. Johnson convened the NSC infrequently, using it mainly for briefings. Instead of relying on the NSC, he made ad hoc use of various consulting arrangements. In 1965, the chief informal forum for Johnson's deliberations on Vietnam was his Tuesday lunches—a small, somewhat shifting group of advisers, the most important of whom were Secretary of State Dean Rusk, Secretary of Defense Robert McNamara, and NSC Special Assistant McGeorge Bundy.

In the first phase of the process that led to the July announcement of an open-ended commitment (the period from late 1964 through the decision to retaliate for the 7 February 1965 attack on the American base at Pleiku), Johnson and his associates were in superficial agreement about the need to defend South Vietnam, but in major disagreement about how to do it. Maxwell Taylor, the U.S. ambassador in Saigon, favored increased air strikes against North Vietnam but was against the introduction of American ground troops. McGeorge Bundy and McNamara favored the use of some U.S. forces, while Rusk at that point seemed reticent about introducing ground combat troops. General William Westmoreland proposed thirty-four battalions of U.S. forces, a request that Ambassador Taylor regarded as "startling." Johnson had reservations about air strikes, preferring to use U.S. unconventional forces.

Following the attack on the U.S. base, Johnson ordered a retaliatory air strike, which soon led to a full-scale air war against North Vietnam. In his memoirs Johnson recalls that his advisers, with the exception of Senate Majority Leader Mansfield, were in virtual agreement.[96] Johnson's recollection, however, did not reflect the differences present among his advisers. George Ball, the under secretary of state, opposed air strikes, for example, but went along in order not to destroy his effectiveness with the group.[97] Douglas Dillon, the treasury secretary, favored further escalation. According to Dillon, "I was the only person to make such a reservation, but I am sure that, *if asked,* [CIA Chief John] McCone and [Joint Chiefs of Staff Chair Earle] Wheeler would have been in full agreement with me."[98] Not only did disagreement among some of his advisers fail to be fully explored, at no time in this period did Johnson raise questions about the broader aims that bombing was meant to accomplish; instead he focused on tactical considerations such as likely targets, damages, and casualties.

The lack of substantive discussion was also apparent in the next phase of escalation: the introduction of American combat troops. The bombing campaign was barely underway when General Westmoreland requested that two Marine battalion teams (3,500 men) be assigned to guard the U.S. base at Da Nang. Ambassador Taylor, who was vehement in his opposition to sending U.S. combat troops, reluctantly agreed to one battalion, but the Joint Chiefs of Staff (JCS) backed Westmoreland, and Johnson agreed to send two. In his memoirs, Taylor notes that such a momentous decision was undertaken without much attention by Johnson and his Washington advisers: "It was curious how hard it had been to get authority for the initiation of the air campaign against the North and how relatively easy to get the marines ashore."[99] According to William Bundy, then assistant secretary of state for Far Eastern affairs, Johnson approved the troop request "with no work by any staffs outside the Pentagon. . . . The matter was presented to the president at a luncheon meeting and approved by him."[100]

From March through June the number of marine battalions increased as other installations needing protection were added to the list. The marines were also authorized to expand the area they patrolled around U.S. bases— first to ten miles, then to thirty miles, and, as of the first of June, to fifty miles; shortly thereafter, Westmoreland was given the authority to use U.S. forces in any way he deemed fit. By early June, 82,000 American troops had been authorized for deployment; this grew to 95,000 by mid-June, 125,000 by early July, and almost 200,000 by late July. Yet, as McGeorge Bundy pointed out to Johnson in a 25 July memorandum, "we have not yet had even a company-level engagement with Viet Cong forces which choose to stand their ground and fight."[101]

Members of Johnson's circle of advisers held a broad spectrum of views, yet the advisory process was so disorderly and Johnson's management of the process so haphazard that they never were channeled into focused debate. Johnson convened few meetings of the NSC before the Pleiku attack, and he held six meetings during the crisis. A meeting on 18 February consisted exclusively of a forty-five-minute briefing by Johnson, Rusk, and McNamara on current developments in Vietnam. The NSC did not meet again until 26 March, when the topic for discussion was how to handle public relations on increasing U.S. involvement. In the interim, the shift from retaliation to ground troops had occurred. There were only four more NSC meetings—all brief—between 1 April and Johnson's announcement in late July of an open-ended military commitment.

Not only was formal machinery inadequate, but the kind of informal advising that existed in 1965 encouraged flawed decision making. In March, Johnson reinstated his Tuesday lunches. Most lunches had only six participants, and many were attended by only three top advisers—Rusk, McNamara, and Bundy. Other participants varied: Under Secretary of State Ball, the newly appointed CIA Director William Raborn, and sometimes Johnson's confidante, Supreme Court Justice Abe Fortas. On only one occasion, 13 April, was JCS Chairman Earle Wheeler in attendance. The shift away from formal meetings of the NSC not only largely excluded Wheeler, but it also excluded, perhaps deliberately, Vice-President Hubert Humphrey, a statutory member of the NSC who had reservations about Johnson's Vietnam policies.[102]

The Tuesday lunches reveal a core group of decision makers whose interpersonal "chemistry" was conducive to escalation, in much the same way the advisers around Kennedy were in agreement on the Bay of Pigs invasion. McNamara was a forceful advocate of his own views (which for much of 1965 favored escalation) at the cost of alternative policy options. According to George Ball, McNamara "brushed . . . caveats aside. . . . It was the quintessential McNamara approach. Once he had made up his mind to go forward, he would push aside the most formidable impediment that might threaten to slow down or deflect him from his determined course."[103]

Secretary of State Rusk was inclined to go along with the others. His experience in the conflict-ridden Truman foreign policy process encouraged him to believe that the secretary of state should not fall into open conflict with the president's other advisers, especially the secretary of defense. Rusk's views, such as they were, were for the president's ears only, and once the president had decided upon a course of action, it was the secretary's duty to carry it out faithfully.

McGeorge Bundy was a policy advocate both in his memoranda to the president and in meetings. His memoranda show him summarizing the views of other advisers, often with advice to Johnson about which should be heeded or ignored and with a particular "spin" that sometimes favored Bundy's own policy views, practices that differed from his behavior as Kennedy's NSC adviser. No Johnson adviser had the "honest broker" role of dispassionately analyzing deliberations and facilitating the full airing of divergent policy views that Eisenhower had assigned to Bundy's predecessors, especially Robert Cutler.

The Tuesday lunches were especially problematic. No notes were kept of most proceedings or decisions. Beyond the core participants, membership varied from week to week. Thus, feedback to the next level of policy makers and implementors was imperfect at best, because subordinates had to rely on whatever word-of-mouth reports might be transmitted to them by the few who were privy to the deliberations; the latter, in turn, might also be flawed since personal recollections can often be imprecise and selective guides to what actually transpired.

Some evidence also suggests that the Tuesday lunches tended to be digressive discussions rather than sharply focused analytic exercises. William Bundy recalls that the meetings he attended were "time wasting." "Johnson would tee off at someone like Arthur Schlesinger or Ken Galbraith. . . . There was a lot of blowing steam and his sense of focusing on an issue was not acute."[104]

Johnson's style of dealing with his advisers in these and other meetings differed from Kennedy's. Although Johnson was no Caligula (as some observers characterized him) and in some meetings seemed attentive to what his advisers had to say, his receptiveness was variable. Strong-minded aides such as Joseph Califano, Douglass Cater, and Harry McPherson pressed Johnson hard with their disagreements, although McPherson reports that he worried, as the war went on, that a direct confrontation would lead him to be "aced out of the whole Vietnam thing."[105] At a 7 February meeting of the NSC, held in the wake of the Pleiku attack, Senate Majority Leader Mansfield expressed reservations about the course Johnson seemed to be embarking upon, triggering an emotional outburst by Johnson on the need to "take America's gun from the mantel." According to William Bundy, Mansfield never again "took this kind of blunt position in an open meeting." At an NSC meeting the next day, Mansfield again seemed prepared to dissent from the consensus forming among Johnson and his advisers and seemed about to read from a memorandum he had prepared. According to Larry O'Brien, who sat next to him, at the last minute Mansfield put the memo away, passing it on to Jack Valenti for delivery to the president privately.[106]

When he did engage his advisers in open discussion, Johnson often failed to focus his questions on matters that needed attention. There is little evidence from the meetings on his Vietnam decision making in 1965, for example, that indicates that specific policy options were put in the larger context of overall American interests and policies in Vietnam. Nor was there much discussion of the political, social, and economic reforms needed. Even the questions Johnson posed were not adequately addressed. There was no sustained attention to issues and no follow-up.[107]

Given the character of Johnson's advisory process in 1965, his decisions were not the product of focused and organized deliberations and clear-cut choices. Unlike Kennedy, Johnson did not remedy the defects that can beset a collegial system of advising; he did not have a Bay of Pigs early in his tenure from which to draw lessons about the strengths and weaknesses of his mode of advising before he encountered a more consequential set of decisions. Perhaps Johnson's Vietnam decision making in 1965 was his Bay of Pigs, but given the momentous nature of the decisions made, he could not easily recover from them, as Kennedy had recovered in 1961.

With even modest changes, Johnson might have had a more effective advisory process. Moreover, there is evidence that Johnson's advisory arrangements were not immutable: his decision in 1968 to bar further escalation and seek negotiations, and perhaps also his decision not to seek reelection, resulted from a changed advisory process. The secretary of defense who replaced McNamara in 1968, Clark Clifford, brought a fresh perspective and tough-minded analytic capacities to his job. Herbert Schandler's analysis of what happened in the Johnson White House in 1968 points to how changes in the advisory process, accompanied by changes in the president's own thinking (to which the process may have contributed), can have an impact on the president's decisions: "After Tet, the 1968 decision-making process functioned properly for the first time. Objectives were matched to the resources required to achieve those objectives, and the strategy being followed was modified when it was seen that the costs, political and material, of attaining those results within a reasonable period of time would be more than the nation was willing to pay."[108]

The experiences of Eisenhower, Nixon, Kennedy, and Johnson reveal the need to tailor formal and collegial styles of management to the organizational setting in which they are applied. Both Eisenhower and Kennedy avoided the weaknesses of their respective management practices by being attentive to how they operated in an organizational context, modifying the structure of their staff system and its internal mode of operations accordingly. Nixon and Johnson, by contrast, were largely inattentive to the institutional presidency and advisory systems on which they relied, with their own individual ways of working and personalities exacerbating the negative tendencies of their management practices.

The experiences of each these presidents as manager, however, may not be wholly explainable by his effort or failure to anticipate how a formal or collegial system will pan out in an organizational context. As we will see in the next chapter, the organizational dynamics of the staff system form another dimension of the institutional presidency that can affect the operation of the White House staff system.

4

THE INSTITUTIONAL PRESIDENCY
Through an Organizational Lens

■ ■ ■

A president's awareness of the strengths and weaknesses of his management of the White House staff—whether formalistic, collegial, or some combination of the two—is an important factor affecting the staff's operations. But this particular lens of analysis—the focus of the preceding chapter—does not take into account the full range of organizational characteristics that may have an impact on the workings of the institutional presidency. It is less directly concerned with what might be termed the dynamics of the organization—that is, how the staff system as a whole operates on a day-to-day basis and the kind of behavior and attitudes that tend to flourish within a complex organization like the White House staff. These are, of course, features of the institutional presidency—its "deep structure," as Heclo aptly terms it—that were discussed in chapter 2: centralization of policy making by the White House to the exclusion of other avenues of information and advice, centralization of power and authority within the staff, and bureaucratization. Let us now consider this aspect of the institutional presidency and ask to what extent it has been the object of presidential concern and attention.

Dealing with Centralization of Policy Making by the White House Staff

As we saw in Chapter 2, one of the effects of relying on the institutional presidency is a tendency to centralize policy-making power in the White House staff. And, as we noted, centralization can have both positive and negative consequences. Members of the White House staff are relatively closely linked to the president and thus relatively likely to reflect his policy views; by contrast, their counterparts outside the White House staff are more likely to feel the tug of their agency's or department's positions and interests. But centralization also has its price: singular reliance on the White House staff can limit the channels of information and advice available to the president.

Fortunately, the experience of recent presidents shows that some have managed to strike a balance between internal and external sources of advice, thereby countering some of the ill effects of centralization. Although a general trend toward centralization of power can be traced back to the Roosevelt presidency, not all presidencies exhibit it to the same degree. Some presidents have recognized that a large staff is a double-edged sword and have devised various ways of dealing with its consequences.

Informal Channels of Information and Advice

Informal channels of information and advice have provided perhaps the most important check on excessive centralization because they free the president from singular reliance on the White House staff. All presidents consult sources outside their immediate staffs, but some presidents seem particularly adept at using these contacts to expand the range and quality of policy options, to challenge their own thinking and that of their staffs, and otherwise to enrich their deliberations.

Although Eisenhower and Kennedy differed in their views about the merits of formally organized decision-making procedures, both ranged widely in their attempts to gather information and advice. According to Arthur Schlesinger, Jr., with Kennedy, "there was an openness to ideas from whatever source. [He was] determined not to become the prisoner of any single information system." Kennedy even used unofficial, nongovernmental sources of advice: "He liked to pit information he got through official channels against information he got from newspaper friends or from foreign visitors or from his own extensive reading; he read the British weeklies for example. In that way he protected himself against exclusive dependence on the information the bureaucracy below saw fit to send up to him."[1]

Kennedy's distrust of bureaucracies and his impatience with formal systems of advice and information, however, discouraged effective use of his cabinet. According to Douglas Dillon, Kennedy's treasury secretary, most cabinet members were "peripheral to his interests, and he didn't see much of them. . . . A number of them resigned: Ribicoff in Health, Education, and Welfare and Postmaster General Day. I don't think he had ever seen the President on a working basis. That's the way Kennedy operated."[2] Thus, while Kennedy developed a range of contacts outside the

White House staff, his preference for more informal, collegial groups and his distrust of more formally organized entities may have prevented effective use of his cabinet as an external source of policy advice.

Eisenhower used both systematic formal and wide-ranging informal channels of contact.[3] His use of informal channels had the effect, as we saw in the last chapter, of remedying some of the defects of relying exclusively on a formal staff system, but it also served to broaden his perspective beyond the White House. In deliberative forums, Eisenhower encouraged presentation of a range of opinion and an open airing of his advisers' views. In a 1967 interview, he reflected on this aspect of his management style:

> I know of only one way in which you can be sure you've done your best to make a wise decision. That is to get all of the people who have a partial and definable responsibility in this particular field, whatever it may be. Get them with their different viewpoints in front of you, and listen to them debate. I do not believe in bringing them in one at a time, and therefore being [more] impressed with the most recent one you hear than by the earlier ones. You must get courageous men, men of strong views, and let them debate and argue with each other. You listen, and you see if there's anything that has been brought up, any idea that changes your view or enriches your view or adds to it.[4]

Effective Use of the Cabinet

Eisenhower's use of the cabinet illustrates a more formal avenue of contact that was largely absent in Kennedy's presidency and reveals the deliberate steps Eisenhower took to make sure the cabinet functioned effectively. Eisenhower's own experience attending cabinet meetings in the Roosevelt and Truman presidencies had impressed upon him the need to "ride herd" on the cabinet and establish more formal procedures for making it function effectively. In his memoirs, Eisenhower recalled that the history of past administrations "recorded much Cabinet bickering, personality conflicts, and end running, tale bearing, and throat cutting."[5] As president, Eisenhower was determined to change this behavior.

At a meeting with his cabinet-designate on 12 January 1953 at the Hotel Commodore in New York City, the president-elect told his associates, "I have had to sit while the Cabinet, so called, went through its gyrations, and there is certainly no more charitable word that you could use with respect to what I have seen." It was Eisenhower's hope, by contrast, to make his own cabinet "a policy body," and "to bring before you and for you to bring up subjects that are worthy of this body as a whole."[6] After taking office, Eisenhower regularly convened cabinet meetings: ten in the first eighty days of his presidency and an average of thirty-four per year over the course of his presidency.[7] Kennedy, by contrast, held only three meetings in his first eighty days in office and even less thereafter.

Part of Eisenhower's efforts at making the cabinet work more effectively were directed at formalizing its procedures. In late 1953, White House aide Maxwell Rabb was made cabinet secretary, and in 1954, after extensive study, a cabinet secretariat was created.

The operations of the cabinet secretariat illustrate how the formal procedures of the Eisenhower presidency avoided the dangers of centralization by enhancing the president's ability to step beyond the White House staff in search of counsel. Committees composed of both departmental representatives and members of the secretariat constituted the first step in bringing matters to the president's attention, thus linking the White House staff and cabinet departments in the development of policy proposals the cabinet and the president would later consider. When policies were ripe for discussion, they would be placed on the cabinet's agenda; the secretariat also saw to it that departments with items on the agenda prepared background papers. Both the agenda and relevant papers were circulated before cabinet meetings were held. The secretariat kept regular minutes of meetings and "records of actions," which listed decisions the president had taken on agenda items. Members of the secretariat also debriefed second-level department officials on what had transpired at cabinet meetings that pertained to their responsibilities. Every three months the secretariat issued "status of action" reports, which summarized departmental efforts at carrying out the president's directives and decisions, and circulated them to all cabinet officers. Thus, although part of the institutional presidency and operating in accordance with formal procedures, the cabinet secretariat facilitated the president's ability to widen his net of information and advice.

Although these formal procedures enhanced the effectiveness of Eisenhower's cabinet compared to those of its predecessors, perhaps of more interest are the more informal aspects of effective operation that Eisenhower fostered. According to Fred Greenstein, Eisenhower urged members of the cabinet "to practice what he had long ago concluded was essential for effective organization—spontaneous mutual coordination." Eisenhower had emphasized this concern at the Hotel Commodore meeting, telling his associates that he hoped "that before we have gone very long each one of you will consider the rest of you here your very best friends in the world so that you can call up and do your own coordinating. That is the perfect way." By "friendship," Greenstein points out, Eisenhower did not mean "bosom companions; his aim was that they develop comfortable, compatible working relationships."[8] Eisenhower had already begun to take steps to build these relationships. He had taken several cabinet designees with him on his trip to Korea in December 1952, and on the sea voyage home they were joined by several more nominees—an optimal setting for developing close relationships, rapport, and mutual understanding. Also, following the Commodore Hotel working sessions, Eisenhower asked his associates to form small dinner groups and discuss mutual interests, rather than convening them all together for a more formal banquet.

Eisenhower recognized the centrifugal pull of cabinet members' interests. But, as Greenstein notes, this could be corrected: "By being consulted . . . Eisenhower's associates were encouraged to think of themselves as part of a collective enterprise rather than as individual entrepreneurs." Also face-to-face contact with the president was advantageous. Cabinet meetings could serve as Eisenhower's "bully pulpit." "It was here," Greenstein observes, "that he personally conveyed the general principles behind his policies, giving them added force by displaying his strength of conviction and 'force of personality'."[9] In a 1967 oral history interview, Eisenhower explained, "One of the big purposes that I wanted to achieve was to make sure that everybody was informed on the workings of the Administration, so that no matter whether you were before Congress, making a speech, or anywhere, we would not be working at opposite ends of the spectrum."[10]

Eisenhower's cabinet meetings also were regularly attended by top White House aides such as Sherman Adams, congressional liaison staffer Wilton Persons, budget director Joseph Dodge, and press secretary James Hagerty. In Eisenhower's view, it was important that White House staff positions be held by persons of stature and that they be on intimate terms with members of the cabinet. Lacking such status, Eisenhower told his cabinet, they "cannot bring . . . problems to the attention of Cabinet officers and get things done on them." He wanted his aides to be able "to walk into the offices of any one of [them] and say, 'Bill, this thing is wrong. We have got to do something.' "[11] Eisenhower was thus concerned not only with making the cabinet operate freely yet harmoniously and productively, but also with establishing smooth working relationships between its members and his White House staff.

Eisenhower was careful, however, not to let his procedures turn into "cabinet government"—that is, exclusive reliance on the cabinet as a source of policy initiatives and as a deliberative forum in which policy choices were made. The cabinet was *a* source of counsel, not *the* place where decisions were made. As Arthur Flemming, Eisenhower's secretary of health, education, and welfare, once recalled, "nothing was ever put to a vote and it was clear that we were talking about these matters as general advisers to him. He is the only person who voted. He is the only person who made a decision." But Flemming also concludes that although the president retained the ultimate power to make policy decisions, "his work with the Cabinet as a collegial group did have an effect on the evolution of policy."[12]

In short, the Eisenhower cabinet complemented the information the president received from his staff; it did not serve as a substitute or replacement for his staff. And, as Greenstein observes, Eisenhower "knew that advice seeking [from the Cabinet] was an effective tool for winning the willing support of those he consulted, even though he might not take their advice."[13]

This careful circumscription of the cabinet's role enabled Eisenhower to avoid the difficulties of Nixon, Carter, and Reagan, who began their presidencies with calls for more reliance on the cabinet. Each failed in his efforts and soon turned to stronger and ultimately ill-fated reliance on the White House staff. The lesson for presidents then is not to abandon their staffs for external sources of information but skillfully to blend what they get from their staffs with what they can garner from other sources.

Two Failures in Dealing with Centralization

The experiences of Eisenhower and Kennedy indicate that presidents can balance the need for centralized control over the policy process, which the White House staff provides, with the need to remain open to other sources of information and advice. The Johnson and Nixon presidencies, by contrast, are cases where the president's contacts outside the staff were largely unproductive—the Johnson experience—or where the president exacerbated the negative consequences of centralization—a problem Nixon's managerial practices generated.

Lyndon Johnson shared Eisenhower's and Kennedy's restiveness about receiving advice from only one channel. He remained in constant contact, usually through incessant telephone calls, with a wide range of informal advisers. Abe Fortas, a longtime confidante and Johnson appointee to the Supreme Court, characterized Johnson as "a pack rat for information and more particularly for points of view. The impression that Johnson did not provoke disagreement and did not obtain a diversity of advice is simply untrue." Johnson was especially uncomfortable when members of his staff took the same position on a difficult issue; that was when, according to Fortas, Johnson was most likely "to ask me to come over and tell him what the other side was."

Johnson, however, did not use his informal contacts to provoke a lively debate. Fortas recalls that there was little "dialogue. . . . Johnson was not the sort of man with whom you had a give and take discussion."[14] Johnson also failed to use his cabinet as a sounding board. According to one Johnson aide, "after awhile he never even bothered to sit down with most of the

Cabinet members even to discuss their major problems and program possibilities." Instead, the aide reports, Johnson turned to his staff for carrying out his departmental concerns: "Johnson wound up using some of his staff as both line managers as well as staff and, I think in retrospect, it frequently didn't work out!"[15]

Nixon's management practices—his emphasis on formalism, his propensity to decide in private, and his low tolerance for conflict and face-to-face discussion—led to increasing centralization of power in his White House, if not to the greatest degree of centralization among recent presidencies. It was Nixon's long-held view that "bringing power to the White House [was necessary] in order to dish it out."[16] Nixon's reliance on Kissinger for foreign policy advice, on Ehrlichman for domestic counsel, and on Haldeman for organizational efficiency blended neatly with his personal needs. But this meshing of the personal and the organizational reinforced the negative tendencies of centralization—particularly presidential isolation— rather than reducing them. Nixon's initial hope of relying on his cabinet, drawn from his experience under Eisenhower, quickly disappeared as the president found himself ill at ease listening to the advice of a George Romney, a John Volpe, or a Walter Hickel. Within the White House staff, the "freethinking outsiders" as Joan Hoff-Wilson calls them—men of new ideas such as Robert Finch and Daniel Patrick Moynihan—fell by the wayside to be replaced by the "political brokers" like Haldeman and Ehrlichman. Only Kissinger survived and prospered, but he was able skillfully to blend the roles of power broker and original thinker and to develop a close personal relationship with the president.

Several observations are suggested by this discussion of how presidents have dealt differently with their common reliance on the White House staff for policy advice. Centralization of power over policy decisions in the White House staff is clearly a trend in the modern presidency; a president needs, as Terry Moe suggests, "the kind of information, expertise, and coordinating capacity that only a large scale organizational apparatus can provide. . . . What he wants is an institutional system responsive to his needs as a political leader."[17] But it is not clear that centralization is the only means for a president to achieve political control. Both Kennedy and Eisenhower pursued leadership strategies that had distinct noncentralizing components and that by most measures were more successful, more politically successful in fact, than those of presidents like Nixon or Johnson, who relied almost exclusively on their staffs. Centralization is an important means of presidential control, but it is not the only means or necessarily the most effective.

The task for presidents, then, is to balance their policy judgments by relying on internal and external sources of policy advice. *Both* can serve the president's need for objective and competent policy analysis, and *both* can be politically responsive. Presidents who lean too far in one direction— excessive reliance on either the cabinet (Carter and Reagan in their first years) or the White House staff (Nixon)—are likely to encounter problems. Presidents who are able to use both and to do so *effectively* are better served.

The Ideal of Multiple Advocacy

Effective use of both internal and external sources of policy advice resembles, albeit in a less organized way, Alexander George's proposal for a system of multiple advocacy—the exposure of the president to a rich and diverse stream of information and advice.[18] Although George is more directly concerned with the question of how to improve the quality of presidential decision making in foreign policy, his multiple advocacy proposal speaks to the need of presidents both to centralize control over the policy process and to avoid the parochial tendencies of bureaucratic politics, and yet to recognize the dangers of exclusive reliance on a limited range of advisers. The premise of multiple advocacy is that exposure to multiple channels of advice improves the president's and his advisers' search for information and their appraisal of it and thereby enables the president to make better policy decisions.

As George argues, some presidents have practiced multiple advocacy, and there is evidence that it has contributed to the quality of their decision making; he cites Eisenhower's 1954 decision not to intervene in Indochina and Lyndon Johnson's 1964 decision not to proceed with a multilateral force for NATO.[19] Multiple advocacy, however, requires great effort on a president's part. It does not simply involve free debate or adversarial proceedings but is a structured, balanced process requiring strong, alert management on the part of the president and his chief advisers. It also has its costs: it can be time consuming and discomforting to persons who dislike active give-and-take, and the premium it places on verbal interaction and, at times, dissent can weaken group cohesion.

Presidents need (and have on occasion had) a range of internal and external sources of advice. Multiple advocacy places decisions in the president's hands and thus recognizes that presidents need to exercise control over the policy process—one of the chief arguments in favor of centralization—and not simply rely on agencies and departments to make decisions presumably in the president's interest. But it avoids exclusive reliance on the staff. To the extent that presidential management of the policy process either achieves multiple advocacy or at least attempts to approximate it, presidents may better be able to attain the positive consequences of centralized control and avoid its dangers.

Dealing with Hierarchy and Internal Centralization

Centralization of power in the White House staff is linked to the second characteristic of the institutional presidency: the development of hierarchy within the White House and the emergence of presidential assistants who wield enormous power. In effect, this is the internal face of centralization: as the White House staff absorbs policy-making power from its surrounding political environment, members of the staff acquire that power in different degrees. Powerful chiefs of staff and special assistants for national security affairs can provide order and coherence to the daily workings and organization of the staff, they can shield the president from mistakes, and they can act as lightning rods to deflect criticism of politically controversial decisions and actions. But they can also act as gatekeepers and become "choke points," preventing the president from receiving information and advice he needs, furthering their own political views and policy agendas, and in extreme cases isolating the president from both his staff and sources of advice outside the White House. How top-level presidential aides have viewed their roles and how presidents have defined those roles have been critical in determining whether it is the positive or negative effects of internal centralization that emerge.

Defining the Job: The Role of the Managerial Custodian

As we saw in chapter 2, highly visible chiefs of staff and NSC special assistants who become policy advocates in their own right have posed the greatest difficulties for recent presidents. By contrast, presidents whose key staffers have defined their role more as manager of the process, concerned with the full and fair flow of advice to the president, have fared better. This accords with Alexander George's observations about what factors contribute to effective presidential decision making. Observing the duties of NSC special assistants since the Eisenhower administration, George notes that the responsibilities of that job have steadily increased. Under Eisenhower, the NSC special assistant was largely a "manager custodian": an "honest broker" of the decision process whose job did not include advancing his own policy views. But beginning in the Kennedy administration and continuing under most of Kennedy's successors, the NSC special assistant has also become the president's chief policy adviser, public spokesman for the administration's foreign policy, political watchdog of the president's power stakes, enforcer of policy decisions, and presidential operative.

Although the addition of these responsibilities may seem natural to most observers, George argues that the quality of presidential decision making has suffered as a result. The assumption of multiple roles has weakened the ability of the NSC special assistant to serve his primary duty as a neutral custodian of the process. Advancing one's own policy views makes it difficult to treat the views of others fairly. The roles of policy spokesman and chief enforcer may compromise the incentive to encourage timely and objective reevaluation of ongoing policy. The role of political watchdog may encourage too much sensitivity to the domestic political implications of particular policy choices. Operational duties such as those of diplomatic negotiator, fact finder, and mediator are likely to be time-consuming "line" responsibilities that distract attention from more immediate duties.

The addition of these other tasks especially may hamper the president's ability to achieve multiple advocacy (or even the lesser goal of balanced formal and informal streams of advice, discussed above). Multiple advocacy involves not merely the willy-nilly presentation of an array of policy views. Rather, it is an organized process in which participants must possess certain bureaucratic and intellectual resources and in which certain rules must prevail. "The mere existence within the policy-making system of actors holding different points of view," George points out, "will not guarantee adequate multisided examination of a policy issue."[20] For multiple advocacy to work, participants must have approximately equal intellectual resources (such as competence, information, and analytic support) and bureaucratic resources (status, power, and standing with the president, as well as persuasion and bargaining skills). Multiple advocacy also requires adequate time for verbal given-and-take and presidential participation to monitor and regulate the process. But most of all it requires that the NSC special assistant fulfill six custodial duties:

1. Balance the resources of those involved in the process

2. Strengthen weaker participants

3. Bring in new participants to argue for unpopular options

4. Establish alternative channels of advice to the president

5. Arrange independent evaluation of policy options

6. Identify and correct malfunctions in the decision process.[21]

For our purposes, George's discussion recognizes the linkage between the structure of the president's system of advising—in this case the presence of multiple channels of information and advice—and the responsibilities of key White House officials to make that system work effectively. Presidents clearly need persons who provide them with substantive advice and even advance their own policy views; and the notion of a managerial custodian is not offered with the claim that all advisers must fit its particulars. But presidents also need persons who are primarily responsible for managing the complex process of decision making and policy implementation that presidents currently face.

Broadening the Application of the Custodian Role

George's concept of the managerial custodian role is also important because it may suggest a more general conception of responsibility that is applicable to other top-level presidential advisers, not just the NSC special assistant, and that may be useful in offsetting the negative aspects of hierarchy and centralization of power within the White House staff. Although discussion of the role of managerial custodian has largely been confined to the area of foreign policy and the responsibilities of the NSC special assistant, it seems equally applicable to the responsibilities of the president's chief of staff.

During the Eisenhower administration, Sherman Adams's duties as chief of staff were similar in many ways to those of Eisenhower's NSC special assistants, although Adams's duties on the domestic policy side did not present the opportunities that Cutler and the other NSC special assistants had to act as neutral broker in an on-going deliberative body like the NSC. Although Adams was reputed to have great discretionary power, to this day it is hard—if not impossible—to identify any substantive policy decisions of the Eisenhower presidency with Adams's own views, save for the incident that brought Adams down. Richard Rovere, a contemporary critic of the Eisenhower presidency, characterized Adams in 1956 as an "efficiency enthusiast" who had "no special knowledge of any national issue, with the possible exception of conservation."[22] Emmet Hughes, who served on Eisenhower's speech-writing staff and later became a critic of his presidency, states, "Notwithstanding descriptions of him through the years as an enigmatic eminence grise, he [Adams] scarcely ever sought to work as a policymaker."[23] In a lengthy diary entry dated 18 January 1954, almost one year after his inauguration, Eisenhower reflected at length on the workings of his cabinet and White House staff. "The staff has performed magnificently," Eisenhower noted. "Sherman Adams has grown into the job that he has, and in a very definite sense has created it as he went along. Honesty, directness, and efficiency have begun to win him friends among people who initially were prone to curse him because he had no time for flattery or cajolery, or even pleasantries over the phone."[24]

The eight former chiefs of staffs who gathered at the University of California at San Diego in 1986 to reflect on twenty-five years of managing the modern presidency also, almost to a man, viewed the proper role of the chief of staff as well as their own duties in that office as properly limited to coordination rather than substantive involvement in the making of policy.

Several of them confessed to having engaged occasionally in subterfuge to prevent the president from taking precipitous and ill-considered actions. But most saw their role in much the same way that Brownlow had prescribed it in 1937 and that George's concept of the managerial custodian sets out; the connections between these views are striking, given the realities of the contemporary White House staff. Commenting on the reflections made at the 1986 meeting, Samuel Kernell observes that

> instead of tales of aggressive management characterized by conflict and confrontation, these chiefs offer less venturesome stories of working mostly as professional coordinators. Almost disinterestedly, they broker policy disagreements among departments, solicit opposing points of view for the president's consideration, assuage the ire of a cabinet member who feels slighted by a colleague or perhaps by the president, and when called on stoically [in the words of Donald Rumsfeld, Gerald Ford's chief of staff] "bear the brunt of hostility" from those whose policy preferences have been rejected, all the while subordinating personal preference and shunning public glory.[25]

This picture of the president's top assistants obviously departs from the conventional wisdom that they are power-hungry, power-wielding usurpers of presidential authority. Their reminiscences may be *post hoc* rationalizations. Some chiefs of staff have indeed been in political business for themselves, as we saw in chapter 2. But as Kernell concludes, there is validity and sincerity in what these particular chiefs of staff say. The explanation of the difference between their account and conventional wisdom may stem from how others interpreted their duties as coordinators. Staffing out a cabinet member's policy suggestions for further study and input may be part of a custodian's duty, but it is likely to be perceived as political interference by the cabinet member with the seemingly good idea. Brokering a process in which some persons win and some must necessarily lose may cast the broker in the unenviable position of seeming to have made the decision. Also, top-level staff members become presidential surrogates for attack and criticism: "Presidential assistants make easy marks, and presidents do not."[26]

Furthermore, according to Carter aide Jack Watson, adopting a neutral policy stance is good strategy: "If you don't act as honest brokers . . . you lose your capability to play, you ultimately cut yourself out over time. As secretary to the cabinet . . . my role was to become trusted by the cabinet, so they knew that I wasn't going to embarrass them in the press. Over time, you have to build that trust. If you don't . . . they are not going to come to you."[27] Good strategy is bolstered by the external perceptions of top aides: if the public sees the chief of staff as a political entrepreneur, then it is all the more necessary that he hew even more closely to the role of neutral coordinator.

Not only have some top-level staff members viewed their roles as fair managers of the policy process, but presidents who have had what are generally regarded as effective staff organizations have tended to recognize it as a managerial task to create such roles and recruit persons to fill its particulars. As one member of Eisenhower's staff observed, "it's the fact that the President picked people like Governor Adams, Bobby Cutler, and Gordon Gray, all men of adequate egos, certainly, but men who also saw their role as strictly being to serve the president." The same observer contrasts Eisenhower's practice in selecting subordinates with Nixon's: Nixon "blew the boat out of the water when he appointed Kissinger . . . because then he was no longer pretending that you had just a staff assistant there working for the President, you had an 'assistant president' for national security affairs."[28]

The Problem of Visibility

The public visibility of top members of the White House staff has tended to undermine their ability to serve the president as neutral brokers and coordinators. The president's special assistant for national security and his chief of staff, as well as other White House staffers, are often the objects of intense media attention; their backgrounds, political views, work habits, and family lives are the subjects of extensive scrutiny and speculation. Lengthy feature stories on them abound in the print media, their off-duty activities are regularly noted in Washington social columns, and they often appear as spokespersons for the administration on Sunday-morning public-affairs shows and as subjects for in-depth stories and interviews on the evening news broadcasts. Such is their notoriety that many write bestseller memoirs once they leave the White House and serve as media commentators and analysts of their successors in office. Brownlow's maxim that members of the White House staff have a "passion for anonymity" has apparently fallen by the wayside.

To some extent this visibility is a natural outcome of the media's search for "the story" and its need to report on the politically powerful. A number of recent chiefs of staff have claimed that they have sought to remain relatively anonymous.[29] H. R. Haldeman—perhaps the prototype of the chief of staff perceived as all powerful—made only one television appearance during his tenure on Nixon's staff; at a staff meeting held before Nixon's inauguration, Haldeman even read aloud Brownlow's maxim about the need for a "passion for anonymity" to the newly assembled staff.

If a top-level official like Haldeman attempts in Brownlowian fashion to remain relatively anonymous but is often unsuccessful, the problem compounds when the president's chief aides actively seek the political limelight. In the 1970s and 1980s, top presidential assistants such as Henry Kissinger and Donald Regan actively sought media attention, often at the expense of the president's political success. Don Regan, for example, was quite amenable to, if not responsible for, the media's depiction of him as Reagan's "prime minister." Numerous articles and news stories during his first months as chief of staff, often substantiated by Regan's own description of his duties, focused on his seeming power in the Reagan White House. But this public visibility of the chief of staff ultimately hurt the president. To take merely one example, after a close defeat by the House of Representatives of a Reagan budget proposal in 1986, the blame was put on Regan. According to Samuel Kernell, "Republican House leaders carped that Chief of Staff Regan had acted as though Congress were his board of directors and he the government's 'chief executive officer'—which is precisely how Regan had recently described his job to a reporter."[30] Regan's battles with others in the administration, most noticeably Nancy Reagan, to become first among equals in the Reagan White House became standard media fare. Regan's understanding of the presidency and his own duties ended up weakening the Reagan presidency and led to Regan's own downfall.

Careful management of the public image of the White House staff has thus become an important task for both presidents and their staff members. Publicly visible staff members are easier targets for criticism and attack than sitting presidents, and the more visible the target, the likelier the attack. Even seemingly innocuous events become newsworthy. During a particularly low period in Carter's presidency, for example, stories about Hamilton Jordan's off-hours behavior surfaced repeatedly in the media.[31] The events may or may not have occurred, but they sent the implicit message of problems at the top level of the Carter White House and reinforced the impression of a presidency that was incompetent and adrift.

Other presidents have fared better, in large measure due to efforts to curb staff members' visibility. All of Eisenhower's assistants, Karl Harr notes, "sought to avoid the press—Bobby Cutler would never even go to a party, he would never even go out in the evening." Harr once proposed to Eisenhower's press secretary, James Hagerty, that Hagerty meet with some of his close friends in the media for an occasional dinner—to talk off the record for background fill-in. Hagerty immediately dismissed the idea: "Young man, that is the dumbest idea I've heard in my life. No, the answer is no." Harr later concluded that "in terms of the President's best interests, he was right."[32]

Franklin Roosevelt was similarly distrustful of aides who emerged as public figures. James Rowe reports that he once encountered FDR's ire when his name began to surface repeatedly in the press. "Didn't I read in the [Washington] Star, in some social column that you were at some cocktail party yesterday?" Roosevelt queried Rowe. "If I read that too often you're going to need another job." According to Rowe, "He made it perfectly clear that there was only one man running for office around there. We did stay away from the newspapermen. Steve Early was the press secretary, and a good one, and he was the man to deal with the press. The rest of us were not out there leaking this or leaking that. We really would have got bounced, I think."[33]

The president occupies a unique position: only he has the power and authority to curb staff members' ambitions for the political limelight and the use of the surreptitious leak to advance their own interests and hurt their opponents. According to one member of the Ford staff, "people tend to reflect the shadow of the man who is leader. There is no factor which affects human behavior more than rewards and penalties. If the President praises reticence, he is going to get reticence. If the President seems to applaud louder voices, he is going to get an infinite supply of them."[34]

Delegating Power

How presidents define the roles of top-level staff members—the degree to which they are honest brokers or policy advocates and the extent to which they are encouraged or discouraged from having a passion for anonymity— is an important element of a broader issue of presidential management of the White House staff: how presidents choose to delegate their powers of office. The degree of authority that presidents delegate to members of their staff is especially likely to affect how much power is centralized in the hands of their top advisers, and presidents have differed significantly in their delegation practices.

Johnson and Nixon stand at the extremes: Johnson with too much personal control and little delegation and Nixon with too much delegation and little personal control. In dealing with his aides, Johnson often established close relationships, but ones that were overly personal, demanding, and in some cases even demeaning. Harry McPherson, who served on Johnson's White House and Senate staffs recalls that Johnson saw his staff "as fungible parts of an army whose purpose was to serve, equip, and sustain its general in his infinite tasks." McPherson recalls one occasion, during Johnson's Senate years, when he had painstakingly prepared a long list of questions for Johnson to raise at a hearing. As Johnson's turn came to speak, he saw Johnson thumbing through his memorandum and then motioning him up to the dias. Excited, McPherson rushed up only to hear Johnson tell him to go back to his office and fetch some orange sourball candy. "I was furious but I did what he said, bringing [the candies] back sealed in an immense manila envelope which, I hoped, he would have trouble opening discreetly." Johnson's interchangeable assignments were legendary: "a speech handed to a chauffeur for comment; senior assistants asked to perform menial jobs of repair or delivery; a young secretary instructed to tell a cabinet member he was a damned fool. Apparently he regarded his staff as an indistinguishable rabble of talents."[35]

The pattern persisted in Johnson's presidency. During a trip to the Philippines, he made a surprise visit to Vietnam without telling McPherson. On his return Johnson was angry at his assistant:

> We get into his car. He wonders why I wasn't there earlier, when he needed me. Nobody told me you were going. We argue heatedly through the narrow streets. I wonder why Lyndon Johnson interrupts a time of high adventure, a coup of wartime leadership, to complain about [my absence]. It is as if nothing can satisfy him that does not exercise the full range of his emotions—triumph, gratitude, resentment toward those who unjustly fail or refuse him.[36]

McPherson's description of the relationship between Johnson and Bill Moyers especially reveals the dangers to an aide's independence—if not psyche—of Johnson's attitude toward subordinates:

> The Johnson-Moyers relationship was essentially father-son. As such it held the potential, for Moyers, of a substantial political inheritance—and the danger that as he became his own man, he would risk Johnson's anger if he strayed from him, submersion by that powerful political personality if he stayed with him, the loss of self-respect if he promoted policies in which he did not believe, and a reputation for disloyalty if he attacked those policies in public or private.[37]

In the Nixon presidency, not only was power centralized in the White House staff, it was in the control of key persons other than the president. Nixon's avoidance of situations that would generate conflict and disagreement and his preference for solitude delegated enormous power to his foreign and domestic staffs in framing his policy agenda, defining his policy options, and carrying out his decisions. According to Joan Hoff-Wilson, policy options, especially in the domestic sphere, abounded in the Nixon administration. But because of his "awkward, stiff, and very private personal style," Nixon may have delegated too much authority to his assistants and created an atmosphere in the White House in which extra-legal activities, "once tacitly approved by the president, may well have encouraged his aides to begin approving their own extralegal activities." Furthermore, Hoff-Wilson observes, Nixon's management style "tend[ed] to minimize the importance of human error or moral considerations." In particular, "when error in judgments resulted in illegal actions, Nixon did not recognize them for what they were because he had long before become inured to the 'underside' . . . of American politics."[38]

Nixon's situation is perhaps ironic given his concerns for reorganization of the White House staff system, his attempts to politicize the executive branch, and his overall goal of centralizing control over the policy process in his staff—bringing power back to the White House. But as Hoff-Wilson points out, excessive preoccupation with the technology and techniques of management may be the root cause of the inability at times, especially during Watergate, of Nixon's staff system to function effectively: "From the beginning of his first term a tendency existed for process to become policy, for organizational reform to become a substitute for more substantive considerations, and for effectiveness to become more important than morality or constitutionality."[39] Nixon's organizational procedures, as A. James Reichley notes, fostered not only isolation of the president but also a "results at any price approach"—which may have contributed to the demise of Nixon's presidency.[40]

In contrast to Johnson and Nixon, both Eisenhower and Kennedy were more effective delegators. In Kennedy's administration, according to Orville Freeman, who as secretary of agriculture saw the staff from the outside, "the presidential assistants in the White House were professionals; they had been with Kennedy a long time, and so could speak for him."

Eisenhower, like Kennedy, recognized the importance of his aides and assistants, as well as other members of his administration, knowing that the president's views and where he stood were important ingredients in the functioning of his administrative team. At the same time, his own broad organizational experience had taught him the necessity of delegating some responsibilities to others. In a letter to Henry Luce written on 8 August 1960, Eisenhower recognized that the responsibilities of the office required the president to delegate power: "The government of the United States has become too big, too complex, and too pervasive in its influence on all our lives for one individual to pretend to direct the details of its important and critical programming. Competent assistants are mandatory; without them the Executive Branch would bog down." But in the same letter, Eisenhower also recognized that the president must continue to exercise care and direction in his delegation so that his team functions loyally and effectively:

> To command the loyalties and dedication and best efforts of capable and outstanding individuals requires patience, understanding, a readiness to delegate, and an acceptance of responsibility for any honest errors—real or apparent—those associates and subordinates might make. Such loyalty from such people cannot be won by shifting responsibility, whining, scolding or demagoguery. Principal subordinates must have confidence that they and their positions are widely respected, and the chief must do his part in assuring that this is so.[41]

According to Fred Greenstein, Eisenhower practiced what social scientists term an "interactionist" conception of leadership; that is, he varied his staff management practices depending on the situation, his own strengths and weaknesses, and those on whom he would rely. With respect to his delegation of authority, as Greenstein observes, "he took care not to delegate in a fashion that would dilute his own ability to keep the actions of his associates in line with his own policies, adjusting the degree of his supervision both to the abilities of his associates and to the extent he believed his own participation in a policy area was necessary."[42] Associates such as John Foster Dulles, Treasury Secretaries George Humphrey and later Robert Anderson, and Attorney General Herbert Brownell could be delegated large amounts of authority where the president did not feel a need to become directly involved; they were cast in the role of "delegates" possessing discretion to carry out the president's goals. Others were more "deputies"—possessing discretion, surely, but within the confines of a clearly defined presidential mission; Budget Director Joseph Dodge and Defense Secretary Charles Wilson fell into this category. Eisenhower had great respect for Dodge, for example, but had his own clear views about the budget priorities of his administration; hence Dodge was kept on a shorter leash. With Wilson, Eisenhower not only wished to retain control over Defense Department policies—an area where he was clearly more competent than Wilson, the former president of General Motors—but he was impatient at Wilson's performance at Defense. Wilson dealt poorly with the press, and his management of the Pentagon did not always fully meet Eisenhower's expectations.[43]

Dealing with Bureaucratization

The tendency of a large presidential staff to acquire the characteristics of a bureaucracy poses one of the most significant challenges to presidents. Complex work routines, paper shuffling, bureaucratic and court politics all work to deflect the staff from effectively serving the president.

In part, creating a staff system that avoids unnecessary meetings and paperwork is likely to be the work of a chief of staff. Indeed the trend toward having a chief of staff, even for presidents like Ford, Carter, and Reagan, who did not initially want one to organize the day-to-day workings of the White House staff, is one response to the difficulty of controlling a large staff organization.

But a chief of staff, even a very effective one like a Sherman Adams or a James Baker, is not enough. Presidents need to do more to make the staff work effectively and avoid the emergence of bureaucratic tendencies. Unfortunately, little in the literature on the American presidency addresses this aspect of the White House staff and this task of presidential leadership. But insight can again be gleaned from the experiences of recent presidents.

Personal Guidance

Some presidents have avoided bureaucratization by exercising personal guidance over the activities of their staff members. John Gardner, who served in several presidencies, notes that Truman and Kennedy were especially skilled at picking their subordinates. Truman's gift was to "surround himself with individuals of exceptional ability." Kennedy had the ability "to draw talent to him. . . . He quickly established ties with the most diverse types—seasoned political operators, nonpolitical academics, military people, civil servants, and so on." But recruiting team members of high caliber is not necessarily a president's first impulse. Instead, presidents tend to favor those who have "an unanswering loyalty to the boss and no power base of their own that would make insubordination feasible. When those criteria prevail, what might have become a leadership team becomes, all too often, a ruling clique or circle of sycophants."[44]

The president's task continues once his team is in place. Milton Eisenhower, who served in the Roosevelt administration and was a close personal adviser to his brother, has emphasized the importance of the president's establishing strong personal bonds with his assistants in order to make them work effectively as a team: "If you want your policies carried out you had better have the top people who are going to carry it out working with you in the formation of policy. They will understand it better. They will feel they have made a contribution to it and with loyalty they will carry it out."[45]

President Eisenhower recognized the importance of cordial working relations among members of his official family. As Fred Greenstein notes, Eisenhower

> was not under the illusion that the official skeleton of an organization was in itself an organism in the absence of muscles, nerves, and vital organs. Rather, he thought in terms of the complementarity of formal and informal organization—of the elements of personal and group psychology that infuse an institution with purpose and motivation. These human relations considerations were if anything more prominent in his leadership theory and practice than was his passion for organization.[46]

Eisenhower's recognition of the importance of informal bonds among his advisers extended to his role as leader of the team. Walter Bedell Smith, his wartime chief of staff and later under secretary of state, observed that Eisenhower's "personality is such that it impresses itself immediately upon senior subordinates as completely frank, completely honest . . . and very considerate. . . . He has great patience and he disdains no advice regardless of source." Smith also recalls a particular technique Eisenhower employed in order to gain candid advice from persons who might otherwise be reticent to speak freely before the president. He assumes "that he himself is lacking in detailed knowledge and liable to make an error and is seeking advice. This is by no means a pose, because he actually values the recommendations and suggestions he receives, although his own better information and sounder judgment might cause them to be disregarded."[47]

Other presidents have been less successful in dealing with subordinates, sometimes going too far in managing the interpersonal and group dynamics of their official family. Orville Freeman, Kennedy's secretary of agriculture, recalls flying back to Washington after being told of Kennedy's assassination and pondering what it would be like to work for Lyndon Johnson. Freeman liked Johnson personally but worried that if he worked too closely with Johnson he would "suck your guts out." Johnson "was a demanding strong person who gave you the feeling that he is putting his tentacles around you and that you are subject to his will on your almost every move."[48]

Nixon's interpersonal behavior differed markedly from Johnson's excessive personalism but was equally problematic. Rather than shape his aides to his will, Nixon exhibited chameleonlike tendencies. According to John Ehrlichman, "he tended to avoid controversy by presenting an aspect of himself which he probably subconsciously calculated would be acceptable to the person that he was dealing with. He could switch around and present the opposite aspect to another person. There were people on the staff with whom he was very profane because he thought that was where he made contact with them. There were other people with whom he would never use a swear word."[49]

Concern for team spirit and other aspects of group dynamics among the president's staff does not mean that presidents must be gentle lambs in dealing with their subordinates. Some presidents have recognized the need to be tough with their staff when they fail to measure up. Eisenhower's aides knew, for example, that his temper would flair—albeit briefly—if they performed poorly. Roosevelt's competitive system worked in no small measure due to the personal attention FDR gave his staff and his ability to use that attention as a lever to discourage poor performance. By contrast, as Maurice Stans (Nixon's secretary of commerce) points out, Nixon could be privately intolerant of the mediocre performance of his subordinates "but lacked the courage to exercise discipline over them." For those who performed well, Stans recalls, Nixon was equally reticent: "he was not given to frequent praise."[50]

Excessive secrecy has also lessened the president's ability to make the lower reaches of the White House staff system work effectively. Ray Cline observes that "the basic remedy is to forgo some of the theoretical advantages of secret deliberations at the top in favor of keeping key staffs informed well enough to have a sense of participation and a clear purpose. If this is done, bureaucratic loyalties would be enlisted, better staff work would reach the top, and a more enlightening rationale would surround and explain key policy decisions."[51]

Bureaucratic and Court Politics: The Problem of Leaking

Where excessive secrecy is practiced at the top and the bulk of the staff feels isolated from policy decisions, behavior such as court politics—currying favor for self-serving reasons—and bureaucratic politics—attempting to further the cause of one's bureaucratic position—are likely to emerge as staff members seek a semblance of prestige and authority that is otherwise denied them. Leaking information to the press and other influential outsiders is an especially prevalent practice that is endemic to all presidencies but likely to be exaggerated under these circumstances.

Not surprisingly, given the high levels of secrecy in the Nixon administration and the general sense of isolation of staff members from the president and from each other—which Nixon deliberately encouraged—leaking was a pressing problem. Nixon seemed to recognize the alienation that some staff members might experience within the system he had created. In a 2 March 1970 memorandum to Haldeman, he noted that "it is very important that everybody down the line *feel* that his recommendations will be given Presidential consideration. Otherwise the quality of work will suffer."[52]

But Nixon's attempts to deal with staff discontent, especially leaking, were ineffective if not heavy handed. In a 16 June 1970 memorandum to both Haldeman and Ehrlichman, he complained about "an increasing number of news reports of columnists indicating that 'White House staffers privately' were raising questions about my activities." Nixon instructed his two aides, "I want the whole staff in the strongest possible terms to be informed that unless they can say something positive about my operations and that of the White House staff they should say nothing. I also would like to get your report on who has been responsible for this kind of statement."[53]

In April 1970, information about a controversial administration report on child care and early education was leaked to the press. In a memo to Haldeman, Nixon surmised that the leak had come from the Department of Health, Education, and Welfare and promptly ordered the following elaborate, orchestrated—and Draconian—response:

> The battle plan will be as follows: You first are to find out how many people the letter was sent to. You will then, of course, discover that the only possible place it could have come from is HEW. You shall then call in Bob Finch [secretary of HEW] and ask him who are the most likely people in his shop who are not on Civil Service who had copies of the letter. He is then to call them in and

say an investigation has revealed that the letter leaked from among them, that he knows that this will be very hard on them and their families, but that we have had too many of these leaks and many have come from HEW. There will probably be six people involved. He is then to tell them that they have 48 hours for one of them to come up and say that he leaked the letter. If they do not he is to ask for the resignation of all six. This is the battle plan. Execute it.

. . . This is the only way to stop leaks, to fire somebody and to fire a group of them like this because if six squeal it isn't going to make any more noise than if one does. Some injustice will be done, but the message will get around that we aren't going to tolerate this kind of deliberate disloyalty. Give me a report on this by Thursday.[54]

Nixon's "battle plan" is startling, not only in its implications for departmental morale—and, needless to say, its effects on those among the six who were innocent of wrongdoing—but also because Nixon's evidence seems inconclusive: "of course," he tells Haldeman, the only possible source is HEW, and he tells Finch to forget about any civil servants as culprits and to assemble a list of those "most likely" to have had access to the information, a number that Nixon believes to be six for reasons that are unclear.[55]

To be fair to Nixon, on other occasions his thoughts about how to deal with leaks appear more productive. In November 1971, reports surfaced in the press that White House staff members took credit for pressuring other members of the administration to make statements or take policy positions. Nixon instructed Haldeman, yet again, "to see to it that not only they but all their subordinates quit talking to the press, even on an off the record basis, unless they have specific instructions to do so." But then he added an interesting suggestion: "I think the way you can stop staff members from having to go out to talk to members of the press with regard to politics or how they influenced this man or that man to do this or that is to have more sessions with them where they can discuss politics and also their other activities completely within the staff." This is one of the few occasions where Nixon thought about the problem of team building or the kind of positive personal loyalty and mutual feeling that preoccupied Eisenhower. Nixon, however, followed his suggestion with the dictum, "We simply need to have a better disciplined staff," as if discipline alone produced an effective White House team.[56]

Nixon also seems to have been reluctant to give credit where credit was due and to acknowledge the work of his staff members. As noted earlier, Maurice Stans recalls that Nixon was reticent to praise members of his administration. The skills of others and the credit they felt due seem to have piqued Nixon on occasion. In a 14 January 1971 memorandum to Haldeman, he complained about members of his press staff who were bragging about their abilities to anticipate reporters' questions and to prep Nixon with answers. Nixon told Haldeman his answers were often spontaneous and that the press staff should point out that they gave him "a great mass of material but that I then proceed to boil it down." Nixon also took issue with his speech-writing staff: "I want to be sure that our speech and research staff gets maximum credit for the enormously effective work that they do. On the other hand, they simply have to recognize that when the President makes a speech—it is his speech and not that of a staff member." Nixon concluded by telling Haldeman (perhaps with an element of self-pity), "If we cannot find staff people who are willing to work on that basis, I, of course, will have to do more of the work myself which would be self-defeating."[57] Nixon's ambivalence provides another interesting contrast with Eisenhower, who often used his aides as lightning rods to absorb blame that might otherwise fall on the president, but by the same token praised them and publicly acknowledged them when they performed well.

Conflict versus Commitment

Dealing with conflicts that arise within the staff presents an especially difficult task for presidents. Whether deliberately or not, some presidents have employed managerial techniques that are responsive to conflicts and their roots in bureaucratic and court politics. One important counter to both tendencies is an ethos that stresses commitment to the president's aims and purposes. Kennedy's "New Frontier" is perhaps the best example: it instilled among his advisers a common set of very unbureaucratic goals. And Kennedy's personal style generated loyalty and trust.

Kennedy was also wary about the intrusion of bureaucratic interests in the advice he received. With respect to his cabinet meetings, for example, Fred Dutton, his liaison to the cabinet, recalls that if Kennedy "caught somebody trying to present what he considered the departmental viewpoint, he would get fairly sharp with his questions and abrupt enough that the advocate knew that he should cut it off." Also, according to Dutton, "unlike what I read of the Roosevelt and Truman administrations, Cabinet members could not lobby the President before and after the meetings. They knew they were there for *Cabinet* meetings."[58]

Members of the administration who appreciated Kennedy's demand for a broader perspective quickly became part of his official family. Kennedy did not restrict his inner counsel to the "Irish Mafia" who had served him earlier in his career, but extended it to new members, such as Treasury Secretary Dillon and Defense Secretary McNamara, neither of whom Kennedy knew well before becoming president and both of whom were nominal Republicans. "In brief," Dutton observes, "he developed new relationships and new reliances among those around him as President."[59]

Eisenhower lacked the youthful vigor of Kennedy and the esprit de corps Kennedy was able to elicit from a staff imbued with the heady goals of the New Frontier. But in less dramatic ways he also encouraged loyalty and commitment. In discussing his role on the White House staff, General Andrew Goodpaster notes that the complex staff arrangements in the Eisenhower presidency, especially in the area of national security, where Goodpaster's duties as staff secretary brought him into frequent contact with the president's national security adviser, might have been a "recipe for friction." They were not, Goodpaster observes, because Eisenhower was a man "to whom and to whose purposes we were all devoted. I think we would have been ashamed of doing anything in our own interest rather than trying to carry out his purposes. So you didn't have these turf battles that have been such an unsavory sight around Washington in later years." Goodpaster especially singled out Eisenhower's role in discouraging this kind of behavior: "He wouldn't have tolerated it for a moment if he thought the serious business of government was being impeded by this kind of— what he would regard as worse than nonsense. It would be quite improper conduct."[60]

Eisenhower recognized that some of the advice he received might be tainted or otherwise biased, a realization that antedated his presidency. In a 14 November 1951 letter to Everett "Swede" Hazlett (a boyhood friend and frequent recipient of lengthy, reflective letters from Eisenhower throughout his life), Eisenhower recognized the strong pull that parochial interests might have on those who advised the president. Reflecting on the Joint Chiefs of Staff, Eisenhower told Hazlett that "our people have, as yet, a lot to learn." "For the Joint Chiefs of Staff to coordinate and balance the great military organism in these days of tension," Eisenhower observed, "requires in each member, selflessness, energy, study, and the broadest kind of viewpoint and comprehension." "Each of these men," he emphasized, "must cease regarding himself as the advocate or special pleader for any particular Service."[61]

A letter Eisenhower wrote on his final day as army chief of staff in 1948 to Defense Secretary James Forrestal illustrates his recognition not only of the problem of parochial interests but of the practical steps that might be taken as remedy:

> The effort should be to promote the concept that the four individuals present, without regard to their respective responsibilities and specific duties, were meeting as a group to talk over broad security problems in an atmosphere of complete friendliness and objectivity. Whenever at such a meeting any individual shows a tendency to become a special pleader, the subject should be skillfully changed and constant effort made to achieve unanimity of conclu-

sion, first upon broad generalities and then gradually brought closer to concrete applications to particular problems. . . . The men composing this staff have reached the pinnacle of their respective careers. They should consider every problem from its broad national viewpoint; but habits of years will have to be overcome by some patience and a sense of humor. If the Secretary habitually and casually brings out into the open, at informal meetings, major controversial issues in the attitude of one seeking general professional assistance so that he may make decisions on the basis of the national welfare, he will eventually profit immeasurably.

Eisenhower's suggestions to Forrestal are particularly interesting in that they not only reveal his understanding of the tendencies at work in organizations, but indicate a number of strands in his leadership style that might be marshaled as a remedy and that he would himself later employ as president: a recognition of the personal strengths and weaknesses of those with whom a leader must deal (they have "reached the pinnacle," "habits of years"); a need to change behavior through the general tone a leader should set ("atmosphere of complete friendliness and objectivity," "patience and a sense of humor"); and the tactic of proceeding indirectly in seeking a leader's goals ("the subject should be skillfully changed . . . and . . . gradually brought . . . to concrete application"). Eisenhower especially stressed the need for a leader to establish close personal bonds to those who would advise and otherwise serve him as a compensatory mechanism: "The work of the Secretary will never be successful unless the principal members of his team are friends. . . . In dealing with problems, friends develop among themselves a natural selflessness that is the outgrowth of their regard for the others. Personal antagonism enjoys the defeat of the opponent—consequently objectivity and selflessness cannot be attained when it is present."[62]

During the first year of his presidency, Eisenhower again reflected on the problem of parochialism, now with reference to the wide range of advisers with whom he dealt. Writing again to Hazlett, Eisenhower saw the necessity for surrounding himself with persons who "are alert for phony agreement and the selfish motive and the untrustworthy individual." "The one thing that must never be forgotten is that when outsiders come in, [they] always have an ax to grind," Eisenhower continued. "Even within government itself, these distorted and selfish views are encountered. For example, you are . . . personally acquainted with some of the inter-service difficulties resulting from granite-like support of a special or parochial viewpoint. These same quarrels I find endlessly in every department of government."[63]

As president, Eisenhower put his thoughts with Hazlett and his advice to Forrestal to work in developing his own "team." He frequently emphasized to his aides, for example, that they worked for him, not their departments, the NSC, Adams, or others on the staff, thereby mitigating some of the effects of bureaucratic and court politics. In fact, the explicit operating norm Eisenhower attempted to instill was that nominal members of departments who served on interdepartmental committees were there to represent the general interest, not the positions of their home departments.

Bradley Patterson, who served on the cabinet secretariat staff, attests to the success of Eisenhower's efforts to counter "parochial viewpoints" especially by using cabinet meetings to build allegiance to the president's program. According to Patterson,

> Cabinet members are beset from every side by Congressional pressures, by the pressures of special constituencies, by the pressures of their bureaucracies . . . all of these pressures tending to grind special axes and sort of turn their heads away from the President who put them in office, and to whom they are responsible. And it actually takes special effort to remind them they are the President's men. . . . The President needs to take all the occasions he can to remind them of what *his* views are. So the Cabinet meeting is the time when he does that.[64]

Similarly, Emmet Hughes recalls that cabinet meetings

> fixed the occasions for exchange of facts and views between a President and department heads. . . . Again and again, the President would seize on some particular matter of legislation or administration as spark for a warm homily on his most personal views. . . . For almost all the persons present, these fervent sermons carried an authority almost scriptural. And they tempered, if they did not alter, some of the Cabinet's own generally more conventional predispositions.[65]

The cabinet secretariat system that Eisenhower created in 1954 also contributed to the effective flow of information to the cabinet and to use of the cabinet as a deliberative forum in the way the president had envisioned it, but now with respect to avoiding the dangers of bureaucratization. On the one hand, the secretariat made sure that items of interest were brought to presidential attention by seeing that they were placed on the cabinet's agenda. In Patterson's words, "this put us . . . in a position of being like a radar set, looking around the whole spectrum of the executive branch and picking up in a sensitive way indications of things that were happening and that were coming toward the President's desk for decision. Or if they weren't coming there, things that ought to be, so that people wouldn't duck them or try to do it . . . unilaterally."[66] On the other hand, the cabinet secretariat took steps to prevent department heads from short-circuiting the process by appealing directly to the president: the secretariat, according to Patterson, "had to dig, wheedle, persuade and finesse Cabinet members to bring to the common table what were clearly common matters, but which department heads, in their century-and-a-half-long tradition, would much prefer to bring privately to the Oval Office. It was only because they knew that Eisenhower wanted it this way and no other that they reluctantly acceded to the Cabinet secretary's or Sherman Adams' agenda-planning."[67] The cabinet secretariat also "rode herd" on departments at the implementation stage of the policy process through its regular status-of-action reports. A system of such regularized reports served to remind Cabinet members and their staffs that they were accountable for their actions in carrying out the president's directives.

Eisenhower valued deliberative forums such as the NSC or the cabinet not only because they weaned participants in the policy process away from parochial perspectives but also because they encouraged them to work together as a team in developing solutions to policy problems, both those at hand and those that might arise without warning in the future. As Robert Cutler, his NSC special assistant, recounts, they accustomed the president's advisers "to working and thinking *together* on hard problems."[68] In 1968, Cutler wrote a brief paper elaborating on Eisenhower's rationale for the NSC process, which he took to the president for approval and editorial comment. In Cutler's words, with Eisenhower's editorial insertion:

> The prime values to Eisenhower of regular, continuous planning experience by the Council and its [Planning] Board lay, first, in the training in planning received by his principal advisors on the Council . . . and, second, in the resultant familiarizing of each Council Member with the others at the Council Table. [DDE insert: Through this practice, the members of the NSC became familiar not only with each other, but with the basic factors of problems that might, on some future date, face the President.] Thus in time of some sudden, explosive crisis, these men would gather to work with and for the President, not as strangers, but as men intimately made familiar through continuing association, with the characters, abilities, and understandings of each colleague at the Council Table. Such training enabled them to act in an emergency, not as mere ciphers and not as yes-men for the President, but as men accustomed to express their own views at the Council Table and join in critical discussion and the resolution of issues before their Chairman, the President.[69]

Although recent presidents have not enjoyed complete success in ensuring that their staff systems overcome the organizational tendencies and dynamics at work in the institutional presidency, the range of their respective experiences offers useful lessons in what a chief executive might or might not do. Most importantly, their experiences suggest that understanding their management practices through an organizational lens—the extent to which they take account of the *institutional* presidency—is likely to be critical in establishing an effective staff system and, ultimately, an effective presidency.

5

JIMMY CARTER
The Travails of Centralized Collegiality

■ ■ ■

This and the next two chapters consider the staff management practices of three recent presidents—Carter, Reagan, and Bush. Their experiences reveal both the dimensions of the institutional presidency that we have examined: how they dealt with the strengths and weaknesses of their respective managerial systems as they operated within an institutional context, the theme of chapter 3, and their strategies for dealing with the more encompassing organizational dynamics of the institutional presidency, the theme of chapter 4. The Carter and Reagan presidencies are especially illuminating because they illustrate two very different types of White House organization and management—the former a variant of a collegial staff arrangement, the latter a more formalistic system—that encountered common difficulties in coping with the organizational dynamics at work in the contemporary White House staff.

Carter and the Institutional Presidency: Through a Managerial Lens

Carter's White House staff presents an interesting variant of collegial staff management as well as a telling commentary on the problems collegial management encounters in an organizational context. Carter campaigned for president, as William Leuchtenburg has observed, "as an outsider who promised to curb the excesses of the imperial presidency,"[1] and he took office with the aim, partly as a response to the Watergate debacle, of fostering a more open White House staff system and a more inclusive policy-making process. Carter hoped to avoid an administration that was strongly based in the White House staff, preferring instead a more decentralized arrangement that reached beyond staff members for counsel. By delegating authority to cabinet officers, Carter hoped to play an active role as the hub of his collegial spokes and wheels; only the most important decisions were to be reserved for presidential attention. Carter initially chose not to appoint a chief of staff, instead giving nine staff members relatively equal access and status, although with different responsibilities. However, decentralization of policy-making responsibility in the cabinet soon proved ill advised. Over time, problems in Carter's collegial system led to increasing formalization of his staff procedures, increasing reliance on his White House aides, and the eventual appointment of a chief of staff. This yielded a unique combination of collegiality and formal procedures, but one that did not effectively serve the president's ends.

Character, Leadership Style, and Centralized Collegiality

Erwin Hargrove, in his seminal study of Carter's leadership style, argues that Carter's practices of staff management were deeply ingrained in his character and drawn from a variety of sources. Carter's emphasis on collegiality had its roots in his training as an engineer and in his moral and religious values. Collegiality meshed with Carter's view, drawn in part from his experience in the navy under Admiral Rickover, that a leader must intimately know the details of his command and duties and be exposed to the views of his subordinates directly rather than rely on what filters up from the hierarchy below.

Carter's background as an engineer also had some effect, particularly in the central role he chose to play in his policy-making process and his predilection to digest enormous amounts of information. "He was an engineer," his secretary of agriculture Bob Bergland once observed, who "delighted in seeing pieces and parts."[2] Furthermore, according to one Carter staff member, "He viewed political problems as cube roots. . . . If you [found] the right answer and [used] your powers of logical deduction that was it. You didn't waste a lot of time persuading people about it." From his moral and religious background, Hargrove observes, Carter thought it possible to achieve "synthesis and balance between seemingly competitive principles and . . . to achieve such balance through study and good will."[3] Carter stood at the intersection of these "moralist" and "engineer" strains, William Lee Miller concludes, and they met "in their shared picture of a world swept clean to be remade by the energetic exertion of the individual will."[4] In addition, according to one Carter aide, "He wasn't going to do the Lord's work on a half-ass basis."[5]

A collegial staff arrangement matched these predilections and put Carter at the center of the policy process in his administration. The spokes of the wheel would radiate from a president who would serve as its hub, not only making decisions but immersing himself in the details of policy and subjecting himself to an array of deliberations. Those spokes would radiate out far for Carter. The isolation of the Nixon White House encouraged his belief that his cabinet officers and their departments should play a vital part in formulating the new policies of his administration. His experience as governor of Georgia led him to believe that cabinet government would work.

Carter also put his collegial management in the service of a leadership style that sought long-run, cost-effective policy solutions that were goal oriented rather than defined by immediate political problems and considerations and that looked to the nation's common good rather than the particular interests of constituency groups. This does not mean that Carter never took the short-run into consideration, failed to address immediate problems in his search for broader goals, or wholly ignored politics. But the former was the main thrust of his leadership style, and it was only partially (and, for Carter, reluctantly) tempered by other considerations. Carter's "politics as public goods" leadership, as Hargrove terms it, or his vision of a "trusteeship" presidency, as Charles O. Jones characterizes it,[6] set a different tone from the incremental and political concerns of a Johnson or a Nixon or the skillful projection of a public image as a public program, which his successor was to employ. Carter's ambition for setting a collegial arrangement at the service of the optimal rather than just the "do-able" was unique; it substituted the aim of a formalistic system—optimality—for the more limited goal of do-ability normally associated with collegial staff arrangements. Its scope, cabinet government rather than a White House–led and –dominated system, also was ambitious. Had it worked, it would have been remarkable.

The Limits of Centralized Collegiality

Carter's intentions notwithstanding, his staff organization and management practices generated many of the shortcomings attributed to collegial systems. They put a heavy burden on the president's time and attention and called for unusual interpersonal skills, which Carter was unable to provide, in mediating differences and maintaining teamwork. As individuals, cabinet members had direct access to the president.[7] But collegial contacts were another matter. Meetings of the cabinet proved unproductive, forcing Carter to work individually with cabinet members or in task forces and placing increasing authority for coordinating the policy process on the White House staff, which was ill-equipped to handle it. In Zbigniew Brzezinski's view, cabinet meetings "were almost useless. The discussions were desultory, there was no coherent theme to them, and after a while they were held less and less frequently. Not wanting to waste time, I used the Cabinet sessions to dispose surreptitiously of my light reading; since they took place on

Monday mornings, I would use them to go through the latest editions of the weekly magazines, carefully hidden on my knees below the edge of the Cabinet table."[8] Bob Bergland, Carter's secretary of agriculture, recalls that Carter "didn't really like to mix it up in a meeting. He didn't like to debate or listen to arguments; he was very uncomfortable in that area. There were a few instances in which I would argue with someone in the Cabinet on the substance of an issue and the President would let the argument go on for awhile, and then he would cut it off."[9]

Overload is endemic in collegial processes and it was manifest in the Carter White House. Carter's initial desire to avoid assigning the tasks and title of chief of staff to one of his aides and his casting of the Domestic Policy Staff, led by Stuart Eizenstat, in the role of coordinator (but with little definition of that role and little authority to perform its demands) thrust increasing numbers of decisions both routine and important upon the president. Carter relished such a central position. More generally, according to one Carter aide, the president in his desire "to have a sense of conquering the office in its every manifestation" took on too much responsibility that might have been delegated more effectively to others: "Broad decisions would be made and then there would be an inability to make a specific decision. . . . people knew that Carter was insisting on making every last decision. . . . What should have happened is the President should have said, 'look . . . you've given me the basic issues, here are my decisions, now go and settle it . . . and don't come back to see me.' " The same aide reports that, although Carter began to delegate more authority to his staff after his first year in office, needed change still did not fully come. The staff had a more central role, but Carter "still loved to hold on to making those last minute decisions, and as much as he complained about them he kept making them."[10]

It is not surprising that Carter encountered the problems he did. Collegial systems are not especially adept at organizing policy analysis or encouraging comprehensive policy development of the sort Carter wanted. Carter's own analytic skills ameliorated, to some extent, these weaknesses. But he lacked the comprehensive vision that could compensate for the coherent policy goals a collegial process often fails to generate. In contrast, as one administration official notes, "he was compulsively oriented in the detail direction." And, according to another, "he was down in the weeds. . . . He did not have a global view of what he wanted."[11] James Fallows, who served for a time on the Carter staff, saw Carter as entirely too "eclectic": he had views on "every issue under the sun but . . . no large view of the relations between them."[12] For biographer Betty Glad, he lacked "a well-thought-out conceptual framework."[13]

Nor was effective remedy provided by the staff system around him.

Carter's collegial arrangements did not provide, as a formal system might have, a way to rank his goals. Instead they played to Carter's sense of being a president of achievement by presenting him with many goals and programs but without a means for ordering them in a comprehensive and politically strategic fashion.

The Limits of "Hands-on" Management

The interpersonal skills necessary to make a collegial staff system function effectively were also wanting in the Carter White House. Carter's own role in his collegial system especially generated difficulties. A president with rather fixed and determined policy views will neither benefit from nor facilitate the give-and-take that is one of the most important products of collegial deliberations.

Brzezinski, his NSC special assistant, found Carter "impatient"; there were "circumstances in which he would make decisions ahead of the NSC coordinating process, prompting me to complain to him." "Moreover," Brzezinski adds, "whenever I tried to relieve him of excessive detail, Carter would show real uneasiness, and I even felt some suspicion, that I was usurping his authority." On one occasion, when Brzezinski complained about the lack of coordination in national security policy making (involving such matters as a decision to change a scheduled seven-power conference to a five-power conference made without Brzezinski's participation, messages to Soviet Foreign Minister Gromyko sent before Brzezinski and Defense Secretary Harold Brown could comment on them, and plans for dealing with the Iran hostage crisis formulated without discussion among Carter's top advisers), Brzezinski recorded in his daily journal that Carter "got really furious. He told me in an icy fashion that I just wanted to be involved in everything. I told him that was not the point. That if he wants to do all the work himself he can, but if he wants issues coordinated for him, he shouldn't encourage this kind of thing. He gave me a rather silent and icy stare."[14]

In meetings, Carter took the lead and was energetic and effective, according to his aides. But it was the effectiveness of a man in control who had his fingers on the answers and knew the details, and who liked to show others that he knew. According to James Fallows, "Carter's performance on first intimate meeting was something special. His intelligence and magnetism banished all thoughts of the limits of his background." But this also had a downside: "Carter's faith was in himself, and in the impression he would create."[15] Yet these may not be the qualities needed to make a collegial system work. Deference to the advice of others, holding back of one's own views, perhaps even a capacity to seem less informed or at least open to education and instruction in order to encourage others to air their views seem more effective in eliciting the kind of advice the president needs in a collegial setting, as Kennedy's experience in the Cuban missile crisis exemplifies. But Carter's interpersonal style was almost the direct opposite. As Hargrove puts it, "At times this skill could cause Carter to show off when he might have been listening. One aide finally discouraged the president from demonstrating his knowledge to experts who were briefing him with the argument that he was intimidating them and depriving himself of information."[16]

Recalling his meetings with his advisers, Carter especially valued his weekly breakfasts with Vice-President Walter Mondale, Secretary of State Cyrus Vance, Defense Secretary Harold Brown, and Brzezinski. But they were meetings in which the president took the lead, surrounded by a small group of top advisers and in a policy area where the president was relatively free from domestic political pressures. Carter described the meetings:

> We didn't have a prepared agenda ahead of time, but Vance, Brown, Brzezinski and I would have the agenda items. I would ordinarily cover almost all of the issues myself and then I would ask for additional ones. I would see them crossing off their lists what I had already brought up. At the conclusion of it Brzezinski would read the decisions we had made or things that were postponed. That was an hour and a half. . . . I think the fact that we could actually make some decisions there was what made it attractive.[17]

Another aspect of Carter's personal style that may have had an effect on his dealings with others was his doggedness in pursuing issues and policies he felt were right. As Carter himself put it: "Once I made a decision I was awfully stubborn about it. . . . Once I get on something I'm awfully hard to change. And that may also be a cause of some of my political failures."[18]

Defects in Formal Procedures

Carter tempered his reliance on a collegial process of advising with a more formal process that emphasized written memoranda, not just verbal deliberations among his advisers; the written record of policy analysis in the Carter White House is more extensive than is usual in collegial systems. At least in the abstract, this combination of formal and informal processes should overcome one of the limitations of purely collegial systems: lack of extensive staff work. But in practice the formal side of Carter's procedures did not always work to his advantage.

Even though staff members such as Brzezinski, Eizenstat, and Jack Watson were designated to act as policy coordinators, Carter insisted on reading approximately three hundred to four hundred pages of information each day.[19] Hargrove observes that "for the most part he preferred to work off paper, checking yes or no to choices the [staff] presented him."[20]

Similarly, Agriculture Secretary Bergland recalls that Carter "liked to have decision memoranda." Uncomfortable with "mixing it up in a meeting," Bergland notes that what Carter really wanted from his associates "was to reduce our arguments to writing. . . . His staff would then produce a letter. It would state who's for and who's against. At the bottom of the letter would be a provision to check yes or no with room for comments."[21]

But Carter's memoranda tended to limit the president's options. As one aide pointed out, while Carter "liked to make a decision on the merits and check the box that seemed to him the best direction for the nation to go and that was an enormous strength," it was "a liability at times because you can't always simply check the right box." Also, as Hargrove observes, extensive reliance on written memoranda can put a tremendous load upon a president, especially in domestic policy, where "the actors shift from issue to issue and the White House must resolve a larger number of questions. The president cannot give intensive study to all of them as he can to a relatively few major foreign policy issues."[22]

Carter's problems with staff work were compounded by his inability, in domestic policy, to develop an effective coordinating role for the Domestic Policy Staff (DPS); according to Colin Campbell, "This state of affairs owed partially to Stuart Eizenstat's eschewing of structure within the Domestic Policy Staff and the lack of experience among DPS members."[23]

The Case of the NSC

In national security policy making, procedures were not the issue, but problems still arose. When Carter took office, he sought to simplify the NSC system that had developed under Kissinger and to reduce both the power and the size of the NSC staff. Carter had hoped to rely on greater input from his secretary of state, Cyrus Vance, in line with his general goal of deemphasizing the White House staff and increasing the policy-making role of the cabinet. In theory, it was Carter's hope that his NSC assistant Brzezinski, would manage NSC operations in the role of a staff coordinator, while Vance would become the administration's chief foreign policy spokesman and adviser.

Brzezinski's efforts appeared to portend a marked improvement in the national security policy–making process. He restructured the complex system that had developed during the Nixon and Ford presidencies, reducing the size of the NSC staff, eliminating the myriad of committees that had proliferated under Kissinger, and attempting to bring cabinet-level participation into the process rather than subcabinet representation, as had been the case. Two standing groups were created: a Policy Review Committee (PRC), which examined foreign policy problems on an issue-by-issue basis and was chaired by a cabinet officer,[24] and a Special Coordination Committee (SCC), chaired by Brzezinski, which focused on arms control, crisis management, and intelligence activities. Brzezinski and his NSC staff were assigned most of the staff work in the process, such as preparing a presidential review memorandum (PRM) on the issue under consideration, gathering information for PRC or SCC sessions, setting agendas for meetings, and coordinating paper flow between the PRC or SCC and the NSC.

Not all policy issues required "full treatment" through the process. In some instances, when consensus prevailed in the PRC or SCC and the president agreed, a presidential directive (PD) based on a PRM would be issued; in other cases the importance of the issue and the degree of disagreement that existed required more careful scrutiny by advisers, including face-to-face meetings with the president. On the most important issues, the latter course was the order of the day, with Carter convening NSC meetings early in his presidency to resolve such issues and then moving, in June 1977, to informal Friday breakfast meetings with Brzezinski and Vance (occasionally also Vice-President Mondale). In 1978, Defense Secretary Brown and Hamilton Jordan of the White House staff were invited to attend, and, toward the end of Carter's presidency, the group had expanded to include Hedley Donovan, Lloyd Cutler, and Jody Powell from the White House staff.

In March 1977, Brzezinski, Vance, and Brown also began to meet on Thursday for lunch. They would discuss issues that would come up the next morning, sometimes "solv[ing] conflicts among themselves without the president's involvement" and "settling issues quickly, at times bypassing the longer deliberations of the PRC and SCC." At least initially, the Thursday lunches were a setting for informal discussion, disposing of minor issues, and facilitating implementation. But over time, they began to intrude into the policy-making functions of the Friday breakfasts, where Carter was present. According to Defense Secretary Brown,

> the first couple of years the Thursday lunches were very informal. We just talked about things. Then, what happened is staffs—the NSC staff, Defense, State—began to see them as a way of getting issues resolved that they had been unable to resolve at a staff level. And so big agendas began to be created and we actually resolved things, but we also lost something. We lost the free interplay and it became more than it had been—a staff-driven exercise. When that happened, the agenda items for the Thursday lunches would provide part of the agenda for Friday, but only part.[25]

It is interesting to note that in his recollections of the Friday breakfasts, Carter recalled, "We didn't have a prepared agenda ahead of time,"[26] which does not square with Brown's account. This raises the question of the extent to which Carter was aware of what transpired at the Thursday sessions of his top advisers (although Brzezinski reports in his memoirs that he kept the president fully informed).[27]

The deliberations of the Friday group, not unlike Lyndon Johnson's Tuesday lunches, were also vexed by a certain casualness in procedures. According to Brzezinski, "there was some disadvantage in the casual way some decisions were made and interpreted. For example, each participant would write down for himself the President's decisions as guidance for implementation. It was only after the flap over the UN vote on Jerusalem in the spring of 1980 that Carter authorized me to provide an authoritative summary of his decisions as guidance for the participants."[28]

Although on paper Brzezinski had created more effective formal procedures (especially in contrast to what was present in domestic policy), the process did not always work to Carter's benefit. When disagreement in the PRC or SCC occurred, according to Alexander Moens's extensive study of Carter's foreign policy making, "the president would deal with it by studying all the position papers or calling a meeting of his advisers. . . . The president listened, encouraged frankness, and did not want to be shielded from unpleasant facts, hard options, or difficult decisions. He absorbed every detail and made the final decision himself." But Carter's advisers, in the first year or so of his presidency, "rarely disagreed," according to Moens, "despite the open decision-making structure." Part of the difficulty may have been Carter's performance in meetings: it discouraged debate and tended to show others what Carter knew; at a minimum Carter did not possess the necessary interpersonal skills to force disagreement out into the open and generate lively discussion. Nor did he learn from his mistakes; as Moens points out, "Unlike Kennedy, who seemed to have learned from the Bay of Pigs Fiasco, to ask tougher questions, Carter does not seem to have learned anything from his early setbacks. SALT II, Human Rights, the Neutron Bomb fiasco and early overtures toward a Geneva Conference for the Middle East are all examples of this lack of self-criticism."[29]

But his top advisers also failed him: although their views about foreign policy often differed, they "did not put the difficult questions on the table," Moens concludes. "To make matters worse, the consensus more often than not was along the lines of Carter's initial policy beliefs. . . . Carter as a result was not fully aware of the limits of his ideals." Lack of substantive disagreement in the president's presence was a constant, Moens argues, in the four cases of Carter's foreign policy decisions he studied at length— intervention in the Ogaden War, normalization of relations with China, the fall of the Shah, and even the "deep cuts" proposal for SALT II, where more substantive divisions existed—and similar problems may also have affected discussions on "human rights, American policy toward Eastern Europe, several aspects of the Middle East negotiations, and American policy toward

Angola, Rhodesia, and Zaire." Carter and his advisers "early on settled into a mode of collegiality and consensus, based more on shared values and beliefs than on rigorous evaluation of expected consequences."[30]

Brzezinski: From Neutral Coordinator to Policy Advocate

Although Brzezinski may have started out hoping to be a neutral coordinator of the national security process, in the vacuum that developed without open debate and disagreement, he increasingly became a more vocal policy advocate, engaging in diplomacy (normalization of relations with China), public speaking (starting in 1978), and policy implementation (Iran). Moens, in part, defends Brzezinski's shift toward policy advocacy and a more active role in the national security process: "What saved the process from becoming a string of consensus meetings was [his] advocacy."[31] He became a counterweight, in effect, offering policy views that breached the consensus and widened the president's range of options; much as Eisenhower's NSC adviser, Robert Cutler, would bring forth policy views that had not been fully or fairly aired, so too did Brzezinski. In Alexander George's terms, his role resembled that of devil's advocate, who argues strongly for the unpopular option, with the added twist that Brzezinski tended to be a committed advocate who did not just rise to the occasion to argue for a position that had been ignored or neglected.

But Brzezinski's advocacy went beyond actions that might be linked to the necessary functions of a managerial custodian, as George sets them out. His advocacy at times compromised the process of full and fair deliberation, even undermining the procedures he had himself created. Brzezinski's strong policy views, compared to Secretary of State Vance's more cautious stance, for example, tended to tilt action away from the Policy Review Committee, which Vance often chaired, to the Special Coordination Committee, Brzezinski's bailiwick. In his own memoirs, Brzezinski notes that "during the early phases of the Carter Administration, the PRC met more frequently. . . . In time, however, the SCC became more active. I used the SCC to shape our policy toward the Persian Gulf, on European security issues, on strategic matters, as well as in determining our response to Soviet aggression. Moreover, right from the very start . . . the SCC was the central organ for shaping our SALT policy."[32] Furthermore, as Colin Campbell observes, "the National Security Council, as such, rarely met; thus the ascendancy of the SCC in relation to the PRC intensified an 'escalator' process whereby cabinet secretaries felt bound to attend the SCC even if a deputy would do just as well." Campbell also found among his respondents the opinion that the SCC "increasingly pandered to the president's preoccupations rather than providing arm's-length preparations of stances and initiatives."[33]

Although Carter potentially had access to a range of advisers and policy views, Brzezinski had the guiding word (at least in the paper flow): he not only prepared the PRMs and controlled the written information reaching the president, but he also "would usually attach a cover memo indicating his analysis of the problem as well as his preference or lack of preference for any of the options."[34] In his memoirs, Brzezinski concedes that "in the latter phases of the administration" he would announce his own interpretation of the discussions of the SCC, "leaving it up to any individual to appeal to the President if he so wished." Brzezinski also prepared periodic (usually weekly) NSC reports for Carter. These contained reports on intelligence and policy implementation, summaries of NSC staff papers, and, according to Brzezinski, "a one-page-long editorial piece by me, entitled 'Opinion.' In it I commented in a freewheeling fashion on the Administration's performance, alerted him to possible problems, conveyed occasionally some criticism, and attempted to impart a global perspective."[35]

Brzezinski was also empowered to issue and sign presidential directives ("once the President had approved their text," he cautions in his memoirs[36]) save for the most important presidential decisions, generally ones dealing with strategic policy. By 1979, Brzezinski was even in a position to exclude some participants from meetings. Moens notes, for example, that he "would quickly change PRC sessions into NSC sessions by bringing in the President, merely to oust the assistant secretaries (from State) whose opinions he did not cherish."[37]

If Brzezinski can be faulted for going too far in his endeavors, so also can Carter for failing to respond to the dysfunction in his national security procedures. Advocacy was needed, but it came at the price of policy coordination, which was necessary to the effective functioning of the policy process. Also, as we shall see shortly, part of Carter's difficulties stemmed from his inability to see the need to resolve conflict among his advisers, his reticence in dealing with unfamiliar sources of counsel, and his failure to respond to bureaucratic and court politics. In contrast to what prevailed in domestic affairs, Carter had an open and, at least on paper, well-organized decision-making process for national security matters, but what he failed to understand and compensate for was its operation within an organizational context.

Nor was the problem simply with Brzezinski's penchant for expressing his own policy views. Advocacy also compromised Carter's Economic Policy Group. According to one of Campbell's respondents, unlike the neutral broker role that had been instrumental in the success of Ford's EPG, "under the current EPG structure, everyone has a policy—a really active position. Thus, the memos that go to the president presumably reflecting the views of all the economic advisers actually state the views of the authors somewhat better. This fact leads to the proliferation of cover memos and counter memos." Furthermore, according to Campbell, "several respondents observed that Stuart Eizenstat's involvement in EPG as a virtual principal belied any claim he or members of the Domestic Policy Staff could make to neutral, process-management roles."[38]

The Eight Decisions Analysis

During Carter's first year in office, an extensive analysis of eight key decisions[39] across a range of foreign and domestic policies was undertaken in order to develop a better understanding of the strengths and weaknesses of Carter's decision-making procedures. According to the summary of the study, "No previous Administration has allowed a detailed study of its ongoing policy-making processes. No previous reorganization study of the Executive Office has ever been permitted to examine the way in which the staff system operates on concrete policy issues."[40] The study's findings reveal the weaknesses of Carter's procedures, especially those of the more formal processes of defining and presenting well-staffed options for the president's consideration.

The summary of the study's findings strongly indicts the administration's decision process; seven of nine chief conclusions point to weaknesses in its operation within an organizational setting:

1. "The Economic Policy group [EPG] is not effective as currently operating. As a result, the President does not always receive a full and systematic staffing of economic issues."

2. "Departmental specialists have demonstrated high competence in support of EOP decision making, but their utilization is inconsistent and inefficient, varying widely across policy areas."

3. "Strong departmental advocacy exists and should be balanced by *early* interdepartmental review by departments, agencies, and EOP units (i.e. structured conflict)."

4. "Political analysis within the EOP, related both to Congress and the broader political environment, is not applied to decision making on a systematic basis."

5. "Follow-up procedures regarding Presidential decisions need to be formalized."

6. "Presidentially-imposed short leadtimes and the intrusion of crises into the EOP decision-making process make the development of better process control mechanisms all the more necessary."

7. "The form and content of written material for the President need to be better planned to enhance the use of the President's finite review time."[41]

Each of these deficiencies in organizational procedure was linked, in turn, to a specific problem that occurred in each of the policy decisions. In the decision to build a breeder reactor, the study found that "the President was provided with uncoordinated decision memoranda over several weeks whose various options allowed the President to make decisions, each of which was slightly inconsistent with its predecessor." These inconsistencies "created ambiguities which afforded 'decision losers' the chance to re-enter their preferred option for another discussion round." Confusion was generated among the EOP staff: "in some cases planned ambiguity creates flexibility; in this case, the ambiguity was unintended and created substantial administrative confusion." In the discussion of the administration's policy regarding quotas for imported footwear, not only was an option discarded only to be resurrected at a subsequent meeting, but "it was not then supported by any written material to structure discussion."[42]

In the White House's deliberations on how to refinance social security, the Economic Policy Group [EPG] was the lead agency; EPG had been created to provide coordination and review the administration's economic policies. But in this instance, according to the study, "the EPG entered the process so late that the alternatives [that] surfaced in the meeting were understaffed by the agencies which advocated them. Had the President wished to choose any other than the HEW proposal, he would probably [have] had to postpone final action." The case study of the breeder reactor raised a related issue, namely the exclusion of relevant participants as well as relevant policy options: "The Science Adviser to the President was screened out of the process until almost the end of the issue. There was almost no opportunity to apply technical advisory skills to an assessment of the decision."[43]

The study also found deficiencies in the formal process of presidential review memoranda, a system designed to develop an orderly identification and researching of policy options. In the administration's discussion of its conventional arms transfer policy, the study found that "the PRM [system] did not adequately identify the issue in the first place. . . . The success of the PRM process is critically dependent upon a careful outlining of the issue(s) at the very outset. Extra resources at the front end may reduce overall effort."[44]

Finally, the study found that there was often confusion about whether the president had made a decision and what that decision entailed. In the breeder reactor case, for example, not only was there disorganization in the process of formulating the administration's policy—"As a consequence of poor issue identification and agency involvement initially, logically related memoranda did not arrive at the Oval Office together"—the eventual decisions "were sufficiently unsynchronized as to confuse affected parties. The confusion over the meaning of the President's decision then resulted in incomplete follow-through and a reopening of the decision process."[45]

Informal Channels

Carter's difficulties in his formal decision procedures were complemented by difficulties besetting his informal channels of information and advice. Like Eisenhower, Carter tapped an informal network of confidantes inside and outside government. These included his wife, Rosalynn, White House aides Jody Powell and Hamilton Jordan, Atlanta lawyer and longtime friend Charles Kirbo, media consultant Gerald Rafshoon, and public opinion analyst Patrick Cadell. Carter trusted these associates and benefited from their ability to be candid with him. But all dated from his Georgia background, and none had extensive Washington experience or detailed knowledge of the nation's political affairs. One informal relationship that bore great fruit for Carter was that with Vice-President Mondale. His weekly lunches with his vice-president, Mondale's intimate involvement in the details of policy making in the Carter White House, and the warm personal ties that developed between them enabled Carter to be exposed to Mondale's political instincts as a Washington insider and knowledgeable participant in congressional politics.

Mondale, however, was almost the lone voice of political experience in the Carter White House. Carter would later bring into his administration such longtime Washington hands as Lloyd Cutler and Edmund Muskie. But his associates from Georgia were by far the majority in his inner circle of counsel, especially before his 1979 reshuffling of the cabinet. Some proved worthy to the challenge, such as Jody Powell as press boss and Eizenstat in the DPS. But, lacking in national-level experience, most of Carter's trusted aides often fell short. As Colin Campbell points out, "dissatisfaction with the administration developed as it became clear that Carter and his most trusted aides were hobbled by inexperience. This defect— lack of familiarity with the Washington scene—presented the administration with very painful learning experiences in virtually all its significant initiatives."[46] One staff member interviewed by Paul Light in his study of the Carter White House singled out this problem: "We spent a great deal of time simply learning how to do things, and even then we made more than our share of mistakes. The president told us that we should do things pretty much the same as we did in Georgia. But Washington isn't Georgia, and the White House isn't the governor's mansion."[47] Paradoxically, in a presidency where, reputedly, Carter himself took on the task of scheduling the White House tennis courts, policy details that counted often went unnoticed. According to one respondent in Campbell's survey of the Carter administration, a couple of guys [in the Ford administration] told me that congressional liaison used to spend hours with Ford deciding which congressional trip went where and who got which airplane and the makeup of the delegation. Now Carter didn't know until he sent Bob Strauss to Egypt as special envoy that we didn't have all the airplanes we need[ed] or that there was any question about who went in what airplane. . . . He didn't know that some had windows and some didn't, which is very important to those people up there.[48]

Carter and the Institutional Presidency: Through an Organizational Lens

Carter began his presidency by practicing a form of centralized collegial management but increasingly moved to a more formalized set of procedures; neither worked effectively. His managerial practices reveal not only the weaknesses of collegial and formalistic staff systems, however, but also the effect of the organizational characteristics of the institutional presidency on the president's staff system. His experience provides, moreover, an interesting case study of how the organizational characteristics of the institutional presidency can be interrelated in their effects, reinforcing each other and compounding the president's managerial task.

Carter's inability to take into account the organizational dynamics of the institutional presidency was striking. As James Sterling Young observes, Carter's "métier is issue politics more than party or institutional politics, and his forte is issue leadership rather than the leadership of institutions or organizations."[49] Carter took few steps that were effective in correcting the problems in his staff system. In fact, his staff organization and management practices tended to exacerbate centralization of power in the White House staff, the development of hierarchy and gatekeeping, and bureaucratic and court politics.

Cabinet Government, Bureaucratic Politics, and Centralization of Power

The administration's extensive study of its early decision-making procedures in eight key foreign and domestic policies is again revealing, but now about how Carter's efforts fared within an organizational context. Undertaken at a point when Carter still had great faith in the possibility of avoiding a policy-making process strongly based on the White House staff by relying instead on substantive input from departments and agencies, the study reveals the intrusion of bureaucratic politics into the administration's deliberations. Little was done, however, to encourage agencies and departments to rise above their parochial perspectives. Slowly but surely the White House staff began to fill the policy gap that the experiment with cabinet government had left, but it did so in ways that centralized control of the policy process in its hands. The shift often veered off into the realm of policy advocacy although Carter had envisioned a more neutral coordinating role for it.

The eight case studies are each replete with evidence of the tendencies of agencies and departments to hew closely to narrow policy perspectives, often reflecting their particular bureaucratic interests. In the decision to fund a breeder reactor, for example, the Energy Research and Development Administration (ERDA) emphasized technologies based on plutonium—on which it had done extensive work—but failed to inform the president about alternative breeder fuel cycles such as thorium, of which it was aware but had not investigated extensively. According to the study, "ERDA failed to provide this advice, and only very late in the process was the Science Adviser, Frank Press, able to point out to the President what was available."[50]

Bureaucratic politics—"standing where you sit"—was an especially prevalent theme in the study's findings. In the decision to raise the minimum wage, the study found that "the Department of Labor adhered through several meetings and memoranda to its position, and provided extensive technical material to support that position." But Labor's representatives "did not discuss alternative options." In the deliberations about how to refinance social security, "the same [was] true of HEW . . . —adherence to a well-staffed agency option." Departmentally backed proposals were well researched and presented, according to the case study, but they tended to "overwhelm the consideration of alternative positions. . . . The President's decision prerogatives are only served if other agency and EOP positions are also requested very early in the issue staffing process." "Since the 'public interest' might be best served by a presidential decision option which is no department's first preference, only continuous scrutiny by the President's advisory staff will ensure the protection of the President's ability to decide."[51]

The prevalence of agencies and departments "standing where they sit" was not an unexpected outcome of Carter's emphasis on cabinet government. As the study notes, "the departments by definition must respond to a narrower mission and constituency than the President's." But Carter's problems were compounded by the inability of White House units charged with coordinating the process—the Economic Policy Group (EPG), the Council of Economic Advisers (CEA), or what was then still the Domestic Council and soon to be reorganized as the Domestic Policy Staff—effectively to meet their responsibilities in expanding the range of the president's policy choices and, in the words of the study, "attempting to assess continuously whether the policy discussion includes representation of the array of interests-at-risk in the issue."[52]

In the decision on the minimum wage, for example, the study reports that the CEA provided adequate technical advice but "no sense of the range of options available to the President, choosing instead to counter the Department of Labor's position with support of their own option." In the footwear imports agreement case study, the EPG was designated as the coordinating agency but failed in its task: the EPG "aligned participants in terms of a narrow set of options." In the decision about whether to increase the minimum wage, the EPG "enabled participants to reflect existing agency positions . . . but did not expand the President's range of options." In the social security refinancing decision, the domestic policy staff "became a strong advocate for a single position, HEW's, though other legitimate options had been presented within the EPG forum." Other proposals were relegated to a secondary status "because they were not developed as extensively on paper."[53]

By way of remedy, the decision analysis recommended that "an approach more consistent with an honest broker role would have involved a fuller presentation of *all* options for the President, with the additional proviso that some options would require additional staffing. In actuality, the proviso was included; a fuller presentation of alternatives was not." The general conclusions of the study also emphasized this point, as well as admonishing the staff for too much policy advocacy: "The advocacy and 'neutral broker' roles performed by the President's policy staffs need to be more carefully delineated; in particular, the President's primary 'issue handlers' should not allow advocacy to compromise their objective presentation of alternative viewpoints regarding policy issues."[54] Carter's efforts to expand the range of his policy advice beyond the White House thus foundered on the inability to counter the bureaucratic perspectives of the agencies and departments to which he turned and the absence of a staff mechanism that could encourage a fuller and fairer consideration of policy views.

Increasing Centralization and the Elusive Goal of Coordination

Carter did over time change his procedures, moving from cabinet-based collegial decision making to more formal procedures and increased reliance on the White House staff. However, neither the NSC staff nor the various domestic policy units were able to achieve an effective role as coordinators, much less as honest brokers of the policy process.

In domestic affairs, according to Hargrove, Carter began to tell members of the cabinet, "Speak with Stu [Eizenstat] if you want to know my mind." According to Eizenstat: "It became clearer and clearer that materials had to flow through my office. . . . You couldn't run a major study on a major issue out of cabinet departments." The administration's effort at welfare reform, Eizenstat notes, was "an excellent example of what happens when the White House doesn't coordinate policy but only participates in agency

run, interagency activities. . . . Agencies can't agree among themselves.
. . . Carter ended up getting a decision memorandum on welfare reform that
was some 60 single-spaced typewritten pages, utterly incomprehensible, in
which the Department of Labor and the Department of HEW could not
even agree on the language to be used in various sections."[55]

By the start of the second year of his presidency, Carter began to move
toward a more centralized coordinating role for the White House staff.
According to Eizenstat, "Carter had begun to slip in the polls. There was
a sense that there was not enough cohesion, that agencies were going off
on their own, that the White House was insufficiently involved in the
coordination of policy, that the President was getting too much reading
material from too many different sources."[56]

Carter increased the responsibilities of the Domestic Policy Staff (DPS)
to coordinate domestic policy, but he kept it on a short leash: it was not
empowered to resolve disputes among departments or other units of the
White House staff. The DPS did act as a manager of the domestic policy
process, but this was within the parameters Carter had set. The DPS
increasingly acted as a facilitator for information going to the president,
developing a presidential review memorandum [PRM] system that had been
used by the NSC staff. The DPS established a policy objective and then
invited relevant agencies and departments to submit memoranda, which
would then be summarized, often in short memos with boxes for Carter to
check. However flawed checking the PRM boxes might have been, it was
an improvement over the sheer confusion and lack of coordination in
Carter's first six months in office.

As Eizenstat notes, he and his staff members were "coordinating the
input of material, we were mediating when possible and ultimately putting
things into decision form."[57] But the DPS did not fully achieve the more
active role of process management of, say, a Cutler in the Eisenhower
process, who did not simply and passively transmit information to the
president but felt free to call others short when there were gaps in information or when policy options were not presented in a fair fashion.

Eizenstat did act as arbitrator among departmental proposals, but often
with less than beneficial effects. When the Energy Department wanted a
20 percent tax credit for the installation of solar energy equipment and the
Treasury Department wanted only a 10 percent credit, Eizenstat split the
difference. Furthermore, according to Hargrove, "some testimony indicates
that Carter was quick to accept compromises the DPS arranged, particularly
if the option paper told him that all the parties agreed to the compromises."[58]
The role of Eizenstat and the DPS, as well as Carter's deference to their
compromises, provides some evidence that his formal procedures may have
manifested one of the predicted effects of formal staff systems—a tendency

to reduce disagreements to lowest common denominator solutions (in this case, splitting differences down the middle and a failure to force policy disagreements up to the level of presidential attention and decision) rather than to serve as an effective coordinator and presidential watchdog.

DPS did fill in one important hole in the Carter process: that of encouraging the president to link policy analysis to political feasibility. Efforts in this area were much needed, given Carter's proclivities not to provide that link himself. Carter tended at times to downplay the political ramifications of his policy choices, in part a function of a leadership strategy that emphasized comprehensive rather than more politically feasible, incremental solutions. As Hargrove points out, "his domestic policy advisers contend[ed] that he did not at first want to hear such [political] advice." But Hargrove notes that Carter increasingly became receptive to "political learning, and his lieutenants describe his growing political sophistication regarding the political actions and compromises necessary to win support for his programs." According to one aide, "Early on, he was very much, 'I only want to know what the best policy is and I'll worry about the politics of it later. You give me the best policy.' . . . He tended to worry much more in the last couple of years about what the public reaction would be and what the political impact would be." Eizenstat and the DPS played an important role in encouraging the president to take politics more seriously: "Eizenstat considered it essential that the DPS, on behalf of the president, test every policy proposal the departments or the DPS itself produced, considering prevailing opinions among Democrats in Congress as well as in the many organized, Washington-based interest groups in the Democratic coalition."[59]

Hamilton Jordan's role as an overall coordinator of the policy process also increased over time, and Jordan eventually assumed the formal title of chief of staff. The development of Jordan's responsibilities reveals the increased centralization of power in the Carter staff and Carter's ongoing problems with a collegial system. In January 1978, in an "eyes only" memo to Carter, Jordan outlined the problems of Carter's staff system:

1. We need better staff coordination. At present staff coordination is practically non-existent. To the extent that any coordination takes place, it is voluntary. Communication among the staff is loose and not structured. We have very little idea or understanding of what each other is doing. There are no staff meetings or opportunities which force us to share our work, our ideas and our problems with each other. . . .

2. Because coordination and communication among the staff is poor, morale among the White House staff is not good. . . .

3. Because no one is in charge (at the staff level), no one is held accountable for their mistakes. . . . The result is that many small problems (which could

be solved) are either ignored or never confronted unless they become big
enough to merit your own attention. . . .

4. There is no formal political input in the foreign policy decision-making
process nor any standard procedure to inform staff members with political
responsibilities once decisions are made. . . .[60]

Jordan suggested that Carter needed a "staff coordinator" who would take
responsibility for each of the shortcomings outlined. On 24 January 1978,
Carter informed senior staff members that Jordan would now serve in that
position, outlining his responsibilities almost verbatim from Jordan's
memo.[61]

In the summer of 1979, Jordan, now chief of staff, again brought to Carter's attention problems in the staff system and proposed major changes in
the decision process of the administration. In particular Jordan noted that
forty persons had direct reporting relationships with Carter and proposed
streamlining this arrangement in a more formalized structure "by putting
people into groups or clusters to report through unit managers" to Jordan or
the president. Jordan also noted that more than two hundred regular meetings of top White House staffers were held each month and needed to be
reduced. Jordan told Carter that "we are looking at the decision-making process within the White House with the view toward developing a system
which will work more effectively for both you and the rest of the staff. . . .
[the] decision-making process deserves serious scrutiny and adjustment."[62]
Each of Jordan's suggestions was marked with an approving check by Carter
or with "good" written in the margin, except for Jordan's proposal to increase the size of the White House staff, which Carter noted with a question
mark.

Isolation, Morale, and Loyalty

As centralization of power in the DPS increased and as Jordan took on
the functions of chief of staff, predictable patterns of presidential isolation
developed, leading to problems of morale and staff loyalty. We have a
"morale problem," Jordan told Carter in 1978. "This is particularly true
with the many young people who did not work in the campaign and/or
began working so late they never developed a personal relationship with
you." Isolation between the president and the staff had also developed:
"Many secretaries, staff assistants and deputies to senior staff members can
complain quite legitimately that they have to read about you and your
programs in the newspaper and that they don't know what is going on. . . .
We can do better communicating with this group of people than we have
to date." Loyalty was also a problem. Many staff members, Jordan told
Carter, "are from Washington and worked on the Hill. These people are
generally bright, energetic and more liberal than you. They want to be in-

volved in everything but feel they know nothing. . . . By and large I don't think we have the complete loyalty of many of these people."[63]

Carter himself was the source of some of these difficulties. Many of the respondents in Campbell's study of the Carter White House "frequently spoke of a pro forma dimension to Carter's accessibility." Two failures, traceable to Carter, emerged. First, "Carter in his personal contact with aides whom he did not know well, avoided overt conflict." According to one of Campbell's respondents, "you have to begin with the personality of the president. In Carter's case, I found him a somewhat shy, withdrawn person, who is guarded in the trust and confidence he places in people." Second, Carter was more at ease with those who had been around him as governor of Georgia and during the campaign; as Campbell's respondent noted, "there is a circle of people he really trusts a lot." But this created rifts among his staff: "the advisers he trusted implicitly, mostly Georgians, demonstrated deep suspicions about both fellow political appointees not in their charmed circle and career officials." As another of Campbell's interviewees stated, "there may be a formal leadership that includes everyone with a stake in the outcome. But then there will be informal ad hoc groups which are not advertised that involve the real heavies. They will meet confidentially in rump sessions and make most of the decisions. . . . This administration . . . tends to pigeonhole people. It does not invite opinions outside your chosen sector. . . . The real difference is that this administration has got that little clutch of Georgians."[64]

Bureaucratization

Carter's problems with loyalty of his White House staff were compounded by interpersonal tensions and bureaucratic politics that developed, especially as staff relationships became more formalized and, as Hamilton Jordan noted, the staff came to include members without prior personal associations with the president. According to Eizenstat, the White House staff should be "a non-turf-interested, presidentially oriented, neutral arbiter, and when it's not there to serve that function . . . then you get a policy muddle."[65] Eizenstat attributes the failure of the Carter staff to meet these expectations to Carter's emphasis on cabinet government. But it is also in part due to something that Eizenstat fails to acknowledge, namely the turf battles, bureaucratic interests, and personal conflicts that can develop within the White House staff. Even among Eizenstat's own DPS staff, competition was rife. According to Campbell, the DPS was a "free-floating" group of "overachievers," lacking the procedures and routines that normally channel staff members' energy. As one of Campbell's respondents put it, "because it is a world of high fliers you will find that there is a lot of competition between people. For instance, I have never worked before this in an atmosphere where information is hoarded. Part of your strength and position comes from hoarding and being very careful about whom you say things to."[66]

Bureaucratic competition was especially marked in the area of foreign policy. Although, as we saw earlier, Brzezinski shifted from a more neutral role as coordinator of the process to a more active stance as a policy advocate in order to widen the range of the president's options, in the final two years of Carter's presidency, bureaucratic competition openly erupted between the NSC staff and the State Department. Part of the difficulty can be traced to Brzezinski's activities. Part also had its source in the way Carter had chosen to organize his foreign policy–making process. Anthony Lake, who directed the State Department's policy-planning staff, notes that Carter's "flexible system . . . depended on collegiality, if it was to work smoothly." But its organization and the actions of those who participated in it "had the effect of undercutting collegiality, as people competed in weekly struggles to decide which agency would take the lead at which meeting."[67]

Carter, for his part, was never able to control the disorganization and rivalry of his foreign policy team, and in April 1980 Vance resigned, in large part, because he felt excluded from the decision leading to the attempt to rescue the American hostages in Iran. Although conflict abated somewhat following Edmund Muskie's appointment as secretary of state, Carter still never developed an effective balance between his two chief sources of foreign policy advice. Even Muskie was to complain, shortly after taking over as secretary of state, that he learned about the administration's decision to alter aspects of its strategy for nuclear war, which Brzezinski had orchestrated, only after reading a newspaper article on it. Furthermore, as Crabb and Mulcahy, observe, "the irony is that although Carter entered office pledged to oppose the Kissinger model of foreign policy making, the actual result was the concentration of nearly as much power in the White House as had been the case in the Nixon administration."[68] As James Sterling Young concludes in his foreword to Erwin Hargrove's *Jimmy Carter as President*, Carter's kind of leadership was not "that of a president trained in the ways of bureaucratic politics."[69]

Since problems of loyalty and bureaucratic politics are endemic to large-scale organizations, Carter's problems were not unique. But his lack of an effective response was. Carter did not effectively manage the breakdown of collegiality among his advisers. As Hargrove points out, "He presumed collegiality to be the fact. . . . It was his nature to expect the best of his lieutenants." Carter was very tolerant of dissent among his associates, "which could be a problem when his associates were not as loyal to him or to the principle of collegiality as he would have liked." According to one aide, Carter was always "surprised at these breakdowns, because he wanted his advisers to be a family and did not think of their relationships as political. He assumed that good personal relations would lead to policy agreement." According to another aide, "the President was reluctant to sanction anyone. . . . He is extraordinarily tolerant, perhaps too much so, of other people's shortcomings."[70]

In short, Carter may have been an engineer, but as Hargrove concludes, he "was not an *institutional* engineer":[71] he did not deal with frictions on the White House staff, was ineffective in managing conflict between the staff and other parts of the policy community, and ended up shouldering the burden of a policy-making process in which effective coordination proved elusive. Carter recognized the dangers of a powerful White House staff, dangers that had haunted his predecessors and had, in part, propelled him into the White House. But he was unable to muster the skills to make the staff serve his own vision of the presidency and the policy goals he chose to pursue. The institutional presidency simply overpowered him, but in this he was not alone: it would soon haunt his successor.

6

RONALD REAGAN
The Travails of Collegial Formalism

. . .

In his 1981 inaugural address to the nation, President Reagan announced a "new beginning." Reagan's objective was bold: to redefine a national political agenda that had been dominated by the Democratic party since Roosevelt's New Deal, restore confidence at home, and reassert American power abroad. Although Reagan, like his predecessor, hoped that the cabinet would play a major role in bringing his "new beginning" to fruition, his mode of governing differed from Carter's. Whereas Carter wedded a collegial system with a significant level of presidential involvement in policy detail—centralized collegiality—Reagan preferred more formal mechanisms for formulating his administration's policies coupled with a strong emphasis on collegial cooperation among his advisers and limited presidential involvement—an arrangement that might be termed collegial formalism. Despite these differences, however, Reagan and his team largely failed, as did their predecessors, to develop an effective staff system.

Reagan and the Institutional Presidency:
Through a Managerial Lens

The basic structure of the policy machinery in place during Reagan's first years as president emerged during his transition to the presidency as a result of discussions among his transition advisers. Reagan's experience as governor of California with strong cabinet government led his advisers, especially transition director Edwin Meese, initially to favor a similar arrangement for his presidency. However, the difficulties Carter experienced with his cabinet and the opposition of Washington "insiders" on the transition team, most notably James Baker, resulted in a compromise.

The proposal had four basic parts. First, instead of relying directly on the entire cabinet as a deliberative body, it organized separate cabinet councils along functional lines and with more limited membership. Second, it reorganized Carter's domestic policy staff as the Office of Policy Development (OPD). The new OPD was designed to serve as the staff support for the new cabinet councils rather than as a separate unit reporting directly to the president. Third, the responsibilities of the chief of staff in previous administrations were divided among Reagan's three top advisers—Ed Meese, James Baker, and Michael Deaver. Finally, national security procedures were revamped. Three senior interagency groups (SIGs) were created and tied more closely to departments: State took the lead in foreign policy, Defense in defense, and the CIA in intelligence; a SIG for international economic policy created a year later was led by Treasury. In addition, NSC special assistant Richard Allen did not have direct access to the president but reported through Ed Meese.

The importance of the formal organization of the Reagan White House is perhaps best captured by Martin Anderson. A longtime Reagan adviser, Anderson served as a special assistant to the president and head of the Office of Policy Development. Like Allen, Anderson reported to the president through Meese, although his duties required frequent attendance at meetings of the cabinet councils. In his memoirs, Anderson observes that

> there were three basic ways to participate in the policy process of the Reagan administration. The first was to talk to him personally and directly. . . . This was the most effective, but opportunities were limited—during the early years only Ed Meese, Jim Baker, and Mike Deaver (and Nancy Reagan) had that option, and later Donald Regan shrank that circle even further. The second was to write and send memoranda. That was not very effective given the way Reagan liked to work. That left the third way—meetings.[1]

In addition to the cabinet councils and the National Security Council, Anderson lists at least ten advisory groups, in many of which he participated, that took part in the Reagan policy process during the time Anderson served on the Reagan staff:

1. Economic policy making by a group of top advisers: Treasury Secretary Don Regan, OMB Director David Stockman, CEA chair Murray Weidenbaum, and Office of Policy Development chief Anderson. The group met every Tuesday morning at 7:30 A.M. for breakfast.

2. Senior staff meetings of the president's top White House advisers at 8:00 A.M. every morning, chaired by Ed Meese, that discussed the entire range of the administration's policy efforts. [According to Michael Deaver, this was preceded by a 7:30 A.M. breakfast in James Baker's office.][2]

3. Meetings of a smaller group of senior staff members that convened in Meese's office following the 8:00 meeting.

4. Meetings at 8:30 with President Reagan of the participants in the 8:00 A.M. meeting.

5. Meetings of the legislative strategy group, which were held daily between 4:30 and 5:30 in the afternoon.

6. Meetings of the budget working group, which functioned as a kind of high-level appeals court to review disputed budget cuts with individual Cabinet members.

7. Meetings of the economic forecasting group, composed of the president's senior economic advisers, which provided long-range economic forecasts for the administration.

8. Meetings of the Presidential Task Force on Regulatory Relief, chaired by Vice President Bush.

9. Meetings of the President's Economic Policy Advisory Board, a group of private citizens who regularly met with the president and advised him on economic issues.

10. Meetings of the President's Foreign Intelligence Advisory Board, a group of distinguished private citizens who oversaw the entire range of U.S. intelligence operations and made recommendations directly to the president.

With the exception of the 8:30 A.M. senior staff meeting and the last two groups, composed of outside advisers, the president was not a participant in these various policy groups. Furthermore, in Anderson's view, most groups failed to generate creative ways of implementing Regan's policy agenda. They became, as is often characteristic of formal bodies insulated from direct presidential involvement, policy "choke points": "It was always much easier to block or derail an idea than to advance one. Anything less than unanimous support in these meetings could stop the making of a new policy in its tracks. Dissent always delayed things and was sometimes fatal. A strong, eloquent objection by even one senior member of a high-level policy group could be serious. And objection by two or more senior players would almost surely kill a new idea."[3]

Other groups also flourished in the Reagan White House. Deaver organized the "Blair House group" shortly after Reagan took office, which focused on long-term communications issues, and in December of 1983 he created a daily "communications strategy meeting," which attempted to orchestrate a "line of the day" strategy for capturing media attention. The White House personnel office organized Wednesday meetings with top administration officials to discuss pending appointments before reviewing them with the president at regular Thursday meetings. During Reagan's first term, the troika (Meese, Baker, and Deaver) and the NSC adviser (William

Clark after Allen's departure) met every Monday with the president for an "issues briefing lunch." And, like all recent presidents, Reagan had a daily national security briefing, which usually followed his early morning meeting with top White House staff members.

Failure of the Cabinet Councils

Establishment of the cabinet councils, the hoped-for centerpiece of the Reagan policy process, was a central task of Reagan's transition planning team. Like Carter, Reagan's advisers hoped that cabinet members would be intimately involved in the policy-making process. Their concerns, however, appear to stem less from mistrust of the White House staff than from a recognition—similar to that embodied in Richard Nixon's "administrative presidency"[4] ten years earlier—that greater cabinet participation at the highest levels of the administration's policy deliberations would enhance the loyalty and support of cabinet officers who would have to carry out the administration's agenda, often at the expense of their own budgets and programmatic authority. Also, like Nixon, who proposed an ill-fated "super cabinet" for reducing the number of departments and subsequently a Domestic Council organized along a limited number of policy-relevant areas, Reagan's advisers recognized that meetings of the entire cabinet would prove unwieldy and carved out separate policy areas with different cabinet representation.

Four major functions were initially identified: economic policy, domestic affairs, budget and management, and political affairs. This functional arrangement had been suggested by Roger Porter of the transition staff, who had served on Ford's economic policy staff. During the transition period, the functional basis of the councils was redefined to accord more closely with the responsibilities of existing cabinet-level departments and areas of public policy. Five cabinet councils were envisioned and in February 1981 formally announced: economic affairs (CCEA), commerce and trade (CCCT), human resources (CCHR), natural resources and the environment (CCNRE), and food and agriculture (CCFA). In January 1982, a council on legal policy (CCLP) was established, and in September 1982, a council on management and administration (CCMA).

The cabinet councils ranged in size from six cabinet officers (human resources and food and agriculture) to ten (commerce and trade), although cabinet members could attend any cabinet council session they wished. The president was nominal chairman of all councils but rarely presided or attended. Of the 190 council meetings held in the first fifteen months of the administration, Reagan attended only 14 percent (26), less than two per month; his attendance varied from 27 percent of the human resources sessions to 7 percent of the economic affairs meetings (see table 6–1 for

Table 6-1 Attendance at Cabinet Council Meetings in First Fifteen Months
of Original Five Councils

Cabinet Council	Total Meetings	President Reagan (%)	Chair Pro Tem (%)	Principal Members (%)	Other Members (%)	Ex Officio (%)
CCEA	100	7	95	53	14	33
CCCT	31	26	97	43	13	41
CCHR	15	27	100	32	7	32
CCNRE	31	16	100	40	9	29
CCFA	10	20	100	20	13	22

Source: Chester Newland, "Executive Office Policy Apparatus: Enforcing the Reagan Agenda," in *The Reagan Presidency and the Government of America,* edited by Lester Salamon and Michael Lund (Washington, D.C.: Urban Institute Press, 1984), 159. Newland's data are from the Office of Planning and Evaluation, Executive Office of the President, *Strategic Evaluation Memorandum #18, Cabinet Councils and Domestic Affairs Management: An Evaluation,* 8 June 1982, 17.

complete data). The cabinet officer with principal responsibilities in a particular area of policy generally served as chairman pro tem of the council.[5] In addition, Meese and Baker of the White House staff and Anderson and Edwin Harper of the Office of Policy Development were ex officio members of all councils. Staff support for each council was provided by a secretariat chaired by an OPD staff member and including the assistant secretaries responsible for policy development in departments represented on the council, with staff work assigned to lower-level OPD officials.

The experiment with the cabinet councils proved short lived. By September 1983, only three of them were active—commerce and trade, management and administration (newly created), and economic affairs. Human resources and legal policy met sporadically, and natural resources and the environment and food and agriculture were dormant.

A study of the cabinet councils undertaken by the White House Office of Planning and Evaluation (OPE) in June 1982 and covering the first fifteen months of the Reagan administration provides some empirical evidence that the councils varied in effectiveness but were generally ineffective in having an impact on policies.

One simple measure of the importance of the work of the councils is attendance at council meetings and frequency of meetings. The data in table 6–1 show a significant drop in participation by members other than the council member designated as chairperson pro tem. Participation rates among the three other council member categories are well under 50 percent, except for the principal members of the most active council, economic affairs.

The same study found that the bulk of matters discussed in cabinet council sessions did not focus on development and formulation of administration policies but on implementing policies that had already been set or on discussions and reviews that led nowhere. Few cabinet council decisions led to matters requiring presidential decision. Drawing on the OPE study, Chester Newland reports that 4.4 percent of agenda items during the first fifteen months of the councils' operations led to immediate presidential policy decisions and that an additional 10.8 percent resulted in later presidential decision. Of the remaining agenda items, 9 percent concerned strategy; 17.7 percent involved a council but not a presidential decision; 30 percent involved review and discussion; 25 percent further study; and 3 percent resulted in postponement. As Newland observes, while the cabinet councils established linkages between the White House staff and the cabinet departments, "the bridging serve[d] not to voice original or challenging inputs from subordinate experts in agencies or elsewhere in the EOP so much as to keep agencies exposed to the EOP's agenda orientation and to provide for agency actions to reconcile policies to it." The policy network, of which the Cabinet councils were designed as a major component, "does not set the general direction; it follows it, working out policy details strictly secondary to the president's fixed views of government."[6]

Other problems beset the cabinet councils. Colin Campbell found in his survey of members of the Reagan administration that "a significant number of respondents wondered if the cabinet council system had not overly channeled conflict in the administration." Some believed that deliberations in the councils became "pro forma, operating under norms of cordiality," and that participants can "lose by criticizing too intensely."[7]

Cabinet officers also devised strategies for bypassing the councils, some staff members assigned to the councils felt, in order "to protect traditional turf from collective scrutiny." They might claim, for example, prerogatives in areas that were set by statute or convention, or they might claim that the danger of leaks in a collective setting threatened national security. During Reagan's second term, Treasury Secretary Baker, who was chair of the Economic Policy Council, bypassed the council by claiming that policy matters were the prerogative of his department; according to Campbell, this was the case "both with tax simplification and efforts to work with the economic secretaries of four other advanced industrial nations toward stabilization of key trading currencies." Campbell also notes that councils themselves could be jealous about their prerogatives. Because there were numerous councils in Reagan's first term and their boundaries unclear, they often competed for pieces of the policy turf: "Overlapping jurisdictions brought considerable confusion to some issue areas." Competition also existed with other parts of the policy process; in the area of trade policy, for example, the statutory Trade Policy Committee, the cabinet council on commerce and trade, and the NSC's senior interagency group on international economic policy all vied for control.[8]

At times, the council system was prevented from examining issues that could have profitably found their way into its deliberations. The OPE study found, for example, that the cabinet councils were not involved in budgetary matters, which were central to the administration's political efforts in 1981 and 1982, the period under review. OMB Director David Stockman attended many cabinet council meetings, but save for last-minute information sessions, budgetary matters were discussed outside the cabinet council structure. The cabinet Council on Economic Affairs, for example, did not even review the FY1983 budget until three days before its formal submission to Congress.

The formal structure of the Reagan policy process during the heyday of the cabinet council system appears to resemble the formalistic advisory arrangements that Richard Tanner Johnson found wanting in the Eisenhower and Nixon White Houses but without the management strategies that Eisenhower used to counter their weaknesses and without Nixon's well-developed political instincts and substantive knowledge of policy. In the Reagan staff system, there was relatively little direct presidential involvement. Few decisions flowed to the presidential level for action. There were no established mechanisms for making sure that disagreements were brought to the president's attention (as, for example, "policy splits" were outlined and emphasized in Eisenhower's NSC procedures). And the emphasis within the councils was apparently on consensus, which may produce the kind of lowest common denominator policy options that Johnson thought were endemic to formal staff arrangements.[9]

Defenders of the Reagan cabinet council system, however, make two arguments worth considering. First, Martin Anderson notes that the cabinet councils may have been useful in at least building some rapport between the White House staff and cabinet officers. The physical requirement that cabinet officers leave their departments and travel frequently to the White House "was a powerful reminder that it was the president's business they were about, not theirs or their department's constituents." The informal contact between the staff and cabinet members that developed during council sessions also was a positive factor. After meetings, council members would sometimes adjourn to neighboring offices for more informal conversation; this enabled "Reagan's advisers to get to know each other personally, intimately. It created, for a while, an unusual degree of harmony between two normally antagonistic groups, the White House staff and the Cabinet."[10] This facet of the Reagan council system resembles Eisenhower's use of cabinet meetings as a method of team building and a strategy for developing mutual cooperation, although with the major difference that, under Reagan, the president was not usually a direct participant and, thus, not a unifying force that could personally encourage their development.

The second defense of the council system is that it worked just as it was designed to work. The argument here is that unlike most presidents, even Franklin Roosevelt, Reagan entered office with a fairly clearly defined political agenda and set of policy goals. Observers such as Newland,[11] who see the impact of the cabinet councils as essentially secondary—that is, filling in the details of policy and devising political means for attaining them—are not, according to this line of argument, detecting failure in the council system but observing its intended, and paradoxically effective, operation.

The logic for this understanding of the Reagan policy process is provided by Ben Heineman: "The administration should have an overall strategy of governing that, among other things, divides the major issues it will face into first-, second-, and third-order initiatives and establishes a time sequence for dealing with them. . . . On first-order initiatives . . . the president makes virtually all significant decisions."[12] Reagan's predetermined political agenda and personal judgment, together with the counsel of his close circle of White House advisers, presumably enabled him to make such decisions, while the cabinet councils and other advisory groups concentrated on the second and third-order issues, which did not require much presidential attention.

James Ceaser takes the argument a step further, arguing not only that Reagan focused on a more select number of policy issues but also that this policy was integrally linked to Reagan's conservative conception of governance. The technocratic, "hands-on" attention to policy detail characteristic of the Carter presidency and the "hands-off," more politically attuned concerns of the Reagan presidency reflect not just different personalities or managerial styles, but, more fundamentally, different conceptions of government: The Reagan administration "viewed governance much less in technical terms and more in political terms. The problem in governing was not just to find the right program but a program that could be put into effect." The means by which the Reagan administration pursued its objectives reflected its "perception of operating in a political environment that required the development of a political strategy based on mobilizing public and congressional support by means of appeals to a few clear-cut ideas."[13]

Given this conception of government, one should not expect a range of innovative policy deliberations churning within the administration's advisory system or a laundry list of legislative proposals sent up for Congress to approve; the Carter administration had both and failed. The emphasis instead is on a more limited, strategically selected set of policy initiatives.

Some evidence can be marshaled to support Ceaser's thesis. Reagan's agenda was bold, but it pursued fewer policy objectives. In Reagan's first year, efforts were largely confined to the area of budget and revenue policy: tax reductions, cuts in domestic spending, and increases in military spending. Reagan aides deliberately attempted to avoid initiatives that would distract from these efforts. I. M. Destler, for example, notes that in 1981 the White House cut short Alexander Haig's attempts to make Central America a primary administration issue: they "did not want to divert attention from the economic program that was [Reagan's] overriding priority."[14] Nor in 1981 did Reagan pursue the conservative but politically divisive social agenda of the "religious right." In 1982, Reagan continued to emphasize the budget but now moved to redefine federal-state relationships in his New Federalism initiative. Next, Reagan turned to Central American policy and, during his second term, relationships with the Soviet Union and his Strategic Defense Initiative, "Star Wars" proposal.

The flaw in this defense of Reagan's policies and procedures is that, while it seems to make strategic sense, few efforts succeeded. On the domestic front, for example, the budget successes of 1981 were followed by congressional resistance in 1982 and thereafter, the 1981 tax cuts were modified by $100 billion in "corrections" in 1982, scandal in the Environmental Protection Agency undermined Reagan's efforts at less stringent environmental regulation, savings and loan industry deregulation would come to haunt Reagan's successor, and Reagan's New Federalism never got off the ground. Reagan did revitalize confidence in the presidency, redressing a spirit of national malaise that had pervaded the Carter years, but success in this area had less to do with policy substance than with Reagan's political style and his skills in managing his political image and dealing with the media.

The problem for Reagan was essentially twofold. First, he had a political agenda, but its details were so broadly drawn as to make it simply an ideology—themes and theories without concrete application. Second, he trusted that the agenda-ideology would suffice for a presidential policy program. The lack of adequate means in place to translate this agenda into concrete programs was illustrated in part by the way the cabinet council system operated. And there was a misplaced faith in its efficacy: as Newland explains, "only after damaging policy failures [did] the administration accede reluctantly to broader political considerations to modify fixed positions. Thus, as an ideology, the Reagan agenda has proved to be a major obstacle to its own implementation."[15]

Donald Regan's memoirs reveal further problems. He notes that despite Reagan's seemingly well-defined economic agenda, the administration's deliberative process was unable to produce the policies necessary to define it in the more concrete terms required for implementation:

> This baffling system, in which the President seldom spoke, while his advisers proposed measures that contradicted his ideas and promises, created uncertainty in a situation that cried out for action. I thought that I understood the President's philosophy. But how did he want it carried out, if at all? Casual exchanges in Cabinet meetings and other large gatherings were not enough to give the necessary guidance, especially at a time when the economy was in distress.

And, at least for Regan, the president's economic agenda was never clear during his tenure as treasury secretary. In a diary entry dated 11 March 1981, he writes: "To this day I have never had so much as a minute alone with Ronald Reagan! Never has he, or anyone else, sat down in private to explain to me what is expected of me, what goals he would like to see me accomplish, what results he wants. . . . How can one do a job if the job is not defined? . . . This is dangerous." Regan obtained most of his views about administration policy, he confesses, "like any other American, by studying [Reagan's] speeches and reading the newspapers."[16]

The cabinet council system was admirable in its intentions. It recognized, as Colin Campbell points out, that "to operate as a team, the cabinet must have group dynamics";[17] that is, it must be structured in such a way as to facilitate honest and lively deliberations by those cabinet members most directly involved in a given policy area. But its procedures and operating norms among participants were not up to the task, nor was there a president at the top of the system who was interested in providing the personal direction and enlisting the commitment of those involved that were necessary to make it work.

In his memoirs, Reagan devotes little attention to the operations of his staff and cabinet. At several points, he states that it was his practice to encourage "Cabinet members to speak frankly and to fight for their points of view," and that he would refrain from entering the debate so as "not to tip my advisers off." But there is little concern about the quality of the advice he received; unlike Eisenhower, who tried to build a sense of teamwork among the cabinet and wean members away from their parochial departmental perspectives, Reagan thought it a good thing that "every member of the Cabinet had to view the problems of the nation and interpret world events from the special vantage point of his or her own job responsibilities, based in part on the advice of specialists in their respective departments."[18]

The weaknesses of Reagan's experiment with his cabinet councils were not unlike those of his predecessor, Jimmy Carter. Carter developed a different mode of reliance on the cabinet, but both presidents lacked the managerial acumen and skills to make their respective systems work effectively.

The Breakdown of Collegial Formalism

As the formal structure of the cabinet councils proved to have less than the expected impact on the policies of the Reagan presidency, power began increasingly to devolve to the White House staff. In effect, the formal structure of the Reagan policy process collapsed inward and in so doing changed the relationships among Reagan's top assistants.

In the original schema developed as part of Reagan's transition efforts, each member of the troika of Reagan's top advisers assumed part of the duties that normally are assigned to the president's chief of staff. Meese, in the role of counsellor to the president, oversaw the cabinet councils, policy development, long-term planning of the Reagan agenda, and, insofar as first NSC special assistant Richard Allen reported through him, national security policy. Michael Deaver, as deputy chief of staff, managed the president's daily schedule, travel plans, personal support functions, the first lady's staff, and the president's public image. James Baker, as nominal chief of staff, had more immediate tasks: the day-to-day management of the White House staff, personnel matters, legal counsel, control over what information reached the president, and responsibilities for the political side of the staff such as press relations and congressional, party, and interest group liaison. The troika also brought together two distinct types of orientation: that of long-standing Reagan loyalists deeply committed to the president's political agenda—Meese and at least initially Deaver—and that of a political pragmatist—Baker.

As the cabinet councils proved unworkable and the OPD went through a succession of directors and failed to develop a critical niche in addressing immediate policy problems, Meese's role began to wither. Meese and Baker were designated co-chairs of the Legislative Strategy Group, which Baker soon came to dominate, and Baker's role as a member of the troika was also broadened when his aide Richard Darman became secretary of the Budget Review Group. In the politics among the troika members, Deaver generally aligned with the more politically adept and increasingly powerful Baker, who soon took on the powers and responsibilities usually assigned to the chief of staff.

Both aspects of the collegial formalism of Reagan's early years as president proved unworkable: not only did the formal structure of reliance on cabinet councils disintegrate, but collegial relationships among Reagan's top advisers began to break down. During the first year of Reagan's presidency, Meese, Baker, and Deaver regularly met in Baker's office for breakfast; by the second year these breakfasts were less frequent. Journalistic accounts during this period emphasized the interpersonal tensions among the troika members, especially Baker and Deaver versus Meese, as the source of problems. But whatever interpersonal competition existed was overshadowed by the unequal distribution of power in the relationship. Meese's emphasis on long-term planning and his continued faith in the cumbersome cabinet councils failed to give him equal impact on the policy-making process; Deaver's personal duties for the president and Baker's political tasks and "here and now" functions made their roles in the process more important.

A Strong Chief of Staff

The shift became complete at the start of Reagan's second term when Meese chose to leave the White House staff for the position of Attorney General and Baker and Treasury Secretary Regan agreed to swap jobs, notifying the president almost as an afterthought. Under Regan's tenure as chief of staff, collegial contacts among the president's top advisers disappeared almost totally, and power within and control over the White House staff passed almost exclusively into Donald Regan's hands.

The developments that took place during Reagan's first term as president—the shift from a collegial form of formalism to the typical formalistic pattern of a system led by a strong chief of staff—were not unique. They reflect, in part, trends in the institutional presidency that can be found in other recent presidencies. But in Reagan's case, there was a crucial difference: little presidential concern about, much less attempt to manage, what was taking place. At least Carter seemed aware of what was transpiring in his presidency. In Reagan's case, it was as if nothing had occurred that was worthy of presidential attention.

Both as a cabinet member and later as chief of staff, Regan saw a chief executive who was essentially unconcerned with the operations of his White House staff or the workings of the broader policy process of his administration. This lack of attention also extended to the absence of substantive interest in the details of policy (where, of course, Reagan differed markedly from Carter) or the making of decisions. According to Regan, the president sent out "few strong signals" to his staff and rarely "made a decision or issued orders." He was "diffident," Regan recalls, hesitating "to ask questions or confess to a lack of knowledge in the presence of strangers. . . . Nearly everyone was a stranger to this shy President except the members of his innermost circle."[19]

Regan's observations are supported by Michael Deaver, a longtime Reagan confidante. Deaver writes: "I often wished he had been more willing to expose his private self to opposing opinions. That he did not, relates, I think, to his sense of security and not, as his critics may contend, to a narrowness of mind."[20] In place of policy direction, Regan opines, the president "seemed to believe that his public statements were all the guidance his private advisers seemed to require. Ronald Reagan's campaign promises *were* his policy. To him, in his extreme simplicity of character and belief, this was obvious."[21]

Regan's awareness of how little impact the president had on most policies of his administration grew as the setting of his own activities moved from the insulated deliberations of the cabinet councils to day-to-day contact as chief of staff with the president. Regan provides an especially telling example of the difficulties that continued to exist in the Reagan White House even under the formalized procedures that he himself sought to instill. In August 1985, Regan prepared for the president a memorandum in which he outlined a course of action for the second term of the Reagan presidency. The document had been prepared by the senior White House staff, including McFarlane of the NSC, and covered three critical areas—economic recovery, foreign policy, and the legislative agenda—over short-, medium-, and long-term time frames.[22] In Regan's view, the paper was simply a first draft, the first stage of what he expected to be a more extensive process of discussion and deliberation, especially because it was more an outline of general goals than a concrete plan of action. Regan expected that the president would read it, decide on his priorities, and call for more detailed suggestions and further deliberation. "Instead, Ronald Reagan read the paper while he was at the ranch and handed it back to me on his return without spoken or written comment," except to say he thought it was "good." "I waited for him to say more. He did not. He had no questions to ask, no objections to raise, no instructions to issue. I realized that the policy that would determine the course of the world's most powerful nation for the next two years . . . had been adopted without amendment. . . . I was surprised that this weighty matter was decided so quickly and with so little ceremony."[23]

Reagan and the Institutional Presidency: Through an Organizational Lens

If Reagan was largely inattentive to the weaknesses in his organization of his staff system and unconcerned about the changes that occurred within it over time, he was even less attentive to, if aware of, the operation of that system within an organizational context. All three of the chief effects of the institutional presidency—centralization of power in the White House staff, development of hierarchy and gatekeeping, and the emergence of bureaucratization—affected the Reagan presidency and over time appear to have increased.

Centralization of Power

With the breakdown of the cabinet council system and the emergence of a strong chief of staff, White House domination of the policy process increased and with it centralization of power in the White House staff. Whereas four persons had free access to the president in his first term—Meese, Deaver, Baker, and (after Allen's departure) NSC special assistant William Clark, then Robert McFarlane—during Donald Regan's tenure the chief of staff had almost exclusive access in domestic affairs and, depending on who one believes, even at times in foreign affairs.

Regan's 1985 draft memo to the president on the administration's economic, national security, and legislative agenda for the coming years reveals Reagan's disinterest in what parties had an impact on his administration's priorities. Not only was Reagan content for his chief of staff to have near exclusive power to define those priorities, he was wholly satisfied with what Regan had done, returning the memo to him without written or oral comment.

In the area of foreign policy, power was less centralized in the White House staff than it had been in previous administrations. No NSC special assistant in the Reagan years emerged as the president's chief foreign policy adviser or spokesman in the way Kissinger had operated in the Nixon presidency or Brzezinski under Carter. Secretary of State George Shultz, an adept Washington insider and a veteran White House staffer, was able to maintain a significant degree of control over the direction of American foreign policy. (White House aides had contributed to the difficulties of his predecessor, Alexander Haig, although Haig's own activities played a major part in his ineffectiveness.)

Shultz's efforts notwithstanding, over time the NSC staff was able to assert more influence over the national security process. For example, the senior interagency groups that had initially been tied to the departments were, by Reagan's second term, under NSC staff control. Writing in 1986, Colin Campbell observes that

> during the current term, only the SIG [senior interagency group] on intelligence remains active. The Crisis Preplanning Group chaired by the NSC staff's director for policy development coordinates the administration's management of major foreign policy emergencies. The Strategic Arms Control Group headed by the assistant to the president for national security affairs has supplanted the SIG on defense. And the Economics Policy Council has absorbed the entire case load of the SIG on International Economic Policy.[24]

The Iran-Contra affair also provided evidence of the increased power—if not at times the subterfuge—of the NSC staff. Robert McFarlane and later John Poindexter overrode the objections of Shultz and Secretary of Defense Casper Weinberger to the arms-for-hostages part of the deal, and they (evidently) kept much of the detail of their operations, especially the transfer of funds to the Nicaraguan Contras, from presidential approval or scrutiny. *The Tower Commission Report* especially singled out the control that NSC assistants McFarlane and Poindexter had over the Iran-Contra affair to the exclusion of other participants in the national security policy process:

> The Iran initiative ran directly counter to the Administration's own policies on terrorism, the Iran/Iraq war, and military support to Iran. This inconsistency was never resolved. . . . The Board believes that failure to deal adequately with these contradictions resulted in large part from the flaws in the manner in which decisions were made. Established procedures for making national security decisions were ignored. Reviews of the initiative by all the NSC principals were too infrequent. The initiatives were not adequately vetted below the cabinet level. Intelligence resources were underutilized. Applicable legal constraints were not adequately addressed. . . . This pattern persisted in the implementation of the Iran initiative. The NSC staff assumed direct operational control. The initiative fell within the traditional jurisdictions of the Departments of State, Defense, and CIA. Yet these agencies were largely ignored. . . . How the initiative was to be carried out never received adequate attention from the NSC principals or a tough working-level review. No periodic evaluation of the progress of the initiative was ever conducted. The result was an unprofessional and, in substantial part, unsatisfactory operation.[25]

Hierarchy and Gatekeeping

The development of hierarchy and gatekeeping also became more pronounced over time in the Reagan White House. Donald Regan's powers as chief of staff were unprecedented, surpassing even those of H. R. Haldeman under Nixon and extending not only into domestic policy but, unprecedentedly, at times into foreign policy. Regan recounts in his memoirs that once he took over as chief of staff, "All duties formerly exercised by Baker, Meese, and Deaver devolved on me—personnel, the coordination of information, the choice of issues, the flow of paper, and the schedule that controlled the President's travel and other movements and determined who would see him and who would not."[26] Regan reduced the number of persons who could walk unannounced into the Oval Office, and he eliminated five of the seven cabinet councils, reorganizing the group into two: a domestic policy council and an economic policy council. Regan also reduced the number of "assistants to the president" from seventeen to eleven.

The president approved Regan's plans under the assumption that they "would streamline operations and simplify the organizational structure."

But as he goes on to note in his memoirs, "I approved the plan not realizing how much it would enlarge Regan's powers at the expense of others on the staff, restrict access to me, and lead to problems later on."[27]

As for Chief of Staff Regan, his behavior was largely determined by the president's passive managerial style and organizational disinterest. Regan saw nothing wrong with assuming the strong powers that had devolved to the chief of staff in the vacuum of the Reagan White House; he also saw no need to take steps to counterbalance any weaknesses on the president's part. In the case of his 1985 memo, for example, Regan did not question what he himself admitted was an inadequate definition of the administration's policy goals in the second term but went along with Reagan's ways of working: "Did the President really want us to do all these things with no more discussion than this? I decided that this must be the case, since always in the past, if he did not say no the answer was yes. . . . I held my tongue."[28]

Regan, a former head of Merrill Lynch without governmental experience before joining the Reagan team, also was encouraged not to challenge Reagan's methods (and to define his own role broadly) by his experience in the corporate world: "To borrow from the vocabulary of corporate practice, I was presenting a plan of action to the chief executive officer of the firm. . . . Once he had signed off, debate ceased and you went to work to carry out the final plan."[29]

Whether this mode of private sector behavior is appropriate to presidential leadership and decision making is a question that apparently did not trouble Regan. Nor did it trouble his "CEO": in his memoirs, President Reagan notes that it was his preference to turn "over the day-to-day details to the specialists," despite the fact that basic contours of policy were sometimes vague if not undefined. That presidents may need to cast their nets to a wider audience than just the chief of staff and his immediate minions also did not factor into the operations of the staff system during Reagan's second term. Reagan ended up with the worst of two worlds: not only a chief of staff presiding powerfully over a staff system from which the president may have been insulated, but a chief of staff who based his behavior on an inappropriate organizational model. Reagan eventually came to realize that "Don thought of himself as a kind of 'deputy president' empowered to make decisions involving the administration. Although I only found out about it later, he resisted having others see me alone and wouldn't forward letters or documents to me unless he saw me first. In short, he wanted to be the *only* conduit to the Oval Office, in effect making that presidential isolation I just complained about more complete."[30]

The president's problems were compounded by the personnel changes Regan made. White House veterans Ed Rollins and Max Friedersdorf returned to the administration at the start of the second term to direct political and governmental affairs and act as legislative liaison. They were gone by the end of the first year under Regan. So, too, was NSC adviser McFarlane. Regan replaced them with officials of less stature and experience but more personal connection and loyalty to the chief of staff. He also "marginalized" Communications Director Patrick Buchanan and Policy Development Chief John Svahn. "Instead of relying upon a quasi-collegial system based on consultation," Campbell states, "Regan turned increasingly to a cadre of advisers who came directly under him." Almost all of these officials, moreover, "had worked for Regan in the Treasury Department and were beholden to him for their rapid career advancement. They function[ed] more as surrogates than as colleagues."[31]

With respect to the other potential gatekeeper role—that of NSC special assistant—those under Reagan had less power as policy advocates than their predecessors. But they were by no means managerial custodians or honest brokers. They were able to exert considerable control over covert operations, for example, extending their roles beyond formulating to implementing administration policies. Reagan himself, during his taped testimony in the trial of John Poindexter in 1990, after he left the presidency, appeared confused about major events in the Iran-Contra episode such as trading arms for hostages and diverting funds from sales of arms to the Contras in Nicaragua; both were long-standing and well-known matters of record in the case and had been major conclusions of Reagan's own Tower Commission charged with investigating the episode during his presidency.[32]

Bureaucratization

With respect to the organizational dynamics of the institutional presidency at levels below those of the president's top advisers, the Reagan experience is mixed. Reagan was successful, perhaps to an extent not seen since Kennedy, in instilling a sense of ideological commitment and personal loyalty among members of his staff. As we saw in chapter 2, John Kessel's study of the Carter and Reagan staffs found a significantly greater degree among the Reagan staffers of both ideological consensus and agreement on specific policy initiatives, which Kessel terms "issue structure."[33]

Ideological and policy agreement in the Reagan staff is not surprising. Reagan's transition team was particularly well organized in its recruitment of persons who were personally committed to the Reagan political agenda and loyal to the president. Nearly one hundred citizen task forces were organized during the transition period. These were dispatched to federal agencies and departments, state and local governments, and the private sector in search of suitable appointees. According to Newland, "Reagan's teams were composed less of substantive policy experts than of ideological campaign workers, many seeking jobs, and they were organized to link

. . . into one agenda implementation network." The transition teams also provided advice on public policy. Those directed at federal agencies, in particular, provided counsel about what programs needed cutbacks, elimination, or deregulation. These reports were kept strictly confidential and forwarded to Martin Anderson, Reagan's designated assistant for policy development. According to Newland, "along with notebook compilations of [Reagan's] campaign promises, . . . on which Anderson and others routinely relied, they provided important initial policy guidance." Thus, with skilled and organized transition planning, Reagan was able to recruit loyal subordinates who were not only ideologically sound but had begun to translate his agenda, to which they were committed, into substantive changes in public policy. Reagan had in place, as Newland crisply phrases it, an "ideological network for agenda enforcement."[34]

But Reagan's staff may have erred too far in the direction of loyalty and ideological agreement. Presidents also need aides and advisers who are familiar with the substantive details and history of federal policy efforts and possess the professional expertise—not just ideological commitment—necessary to the formulation of sound policy. Too much emphasis on ideology and loyalty may prevent staff members from developing linkages to those with such skills, leading, as Newland observes, to the "insulation of the policy process from career service perspectives and from professional expertise" and the failure to obtain a "workable balance of policy involvement between Congress, the agencies, and the EOP."[35]

Strong ideological commitment also led some staff members to ignore the procedures that had been established in the Reagan White House. Campbell found, for example, in his interviews with staff members that "ideologically oriented officials in the NSC staff and the OPD used their status as true-blue Reaganites to short-circuit the process by winning over the president through sympathetic contact in the West Wing of the White House." This practice subsided somewhat with the appointment of Edwin L. Harper, a veteran of the Ford White House, in place of the more ideological Martin Anderson as head of the OPD, and with the increasing influence of Chief of Staff James Baker and his more pragmatic associates. But it still evidently persisted in the NSC. According to one of Campbell's respondents, "there are still cats on the NSC staff who are ideologues. They have their own personal agenda. Their mission in life is not to lay out arguments but to get their will done."[36]

Not all members of the Reagan staff were ideologues and policy advocates by any means. Part of the success of the Cabinet Council on Economic Affairs can be attributed to the work of Roger Porter, its executive secretary, and his attempts to be a neutral "honest broker," a role he had ably performed in the Ford White House for the Economic Policy Board."[37]

According to Campbell, "virtually every respondent in a position to assess the operation of the CCEA made a point of stressing Porter's effectiveness. . . . They recognized that Porter could become acquisitive in his zeal to have economic issues 'roundtabled.' " Campbell's respondents saw Porter as the "broker par excellence." As one observed: "His role is genuinely that of an honest broker. He will assure that papers are well written, that— when decision papers—they offer very clear choices that are presented in as unbiased way as possible, and they'll often be written or at least reviewed by a work group."[38]

A presumption of loyalty may also lead to a false sense of trust that the bulk of the White House staff is serving the president's interests and that bureaucratic and court politics are not at work among the president's staff. There is little evidence to suggest that the Reagan administration was more successful than others in countering these general tendencies in organizations. If anything, the politics of the well-placed leak to the press, bureaucratic competition and intrigue, and currying favor with superiors was rife in the Reagan presidency.

Not all the staff assigned to the councils followed Porter's example as a neutral broker, for example. Some evidently became captive to the chairman pro tem and the views of their cabinet departments. According to one of Campbell's respondents who wished to keep his council affiliation anonymous, one executive secretary "views himself as working for the chairman pro tem [the cabinet officer heading the council]. The papers that go to his cabinet council are not necessarily unbiased. They may be written by the chairman pro tem's department. They may not present the other side of the issue. He doesn't view himself as an honest broker. He would like to be, but feels constrained by his chairman."[39]

The case of Richard Darman provides some testimony for each of these tendencies as well as for their mutually reinforcing relationship.[40] Baker initially gave Darman the title White House staff secretary, which Darman evidently found demeaning and had changed, before his swearing in, to deputy assistant to the president. Darman chose to downplay this title, however, reasoning that "in order to be upwardly mobile, he must associate himself with each of the three White House loyalists and not be seen simply as a Baker loyalist." Darman took Meese deputy Craig Fuller, who had been a member of Deaver's Los Angeles public relations firm, under his wing and successfully promoted the idea that Fuller should attend virtually all high-level staff meetings. Because Fuller attended such meetings as Meese's deputy, according to informal White House protocol Darman should also attend as Baker's deputy. Darman was "unhesitating about promoting his own efforts and denigrating the work of others." According to a White House staff member, "Darman's vendettas have sometimes strengthened his own position more than they have strengthened the over-all capacity of the White House to serve the President. 'His reputation for going after people is really something.' "

Michael Deaver also discusses Darman's role on the staff, as well as general tensions among members of Reagan's team: "The White House staff was split right down the middle between the moderates and the conservatives. Dick Darman, who had worked for Baker, was clearly a pragmatic guy. When [NSC adviser William] Clark suspected Dick of leaking some piece of information, he changed the computer codes on the entry lock to the NSC briefing room, the Situation Room, so Darman could not get in. In retaliation, Darman had a coded entry installed on his office door."[41] Deaver goes on to describe the mood in the White House at the time as "a period of semi-rampant paranoia."

Both Martin Anderson and Donald Regan—hardly allies—also report numerous examples of similar behavior. Regan's own fall from power was in great measure attributable to the campaign depicting his faults and his weakening powers as chief of staff waged in the media by his opponents in the administration. Although Regan had wanted to leave the White House staff long before the Iran-Contra scandal broke, he found out through news sources that the president had decided to accept his resignation well before he had finally chosen a date of departure; the news leaks were intended to drive Regan from power even sooner than he had contemplated and perhaps implicitly to link him to the Iran-Contra affair (the Tower Commission Report had been issued only days before the leak was made).

President Reagan's problems were compounded by his trust in his subor-dinates' loyalty. It was, according to Donald Regan, a "degree of trust" that was "unprecedented in modern American history." But it was, Regan goes on to note, a trust that "was betrayed in shocking fashion. When that happened Reagan seldom criticized, seldom complained, never scolded."[42] According to another source, President Reagan "frequently expressed irrita-tion over the steady flow of leaked stories depicting strife among his staff." But there was "no noticeable disciplinary action to stem the tide even though some of the sources [were] fairly obvious."[43]

Comparison of Reagan's difficulties with those of Carter is instructive. Although the degree of their personal involvement in the policy processes of their presidencies obviously differed and the specific modes of organizing their respective staff systems were dissimilar, both sought to widen their circle of counsel beyond the immediate White House staff, especially by revitalizing the use of the cabinet, albeit in different ways. Both also developed new procedures and means for policy making with which they felt comfortable and which would mesh with their broader political and ideological goals. Yet both had an inability to remedy the weaknesses that developed in their staff arrangements, and both failed to take steps to make their system work within an organizational context. In short, despite the intentions of these two very different presidents, the forces at work in the institutional presidency—centralization of power, hierarchy, and bureaucratization—emerged under both, and each proved ill equipped to harness them.

7

GEORGE BUSH IN MIDSTREAM

■ ■ ■

Characterizing the staff operations of sitting presidents is risky because few reliable sources of data are available and the track record is incomplete. But several trends in the Bush White House can be discerned: a president pursuing different managerial strategies in foreign and domestic affairs—and with different records of success. Especially on the domestic front, Bush began propitiously but encountered increasing difficulty with the emergence of a strong White House chief of staff. Effective management of the institutional presidency increasingly proved elusive.

Bush and the Institutional Presidency: Through a Managerial Lens

Bush began his presidency in January 1989 by bringing on board his staff a group of professional and experienced policy advisers. Twenty-four of twenty-nine top staffers had prior White House experience, advanced academic degrees, and, despite their relative youth, impressive résumés.[1] Although, unlike Reagan or Carter, Bush did not enter the presidency with talk about giving the cabinet a strong role in his policy decisions, he assembled a group of experienced cabinet officers—many of whom had served in previous administrations and were in several cases close friends of the president—and gave them a great deal of leeway in conducting the affairs of their departments as well as direct personal access to the president.[2] Furthermore, as journalist Burt Solomon observes, Bush by and large "filled his administration with practical men and women who are generally conservative but not obsessively so, who tend to be—as he is—civil, cautious and conciliatory. They like to face problems and solve them using a few shared values—prudence, marketplace wisdom, compassion in word if not in deed—as their guide."[3] With the exception of White House Chief of Staff John Sununu, Bush avoided appointing publicly outspoken policy advocates and hired few ideological crusaders, a marked contrast to Reagan's initial record. Bush retained the cabinet council system of the later Reagan years, with three councils: on economic policy, domestic policy, and national security policy. But unlike his predecessor, who relied on largely formal decision procedures, Bush has used the councils as only one among a number of channels of advice. They have been complemented by extensive informal means of access to the Oval Office. Over time, however, Bush's economic and domestic policy units began to atrophy as they were supplanted by a powerful chief of staff.

Economic and Domestic Policy: Formal Procedures and Informal Networks

At the start of his presidency, Bush developed staff procedures designed to refine a range of domestic policy options and argue them out vigorously in front of him. Bush's special assistant for domestic and economic policy, Roger Porter, was assigned the task of coordinating the work of the Domestic and Economic Policy Councils and chairing working groups composed of White House staff members and representatives from the OMB and relevant agencies and departments. The main duty of the working groups has been to prepare policy options papers, which are passed to the relevant councils and other interested parties for discussion (a process Bush staffers have termed "shopping it around"). Each council has usually convened every week for an hour or so, more frequently when an issue has been pressing or controversial; discussions of certain policy issues have often consumed several sessions (ten in the case of the Domestic Policy Council's discussion of clean air legislation in 1989).[4] Although Bush did not attend all council meetings, when the system was fully functioning in his first year as president, he was perceived to be an active participant at key points in the process (dubbed "scheduled train wrecks") when issues were reportedly hotly debated. "He doesn't want filters," according to one participant. "He actually wants to sit there at the table and listen to [OMB Director Richard] Darman fight with [Environmental Protection Agency Administrator William] Reilly."[5] Thus, unlike Nixon or Carter, Bush has not relied largely on written option papers and, unlike Reagan, he has preferred to have disagreements argued out in front of him.

Initial reports coming from the Bush White House depicted a well-crafted and functioning system. Staff members, Porter in particular, were reported to subscribe (at least in principle) to the tenets of multiple advocacy and to a role for key staff members as "honest brokers" in the process, views that accord with Porter's prescriptions, based on his experience during the Ford administration as coordinator of the Economic Policy Board, set out in his book *Presidential Decision Making*. But the White House staff increasingly played a proactive role in the policy process, as one journalist noted in 1989, "fashioning options, brokering disagreements, controlling the paperwork, molding legislative details, and usually having the last word before Bush decides."[6] With John Sununu's ascendance to prominence, the council system began to atrophy and an honest-broker mentality was edged out by policy advocacy and institutional partisanship on the part of Sununu and those staff members closest to him.

Thus, controversial issues, such as federal funding for the arts and fiscal policy, were sometimes not entrusted to the council system but have been taken up directly by Bush's top aides in consultation with the president. Bush's May 1990 decision to convene a summit with congressional leaders to resolve differences over the budget, for example, was made by the president and high-level White House staffers, Sununu most notably. Similarly, administration policies in dealing with the greenhouse effect were thrashed out, in 1989, among Bush, John Sununu, OMB Director Darman, and EPA Administrator Reilly after the formal policy review process was seen as unproductive.[7]

These more formal deliberate forums have generally had fluid membership, with staff members who express interest in particular policy areas invited to participate. For example, White House Counsel C. Boyden Gray, whose usual duties are those of the president's chief in-house legal adviser, was involved in the 1990 dispute over funding for the arts, an area where Gray had a personal interest. Similarly, James C. Cicconi, Bush's staff secretary, has been on hand for discussions of civil rights issues, an area where he has expressed personal concerns. And Vice-President Quayle has been a major participant in space policy, efforts to deal with economic competitiveness, legislative strategy, and foreign policy crisis management, most notably the Panama crisis and the Persian Gulf War.[8]

Bush has often complemented the formal domestic council process or meetings with his top aides by a wide range of informal contacts. After cabinet and staff meetings, "Bush repairs to the Oval Office and widens his net," inviting staff assistants in for further discussion or telephoning his "sources" on Capitol Hill and other Washington influentials.[9] In foreign policy matters, Bush has frequently relied on intense personal diplomacy with world leaders, generally over the telephone ("Rolodex diplomacy" as it has come to be termed in Washington circles). According to one report, "This diplomacy is a central part of Mr. Bush's decision-making style: He develops personal friendship with world leaders [and] talks to them with great frequency as he weighs his options." However, within administration circles, Bush has generally held his cards tightly, making his final judgments "in a highly informal and secretive setting with only a few aides in the know."[10]

Compared to both the Carter and the Reagan administrations, Bush has had better success in keeping cabinet officers involved in the policy process. Bush has created, according to one journalistic report based on extensive interviews with the White House staff and cabinet officers, "a system in his own image that steers toward a middle course, and that seems to offer many different players a seat at the table and just as many different ways to make their mark."[11] Bush has generously delegated responsibility to his cabinet officers, permitting them to establish whatever patterns of contact with the White House they are most comfortable with. At times this has worked—for example, a proposal for clean air legislation worked out by Energy Secretary James Watkins and EPA Administrator Reilly and then sent to the policy council for discussion—but on other occasions it has backfired. Three notable slip-ups occurred during Bush's first six months as president. Commerce Secretary Robert Mosbacher lifted restrictions on sales of midsize computers to the Eastern Bloc, only to have Bush reopen the discussion after objections by Defense Secretary Richard Cheney. Veterans Affairs Secretary Edward Derwinski decided not to appeal a federal court decision against his department's position on Vietnam-era veterans seeking compensation for exposure to the defoliant Agent Orange; Derwinski made the decision himself without telling the president he was reversing a decade of governmental policy. EPA Administrator Reilly announced efforts virtually to ban the use of asbestos by 1997, which took White House officials by surprise; as it turned out, Reilly had advised the White House beforehand of his actions in a regular weekly report, and the ban on asbestos came after a lengthy regulatory review process. In late 1990, Bush's commitment to civil rights efforts suffered an embarrassing setback following an Education Department ruling, which the White House later rescinded, that college scholarships designated exclusively for minority students were not permissible.

A Strong Chief of Staff

Not surprisingly in light of such incidents, especially those during the first months of Bush's presidency, the White House staff quickly became a focal point of Bush's decision-making process, with Chief of Staff Sununu emerging as a key player. Republican National Chairman Lee Atwater was forestalled by illness in his attempts to broaden political advice coming to the president by establishing closer links to the Republican party apparatus and weakening the White House political office. Under President Reagan, the White House political affairs office had broad patronage powers and was the chief conduit of political advice to the president, but when Bush took office, its powers were limited to administrative and public relations matters and political affairs were handled by Atwater and his staff. Before he was stricken with a brain tumor, Atwater had also emerged as a close political adviser to Bush, meeting daily with the chief of staff and partaking in frequent conversations and meetings with the president. In the vacuum left by Atwater's illness and subsequent death, political advice once again began to move back within the White House staff.

Perhaps the most important centralizing tendency at work in the first three years of the Bush administration was the increasing power wielded by Chief of Staff John Sununu, former governor of New Hampshire and key Bush supporter during the 1988 campaign for the Republican party nomination, who served as chief of staff until December 3, 1991. On taking over as chief of staff, Sununu scuttled a plan to bring Bush pollster and political strategist Robert Teeter on board as counselor to the president and Sununu's equal; Teeter retired to the private sector. Following Atwater's illness, Sununu's deputy chief of staff in New Hampshire, David Carney, was named to fill a vacancy heading the White House political office. Carney and Sununu's executive assistant, Edward Rogers, emerged as Bush's top in-house political advisers. According to one source, "The two meet with the White House political staff every morning and divvy up duties, Carney supervising the political office day to day and Rogers shepherding relations with Republican strategists and ensuring that Bush aides remain sensitive to political needs."[12] Although strategy for the 1990 midterm election was devised by a wider policy group, including OMB Director Darman and Teeter, who was brought in as a consultant, it was essentially run out of Sununu's shop. Legislative liaison with Congress was also more directly controlled by Sununu than it was by Reagan's chiefs of staff. Unlike Reagan's practice, meetings of the White House legislative liaison staff were not regularly held but occurred only when Sununu felt them needed. Nor, to date, has Bush created a legislative strategy group of the sort that played a major role in the Reagan White House; instead Sununu and Darman, or Sununu's immediate staff, fashioned strategies and tactics for dealing with Congress on an ad hoc basis at the 7:30 A.M. meeting of senior aides.

Sununu's role as chief of staff resembled that of his powerful predecessors. He, along with NSC adviser Brent Scowcroft, generally met with Bush from 8:00 A.M. to about 9:30 every working day and then again from 4:30 to about 5:00 P.M.; in between Sununu usually saw Bush ten times, spending on average about 35 to 45 percent of his working day with the president.[13] Sununu was not reluctant to make his views on policy known to the president. More than a process manager, he became a personal adviser to the president, akin to a Don Regan rather than a Sherman Adams. Also like Regan, Sununu was not reluctant to involve himself in foreign policy matters, particularly if they had bearing on the president's standing with the public.

Sununu was very much a "hands-on" chief of staff, immersing himself in policy detail. In the April 1990 White House conference on the greenhouse effect, a topic in which Sununu was personally interested, his attention to detail, according to some reports, approached the obsessive: Sununu insisted on personally approving "virtually every decision," according to one White House official, including who was invited, what was on the agenda, what the order of speeches would be, and how papers would be distributed.[14] Sununu then personally edited the president's speech on global warming, toning down passages he felt were too proenvironmentalist but insisting the changes reflected President Bush's views.[15] Sununu was also a strong policy advocate on other environmental issues, such as the Clean Air Act, legislation on physical access for the disabled, federal policies on funding abortions, telecommunications policy, and budget negotiations with Congress. According to some administration sources, Sununu's strong interest in policy matters sometimes intimidated other senior policy advisers, both on the staff and in the cabinet, who occasionally delegated working with Sununu to their deputies.

Unlike Regan, however, Sununu worked for a president who has been inclined to immerse himself in policy detail, thus counteracting any tendency for the chief of staff to be touted as the president's prime minister. Sununu also took in stride Bush's penchant to deal with staff aides and cabinet officers directly. Although he has a sizable ego and relished media attention, Sununu did not resent Bush's penchant for wider policy advice and was generally regarded as accessible by members of the staff.[16]

Sununu's personality and operating style, however, sometimes alienated other members of the White House staff, the Cabinet, and members of Congress. As the self-styled "pit bull" of the Bush White House, Sununu's questionable practices—most notably frequent use of White House transportation for personal purposes—and his often abrasive and arrogant behavior in dealing with others generated enmity. Even William Bennett, Bush's former drug czar and prominent conservative supporter of Sununu during his last days as chief of staff, remarked in the aftermath of Sununu's resignation that "From talking to assistant secretaries and lower level people in the White House, it's clear they never forgave him for showing them the error in their memo in front of five other people."[17]

Sununu's relationships with Congress, even members of his own party, were also not particularly cordial; critics charged him with failing to understand the differences between the pliable New Hampshire state legislature and the federal Congress and with being ham-handed in congressional negotiations, sometimes even threatening recalcitrant Republicans with electoral retribution by the president.[18] Aspects of Sununu's role, however, may have been deliberate: playing "bad cop" to Bush's "good cop" and acting as the president's lightning rod for politically difficult decisions. Sununu's willingness to take bold and often controversial positions may also have served as a useful complement to Bush' usually risk-averse political instincts, and he bolstered the president's often wavering support among the Republican right wing.

Predicted conflict with OMB Director Darman, a longtime Washington insider and skilled political and bureaucratic operative, failed to materialize, and Sununu and Darman even developed a cordial if not friendly working relationship,[19] often meeting before the 7:30 A.M. senior staff meeting to discuss strategy. When Sununu and Darman agreed on a policy issue, however, other advisers often ducked an open confrontation with them, perceiving that their combined efforts were too strong to oppose.

The advice of Sununu and Darman was also sometimes politically damaging to the president. In the ill-fated 1990 budget negotiations with Congress over the FY1991 budget, Sununu and Darman miscalculated the opposition of conservative Republicans to revenue increases and were viewed as heavy handed in their treatment of Republican members who opposed the package that had been negotiated with congressional leaders. The administration appeared unprepared for the defeat, and in its aftermath sent out conflicting signals on where it wished to proceed. In a 9 October 1990 news conference, for example, Bush indicated he might trade higher income taxes for a cut in capital gains taxes, but shortly thereafter press secretary Marlin Fitzwater, apparently at Sununu's instigation, told reporters that such a deal was off the table. The air of chaos, according to one Republican strategist, made "the Keystone Kops look like they've got their [expletive deleted] together."[20]

Bush has not, of course, pursued an ambitious domestic policy agenda. With the exception of the budget, Bush's major domestic policy initiatives have involved policies that require little federal funding. Bush's fall 1989 "education summit" with the nation's governors led to recommendations that were largely the province of state and local governments to carry out— and fund; costs for the clean air initiatives were passed on to the private sector; Bush's child care proposal envisioned tax incentives rather than federal assistance as a means of funding, and met congressional resistance for that reason; and Bush consented to support legislation on physical access for the disabled with the proviso that its costs would be borne by employers. The danger that Bush faces is whether in times of economic downturn and increasing congressional opposition, when adept compromise, bargaining, and accommodations are the order of the day, a system with a powerful chief of staff will be able to meet the president's policy needs.

Bush has, however, widened his net of domestic policy advice, resuscitating several White House units that had become almost dormant during the Reagan years. The Council on Environmental Quality, which was subjected to severe staff and budget cuts in the 1980s, had its budget doubled during Bush's first year in office and saw its staff increase in size from seventeen to approximately forty. The White House consumer affairs staff was also rejuvenated and given increased responsibilities in the area of privacy protection.[21] The Council of Economic Advisers regained status lost during the Reagan years as a key source of economic advice to the president. Its chairman, Stanford economist Michael Boskin, became a central participant in the administration's high-level economic policy councils, enjoyed an occasional game of tennis with the president, and received late-night, follow-up telephone calls from him.[22] Bush's Office of National Drug Control Policy, however, has been a more mixed success. Initially led by Reagan's vocal secretary of education, William Bennett, drug policy enjoyed increased funding and, for a time, increased visibility. But Bennett did not receive cabinet-level status as he had originally requested, nor did he receive powers to demand specific action from government agencies whose operations touch on drug control; after nineteen months on the White House staff, Bennett resigned.

Foreign Policy: Restricted Collegiality

Less is known about Bush's decision making in foreign affairs, but procedures there appear to differ from those in domestic policy. Bush has been more ad hoc in his foreign policy decision making, has consulted with fewer sources (except for foreign leaders, whom he consults extensively), and has often been secretive.[23] But his own extensive experience in foreign affairs, plus his innate caution and concern to avoid mistakes, may compensate for any narrowing of the foreign policy advice net. Bush has provided more personal direction over foreign policy decision making than Reagan did. Bush also has enjoyed the services of two competent chief advisers— Secretary of State Baker and NSC Special Assistant Brent Scowcroft—who have established a cooperative working relationship with each other and the president. During the Persian Gulf crisis, they were joined by two other skilled advisers—Secretary of Defense Richard Cheney and General Colin Powell, chairman of the Joint Chiefs of Staff—plus Robert Gates (Scowcroft's deputy), Chief of Staff Sununu, and Vice-President Quayle.

Scowcroft has deliberately pursued a less visible and less proactive role than most of his predecessors as NSC special assistant. He has avoided becoming a policy advocate who seeks to become the president's chief policy adviser. At the same time,he has not confined his role to that of managerial custodian/honest broker, as he did as NSC assistant during the Ford presidency with an activist and assertive secretary of state, Henry Kissinger. Scowcroft has spent more time with Bush than any other senior official in the administration, and reports indicate that he has freely expressed his views to the president but has made it clear to Bush when he is doing so.

According to Kevin Mulachy, Scowcroft's performance so far has fit the role of a presidential "counselor," "in actively guarding the president's interests in the policy-making process and advocating personal policy preferences, if convinced that a department proposal is inimicable to the president's interests. General Scowcroft has been particularly distinguished as a full partner with the secretaries of State and Defense, but without usurping their departmental prerogatives or presuming to be the sole instrument of the president's will."[24]

In his dealings with the president, "Scowcroft decided not to do what he expected Bush would do—drive the policy, broker the deals, knock heads together when necessary and call crisis meetings. . . . Scowcroft has instead tried to be the wise man in the mix." Scowcroft has not defined his role as the president's personal counselor without costs. Much of the day-to-day management of the NSC staff has been delegated to his assistant, Robert Gates, (until 1991, when he became CIA director), and when Scowcroft returns to his own desk from meeting with Bush in the Oval Office, "often at the end of the day, paperwork can be piled high. . . . Staff members often complain that Scowcroft has too little time for them and often fails to stay on top of unfolding events."[25] Some administration officials also have complained that Scowcroft "pays more attention to his personal relationship with the President than to organization, turning the security council [staff] from a well-spring of policy initiative to a lesser clearinghouse of information."[26]

Scowcroft in the Bush White House thus differed markedly from his domestic policy counterpart, Chief of Staff Sununu. Scowcroft has avoided the political limelight and deferred to the secretary of state as the chief spokesman of administration policy. This accords with one of the recommendations of the Tower commission, of which Scowcroft was one of the three principal members, that "the national security adviser should generally operate off stage."[27]

Whether that same deference has occurred in the administration's private councils is not clear, however; some reports indicate that Secretary of State Baker and a tightly knit group of assistants in the State Department have often set the national security agenda with little input from the NSC staff.[28] Detailed knowledge of foreign policy and a comprehensive vision of America's place in world affairs have not, however, been Baker's strong suit; the general perception of Baker has been that he is "long on politics and short on policy." Furthermore, unlike George Shultz, who relied on State Department careerists for senior personnel and policy advice, Baker has been relatively cool toward his department's professionals, making it "clear from the start that he intended to be President Bush's man at the State Department and not the State Department's man at the White House."[29]

Scowcroft has streamlined the NSC staff system, again drawing on his experience on the Tower commission. A new three-tiered system was established to replace the numerous interagency committees of the Reagan years, which numbered six dozen at one point by some estimates. At the highest decisional level is the National Security Council, dubbed the "Principals Committee," which (in departure from the practice of other administrations) Scowcroft chairs in the president's absence. At the second level is a "Deputies Committee" composed of second-level department and NSC staff members, which, as the situation demands, brings in representatives of agencies that are not formally represented on the council level. This tier is reminiscent of Eisenhower's Planning Board and essentially defines policy alternatives for presentation to the NSC. At the third level are approximately twelve "policy coordination committees," which examine and develop policy proposals for discussion by the Deputies Committee. These working groups are composed of midlevel department and NSC staff officials, with an NSC staff member serving as executive secretary of each group.[30] No implementation mechanism comparable to the Eisenhower Operations Coordinating Board, however, has been established.

The ability of Scowcroft and Baker to avoid personal and political rivalries, plus Bush's own "hands-on" management of foreign policy, have undoubtedly improved the functioning of national security policy making, at least in comparison with the Carter and Reagan years. Whether it has led and will lead to better foreign policy is an open question. "Groupthink" is always a danger among a small number of like-minded advisers, and isolation from the information and advice of policy experts who are "out of the loop" (especially lower-level NSC staffers) can prevent useful counsel from reaching the president.

Some slip-ups have occurred. An abortive 3 October 1989 coup in Panama against the government of strongman General Manuel Noriega took Bush and his advisers by surprise. As Elizabeth Drew notes, "this most experienced of administrations . . . was utterly unprepared for a fairly predictable crisis and stumbled its way through it. . . . Even if the administration came out at the right place . . . in deciding not to use force to help the coup succeed or to nab Panamanian leader Manuel Noriega while he was being held by the rebels, it got there by a very strange route."[31]

Bush handled the crisis "in a characteristic manner—informally, with only a small circle of trusted senior advisers, sometimes just talking with them on the telephone." According to one administration source, "For ten months they've had this collegial, informal atmosphere. They just continued as they had. They took in the facts as they needed them. They shut out the bureaucracy. The flow of information into them should have been more organized. There should have been a central collection point."[32] The eventual invasion of Panama in December 1989 was deemed an overall success but was plagued by failures in intelligence gathering and communication (and embarrassment in the days following the coup in not being able to locate General Noriega) that might have been corrected had better procedures been in place.[33]

War in the Persian Gulf

Bush's most ambitious foreign policy initiative—his military response to the invasion of Kuwait by President Saddam Hussein of Iraq on 2 August 1990—enlisted the support of the world community, including such unlikely allies as Syria and the Soviet Union, in thwarting and ultimately defeating Hussein. The American military presence at the height of the war exceeded 540,000 ground, sea, and air forces; it was the largest buildup since the height of the Vietnam War and the quickest introduction of such a large number of U.S. forces since World War II.

The White House was largely unprepared for Hussein's move, despite intelligence reports that the Iraqis were massing a large military force on the Kuwait border.[34] Earlier in the summer, Colin Powell, Bush's chairman of the Joint Chiefs of Staff and formerly Reagan's NSC assistant, had returned to Washington from a Mideast tour optimistic about prospects for peace in the region. As reports of an Iraqi buildup filtered in, Powell commissioned the U.S. Central Command to develop a two-tiered plan for an American response to an outbreak of war; one tier was defensive, the other retaliatory. But on 30 July, when the Iraqi force reached 100,000 troops, "no alarm bells went off at the Pentagon." On 1 August, a few hours before the invasion, Powell met with his top commanders to consider the situation and concluded that Iraq now had the intent and capability to invade Kuwait. But according to one senior Pentagon official, "no one said, 'This is it, god damn it, he [Hussein] is coming.' "

Although surprised by the extent of Hussein's invasion, if not perhaps by the reality of it, Bush and his top advisers decided to intervene militarily. Bush settled on a military response almost immediately following the invasion, spurred in part by fear that Hussein might invade Saudi Arabia or eventually attack Israel.[35] Essentially "starting from zero," according to one Air Force general,[36] the White House updated a general contingency plan for introducing military force in the Mideast, Op Plan 90–1002, which envisioned neither Iraq as an adversary nor the loss of Kuwait. Bush requested that military options be fully presented to him at Camp David on Saturday, 4 August. But before meeting with his advisers back at the White House late on Sunday, 5 August, Bush vowed to reporters that an Iraqi invasion "will not stand." An hour later, he approved the first deployment of American combat forces.

Not only had the White House misguessed Hussein's action, but Bush decided to intervene, according to the *Washington Post*, "despite the lack of a detailed war plan for fighting Iraq or a strong initial recommendation from his military advisers to commit U.S. forces to Saudi Arabia." Diplomatic and other alternatives, including more limited military responses, were either not considered or briefly discussed, then dismissed: "By all accounts, it was President Bush's gut instincts that drove the rapid American commitment of forces to Saudi Arabia."[37] Bush also limited his own hand in dealing with Hussein by telling the press, the public, and Hussein that the invasion "will not stand," making a partial Iraqi withdrawal from Kuwait as a basis for a negotiated settlement difficult for him to accept at a later date.

As it turned out, Bush's strategy in demanding Iraq's complete withdrawal from Kuwait and its acceptance of all United Nations resolutions paid off, at least in the sense of securing a military victory over Hussein. The technical superiority of the American-led coalition forces coupled with an effective economic embargo wreaked near destruction on Hussein's military infrastructure and Iraq's economy. An air campaign that began on 16 January 1991—encompassing more than one hundred thousand air sorties against militarily significant targets in Iraq and Kuwait—prepared the way for a ground assault by coalition forces on 23 February. In less than one hundred hours, Hussein's army faced total military defeat, suffering tens of thousands of casualties, estimates of from 50,000 to 100,000 troops taken prisoner of war, and near total destruction of arms, tanks, and other equipment.

The victory of coalition forces against Iraq was hailed in the press and the public as a personal triumph for George Bush. From a military standpoint, this assessment cannot be denied. Bush's efforts during the crisis to seek a negotiated settlement within the terms of the United Nations resolutions plus his resolve and determination to move toward the firm application of force when diplomacy proved unproductive were critical elements in ending Iraq's occupation of Kuwait with little loss of life among coalition forces: fewer than one hundred Americans were killed in combat-related incidents from the onset of "Operation Desert Storm" with the air war in January through its culmination in victory by the end of February (approximately fifty Americans were killed during the ground war phase), approximately fifty Americans were killed in noncombat incidents, and an additional 105 casualties were sustained before the start of Desert Storm during the "Desert Shield" phase of operations from August to mid-January. The domestic political consequences of the victory were also astounding: Bush's approval rating at the end of the war stood at 87 percent, the highest ever recorded and matched only by Harry Truman's popularity after World War II.[38] As one *New York Times* correspondent put it, "the power of principle, the stark and vivid definition of purpose, allowed Mr. Bush to reverse the conventional wisdom and turn a conflict that no one wanted at the outset into the most popular American war since the one he fought in himself."[39]

The long-term consequences of the coalition strategy in defeating Hussein are more uncertain. Hussein remained in power, and Iraq's nuclear and chemical weapons capability apparently was not fully destroyed. The course of political developments in the Mideast was dramatically altered by the war and Hussein's defeat; its future direction cannot be predicted. So too with the effects on the regional—perhaps even the global—environment of Hussein's futile activities during the war: it will take many years even to assess, much less remedy, his deliberate massive oil spills in the Persian Gulf and, especially, his setting on fire six hundred of Kuwait's nine hundred oil wells.

Much also remains to be discovered about the Bush decision-making process during the crisis. Was the anticipation of an attack by Hussein on Saudi Arabia justified?[40] What role did the decision process play in altering American war plans during October 1990 from a frontal attack on Iraqi forces in Kuwait, which the military initially presented, to the flanking operation that brought swift victory in February?[41] What role did it play in the crucial timing of the air campaign and the ground war? What role did it play in creating and holding together a difficult coalition of Western and Arab forces and in restraining Israel from involvement—which might have split the coalition—despite the bombing of that nation by Iraqi scud missiles? Early assessments suggest a careful deliberative process once the decision to intervene was made, coupled with the benefit of Bush's extensive contacts with other world leaders. But time will tell whether this is an adequate characterization, as well as answer lingering questions about whether military operations might have been avoided if Arab states had at the outset of the crisis brokered a diplomatic solution without American involvement, and, more broadly, whether victory was due simply to overwhelming and superior American technology rather than to particular strategic decisions.

Beyond responding to particular crises like those in Panama or Kuwait, Bush and his advisers did not conduct a comprehensive review of American foreign policy during his first two years as president, nor have they had the ideological commitment of Reagan or the overall conception of world order that Carter at least sought to develop (notwithstanding talk of a vague "New World Order"). Instead, foreign policy in the Bush administration has been incremental, pragmatic, and largely reactive. Given a rapidly changing international context and the United States' uncertain place in it, such caution may be appropriate, but it may also lead to missed opportunities and undue constraint by the march of world events.

Bush and the Institutional Presidency: Through an Organizational Lens

Although some aspects of Bush's formal decision-making procedures in both foreign and domestic policy may be wanting, he has shown a salutary ability to create positive informal relationships among staff members and has placed strong emphasis on collegiality. Part of Bush's success stems from his staff appointments. Many on his staff have had past experience in Bush's political campaigns and on the Ford and Reagan staffs and are well known by the president. Perhaps more important, many have worked together in the past, thus reducing tendencies for bureaucratic jockeying and court intrigue; according to Edward Rogers, Sununu's executive assistant, when turf battles have occurred, they have generally been quickly settled by comrades who engage in "good-natured confrontation" rather than continued intramural bickering.[42] Bush staff members have also been less ideological than some of their predecessors in the Reagan administration. And with the exception of Sununu and Darman, they have been less publicly visible.

Bush has not been confrontational, nor has he been willing to wield a stick on erring staff members. Instead he has preferred to reward performance by including staff members in his endless flow of handwritten notes and frequent invitations to formal and informal social occasions; Bush also has been in the habit of having lunch weekly in the White House staff mess. The atmosphere Bush has sought to create with his staff has been of positive consequence; as John Sununu points out, "he's got such a way of letting you know he'd like something changed. He almost creates a climate [in] which you come to a mutual decision to make a change."[43] Thus, "the Bush White House's vaunted collegiality, though it's hardly perfect, 'isn't bad,' said one middle-level adviser who came from academia expecting the worst. In manners and organization alike, this White House is pervaded by an informality that reflects the man who sleeps in the presidential bed."[44] According to CEA chair Boskin, "I feel very much part of a team assisting the president and I'm lucky to have such terrific teammates."[45]

Bush's attempts at showing continued personal trust in aides who have suffered setbacks or who are perceived to be in disfavor has reinforced a sense of collegiality and reduced the temptation to engage in bureaucratic politics and court intrigue. For example, he was seen to throw his arm around OMB Director Darman in the aftermath of the budget fiasco in the fall of 1990. Similarly, as the Persian Gulf War came to a close in February 1991, reports surfaced that Secretary of State Baker was in low standing because he had purportedly favored negotiation with the Iraqis and Soviet efforts to secure a face-saving end to the war. Media stories about the NSC gaining the upper hand over the State Department reportedly "upset" Bush, who made a pointed effort to include Baker in a visit to Camp David on the eve of ground operations against Iraq.[46]

Bush's penchant for direct contact with his aides may be especially important to the sense of teamwork that has so far developed among his staff. Lack of access to the president, as we noted in chapter 4, contributes to bureaucratic infighting and court intrigue. Yet by all accounts Bush has been a remarkably accessible president, not unlike John Kennedy. According to Bonnie Newman, assistant to the president for management and administration, "he picks up the phone and calls or walks down the hall." Andrew Card, who served as Sununu's deputy, says Bush "is not one to stay in a box."[47] In short, Bush has practiced what one aide has termed "a theology" of collegiality that "tends to [be] self-reinforcing."[48]

Collegiality also has extended to members of the cabinet, several of whom—Treasury Secretary Brady, Secretary of State Baker, Defense Secretary Cheney, and Commerce Secretary Mosbacher—have been longtime associates if not personal friends of Bush and each other. These informal linkages have reduced the turf battles that normally occur among cabinet officers and have strengthened the role of these persons as informal advisers to the president. Nor have the ups and downs of particular cabinet members so far affected their standing with the president; for example, Nicholas Brady's plan to impose a fee on savings and loan depositors was aborted, but the event did not diminish Brady's standing with the president or encourage other cabinet officers to encroach on Brady's turf.[49]

The jury on Bush's White House management is still out. Critical details about its internal operations, as opposed to those reported in the press or in interviews with participants, remain unknown, and its success or failure cannot be judged while the political events it deals with are still unfolding. But a mixed verdict appears likely: generally high marks in foreign policy but a spotty record on the domestic front. Bush's experience to date offers, however, a number of interesting lessons about managing the institutional presidency.

It suggests, at the most general level, that presidents can (and may need to) pursue different managerial strategies depending upon the particular area of policy and the president's own strengths and weaknesses as a decision maker in those differing domains. Bush's foreign and domestic policy systems clearly differ in organization and style. Bush has especially benefited from a foreign policy system that generally complements his own strengths as a knowledgeable world leader with an extensive network of contacts both at home and abroad. Its seeming limitations may be its inability to check Bush's penchant for decisive—but perhaps not fully considered—action at key moments of crises and the possibility of acquiescence among the president's top advisers when faced with a determined commander-in-chief.

On the domestic front, Bush has relied on a different approach with less measurable success: generally open and fluid decision-making procedures at the start of his presidency but their gradual atrophy under a strong chief of staff. These evolving arrangements did enable him, during his first two and a half years as president, to respond (or at least appear to respond) selectively to domestic issues while pursuing, in Bush's view, more important foreign policy concerns. But by the end of Bush's third year in office, the pressing, inescapable problem of economic recovery and perceived inaction on other policy problems, health care most notably, fostered a sense of drift and uncertainty. John Sununu's role as a powerful but controversial chief of staff especially compounded Bush's difficulties.

But the management problem that Bush faces in domestic and economic policy is less a matter of procedures and staff organization. It is, rather, the managerial skill in making them work effectively: presidential vigilance in reining in a powerful chief of staff—only belatedly and reluctantly done—and responding in a timely fashion to those domestic policy concerns that require presidential attention and intervention. Bush's replacement of Sununu with Transportation Secretary Samuel Skinner may provide the kind of chief of staff long needed: a knowledgeable and politically skilled chief assistant but one less inclined to act as an abrasive policy advocate. But even then, Bush may falter over the chief failing of all systems of White House organization and management: they can aid the process of full, informed, and fair policy choice but they cannot guarantee that the right policies and programs will emerge and meet the needs of the times. The "vision thing" haunts still again.

CONCLUSION

■ ■ ■

This book began with the assertion that studies of the White House staff essentially fall into two camps: one that emphasizes certain institutional features of the presidency that transcend particular administrations, and another that notes striking variation from administration to administration depending on personalities, managerial styles, and organizational proclivities of individual presidents. One general conclusion to be drawn from this study is that both approaches are in part right.

On the one hand, the institutional traits we noted in chapter 2—centralization of policy making by the White House staff, centralization of power and authority within the staff, and various manifestations of bureaucratic behavior—recur across White House staff systems with different organizational structures and under the leadership of presidents exhibiting a range of managerial styles and practices. Analysis of the Carter and Reagan presidencies especially suggests the importance of the institutional presidency as a determining factor. Ineffective staff organization and management tended to exacerbate the weaknesses of both presidents' White House staffs. Carter and Reagan differed markedly in their organization of their staff systems and in their daily dealings with their staffs, but they shared the vexation of being unable to cope with the challenges that an institutional presidency presents to modern presidents.

On the other hand, however, the managerial practices of individual presidents also seem to count. Variation in the operations and procedures of particular staff systems—variation affecting presidential performance—is too great to be attributed simply to institutional forces. This is especially true when we "hold constant" basic patterns of staff organization: presidents with formally organized staff systems, such as Eisenhower and Nixon, fared quite differently with their staffs; so too did Kennedy and Johnson, though both had collegial staff arrangements. In each case, differences in managerial styles and practices are central factors in accounting for the different track records and experiences of these presidents.

But the study suggests more than just the notion that both approaches are in some sense right: the interaction of "the man" and "the office" is also vitally important. As we saw in chapter 3, the extent to which presidents tailor their staff organization and management practices, whether formal or collegial, to an institutional context bears consequences on their effective operation. And as we saw in chapter 4, the extent to which they are cognizant of those features of the institutional presidency that transcend particular patterns of staff organization and incorporate this awareness into their management strategies also significantly affects their success in dealing with their staffs.

The institutional presidency clearly presents a challenge to contemporary occupants of the Oval Office: it can work for or against them. And it is a challenge that is not likely to go away: given the great demands and expectations placed upon the presidency and the complexity of those policy problems, both foreign and domestic, to which the chief executive is expected to respond, contemporary presidents must turn to others for aid and assistance, whether for policy advice or to implement policy choices. Given this context, which is unlikely to change in the near future, the president's staff system can powerfully affect his performance in office. Some presidents have responded successfully to the need to turn to others for information and advice and occasionally to delegate their authority, and others have not. Useful lessons can be drawn from both sets of experiences, as we have seen.

That said, it must still be borne in mind that the arguments of the preceding chapters and the general point that the White House staff and its effective management are significant isolate only one set of factors that is likely to have an impact on how today's presidency fares. Let us briefly consider others.

Organizational Choice beyond Staff Management?

One issue is whether more can be said about the respective merits of collegial, formal, and competitive systems. In chapter 3, it was suggested that the decision to organize a collegial or formal staff structure is essentially a matter of presidential inclination: personal styles of interaction generally determine which of the two major modes of organizing the White House staff a president favors. This accords with the insight of most observers of the presidency that the president's staff must essentially fit him like a suit of clothes. But as we saw in that chapter, it is also plausible to reason that the relationship is more complex. If particular features of either a collegial or a formal staff system should be tailored in light of their predictable consequences in a (largely) institutional context—the argument of chapter 3—then perhaps the more basic decision to select either a collegial or a formal system (or whatever other organizational arrangement is possible) should be regarded as more than a matter of personal comfort and predilection. Indeed, it is plausible to imagine presidents who might naturally favor one or the other basic system faring better by selecting the unfavored alternative. Presidents might feel discomfort with the fit, but their discomfort might heighten their vigilance over its deficiencies; "fit" and "comfort" might lull into false complacency, while unfamiliarity and discomfort might facilitate correction.

Karen Hult and Charles Walcott[1] provide more general insight into the utility of particular advisory arrangements. Drawing on the work of sociologists James Thompson and Arthur Tuden,[2] Hult and Walcott suggest, first, that the design of organizational structures involves something more than developing norms for dividing, coordinating, and supervising work and responding to discrete problems. These essentially administrative tasks must be complemented by a recognition of what might be termed the "political dimension" of the policy process—which they term "governance"—entailing the discovery and articulation of goals, coping with controversy and uncertainty, and generating legitimacy and commitment. Second, different staff arrangements ("governance structures," in their phraseology) become appropriate depending on the degree of certainty, uncertainty, and controversy along two dimensions: preferences about outcomes or goals, and beliefs about causation (i.e., the means used to produce policy goals). Collegial arrangements, they argue, are appropriate where outcomes are certain but beliefs about causation are uncertain (and vice versa). Hierarchical staff systems—presumably including those I term formal—work best when both outcomes and causation beliefs are certain. Multiple advocacy fits best when outcomes are uncertain and beliefs about causation are controversial.[3]

Although Hult and Walcott's discussion requires more consideration than can be given here, their concern about the appropriateness of staff arrangements in light of goals or outcomes desired and beliefs about causation provide an important set of issues that, plausibly, should be considered in the selection of a staff structure. The preceding chapters have emphasized the need for attention to institutional factors that can deflect a staff system away from its presidentially intended purposes; Hult and Walcott alert us to some of the factors inherent in certain policy choices that also appear to be critical in the design of effective staff structures.

Indeed, one can think of other considerations that might also be taken into account profitably. Alexander George, for example, while emphasizing the importance of rational decision making as a goal of staff and advisory systems, notes that presidents must fill emotional needs in order to cope with the strain of making difficult, if not on occasion fateful, policy choices; presidents must gain understanding and support for their actions within their circle of advisers; they must obtain political support and legitimacy for their decisions from the wider audience of Congress and the public; and, following the suit of clothes analogy, they must satisfy their own cognitive needs in selecting an advisory system.[4] Advisory arrangements clearly differ in their ability to satisfy these and other needs decision makers have in organizing their staff systems and the processes they use to make policy decisions.

The problem in thinking about how these concerns affect the organization of a presidency is that it is often difficult beforehand to anticipate how they will be met by a particular staff arrangement. In Hult and Walcott's schema, for example, while the degree of controversy or disagreement about goals or causation may be known beforehand, it is often the case that certainty, disagreement, or controversy only emerge in situ, that is as particular policies are under consideration within a preexisting staff arrangement. Because it is the policy process itself that generates this "political" dimension, one could be at a loss to anticipate its contours and implications before the fact. Furthermore, even if various facts about the "political" dimension can be ascertained beforehand, most decisions that reach the level of presidential choice are precisely those marked by disagreement or controversy; interestingly enough, Hult and Walcott's call in this situation for a decision setting that is "indeterminate," a structure that emphasizes fairness and facilitates representation, offers only limited guidance.

Given the policy terrain in which most presidents operate most of the time, plus the difficulty of determining how particular organizational arrangements fare in incorporating the concerns that George and Walcott and Hult raise, perhaps the best counsel is to come back where we started: selection of a staff system and managerial practices based on the president's perception of his cognitive and emotional needs but flexibly tailored to take account of the strengths and weaknesses of the system chosen as it operates within an institutional context. Furthermore, the relationship between structure and style, on the one hand, and institutional context, on the other, does not necessarily ignore the concerns raised by Hult and Walcott or those that inform George's analysis. By alerting decision makers to a powerful set of factors that can detract from effective staff management and decision making (or in some cases enhance them), this approach may enable them to determine when in fact disagreement and controversy over ends and means, Hult and Walcott's concern, is legitimate and when they have their source in bureaucratic or court politics, for example. With respect to George's concerns, an institutional approach may be helpful to presidents in crafting a staff structure and managing it on a daily basis so that it fulfills their legitimate needs for emotional support, understanding within the staff system for their policies, and legitimacy with Congress and the public without leading, respectively, to obsequiousness, tunnel vision, and political hypersensitivity.

Responsive Competence?

A concern for viewing management of the White House staff system through the lens of the institutional presidency also differs from two other issues about White House staff management that are prominent in the literature: Hugh Heclo's concern for the loss of "neutral competence" of the White House staff and Terry Moe's conclusion that the recent evolution of the staff system is best understood in terms of a presidential quest for "responsive competence." Both bear descriptive and prescriptive implications about the institutional presidency that differ somewhat from the argument of this book and deserve further attention.

Let us begin with responsive competence. Like many observers of the institutional presidency, Moe notes that presidents' attention to the White House staff is driven by the need to respond to a political environment that sets expectations on their performance in office but provides few means to carry out tasks. But, Moe continues, presidents are not interested in organizational "efficiency or effectiveness or coordination per se." It is political control they seek: *centralization* of decision-making power in the White House staff and, especially, *politicization* of the staff system (as well as other parts of the executive branch) through the appointment of political loyalists rather than professional experts. Taken together, centralization and politicization form what Moe terms a strategy of "responsive competence," which in his view not only describes the underlying dynamics of the presidency and the place of the staff within it but also sets a prescriptive agenda for presidents eager to make their political mark. In short, according to Moe, "whatever his particular policy objectives, whatever his personality and style, the modern president is driven by . . . formidable expectations to seek control over the structures and processes of government. . . . What he wants is an institutional system responsive to his needs as a political leader."[5]

Moe's concept of responsive competence describes an important force at work in the development of the president's staff resources. Centralization of power in the White House staff—especially as a locus of presidential policy making—has been, as we have seen, a characteristic of the institutional presidency almost since its inception. And, although politicization is a strategic response practiced only by some presidents, it too is often present in particular administrations during this period.

But do responsive competence and its twin components, centralization and politicization, provide a *full* descriptive account of the dynamic of forces at work in the development of the institutional presidency? The Nixon and Reagan administrations fit the pattern most closely with respect to politicization. Both presidents took extensive measures to ensure that presidential loyalists were appointed to White House positions and to available slots for political appointees in the agencies and departments.

With respect to centralization, the picture is less clear. Nixon was especially successful, the demise of his ambitious plan for a powerful Domestic Council notwithstanding, in centralizing control over policy making in his White House staff. But Reagan's experiment with cabinet councils seems more decentralist in its intent, while the centralization that took place in the later years of his presidency seems to have resulted more from the efforts of a power-seeking chief of staff than from a president seeking political control (indeed, it even seems reasonable to argue that Reagan himself was not aware of the need for political control, much less did he attempt to attain it). Furthermore, foreign policy in the Reagan presidency was heavily influenced by Secretary of State George Shultz and his department, and Reagan's White House national security advisers were not as influential as Henry Kissinger had been under Nixon. The NSC adviser and his staff were heavily involved in policy implementation, not just policy formulation, though to what seems to have been negative effect, especially as it may have contributed to the Iran-Contra debacle.

Other presidents fit the centralization and politicization pattern less neatly: the degree of centralization and politicization is often less marked, and in particular, their linkage to the goal of political control—*responsive* competence—is more tenuous. Both Kennedy and Johnson, mistrustful of the bureaucracy, attempted to ensure some measure of centralized, White House control over domestic policy. Yet in neither presidency does centralization seem clearly linked to the ends of responsive competence, as Moe's formula would have it. In both administrations, for example, tendencies toward White House staff centralization existed hand-in-hand with decentralist tendencies: both presidents picked their foreign policy advisers from departments, not just from the White House staff, and both maintained extensive informal contacts with other foreign policy experts both in and out of government.

The purpose of centralization is also not always clearly linked to a presidential desire for *political* control. For Kennedy, the particular institutional arrangements he favored were largely a response to information gathering and deliberating channels he felt comfortable with. Moreover, these arrangements evolved over time in response to the lessons he and his advisers drew from past decision-making experiences. The changes in Kennedy's decision-making practices in the aftermath of the Bay of Pigs fiasco, for example, were not driven by a need for greater political control, which underlies responsive competence, but by a need for more reliable information and more capable modes of deliberation: hence, learned or rational competence rather than responsive competence. For Lyndon Johnson, a need for political control over processes crucial to the success of his presidency was obviously more ingrained to a style of leadership that had developed from his long experience in Congress. But for Johnson such control may have derived more from needs for personal control rather than for political control, more from his psychological needs rather than from a calculated assessment of and response to the institutional barriers to his leadership.

The Eisenhower presidency is an especially notable exception to the claim that presidents seek responsive competence through centralization and politicization or that the aim of the latter is to produce the former. With respect to politicization, although the number of Republican appointees clearly increased once Eisenhower took office, few observers of Eisenhower's presidency have noted any marked tendencies to politicize the staff or political appointees in the bureaucracy. If anything, Eisenhower's appointments more closely resemble the search for neutral competence, which is generally viewed as opposed to politicization, or as an attempt to bring personal associates on board.

Eisenhower did introduce more formal organization to the White House staff. Yet the decision process and day-to-day workings of the administration were not centralized, if we mean by centralization a process whereby most significant decisions and effective control over operations devolve upon the White House staff. In foreign policy, Secretary of State John Foster Dulles was in daily contact with the president and had more substantive influence over policy than the NSC special assistant. It was Eisenhower's practice, as we have seen, to use the latter not as a source of policy advice, but as a manager of the advisory process whose role was to sharpen debate, identify policy disagreements, and provide adequate staff analysis by both the White House and sources outside it. Both the NSC Planning Board and the NSC Operations Coordinating Board, the organizational entities at the core of the NSC staff process, included representatives from relevant agencies and departments, such as State and Defense, as well as members of the NSC staff. Eisenhower also relied on an extensive but informal network of advisers and confidantes from both the public and private spheres.

Eisenhower's decision-making apparatus, although centralized and highly organized, cannot therefore be considered an example of responsive competence. Insofar as Eisenhower centralized at all, he did not do so to exert greater political control. Rather, his purpose in creating orderly organizational structures and processes was to maximize the quality of information and advice available to the president and to encourage the integrity of his deliberations—what might be characterized as rational or organizational competence rather than responsive competence.

As a descriptive observation about the underlying dynamics of the White House staff system, a quest for politicization does not adequately character-ize presidential intentions. So too with its prescriptive implications. Con-sider the most prominent example: the OMB. Although politicization of the OMB has strengthened presidential control over the office, its usefulness to presidents has declined accordingly; as it has been transformed from a professional arm of the EOP to another, de facto part of the president's personal staff, its relationship with Congress and with other parts of the executive branch have suffered because it is perceived to be part of the "president's team." Its ability to provide the president with the kind of advice he needs has also been compromised. As Elmer Staats observes, "now instead of a nonpolitical director and deputy director which we obtained in the Truman period, you have a political director and associate directors, all confirmed by the Senate and they are all regarded as political appointees. . . . The career people are now down about four levels in the hierarchy." The result of these changes, according to Staats, is that "people who are digging into the programs of the agencies don't have direct access to the director. That was something we insisted on. And we would take those people with us when we went to see the President on budget deci-sions."[6] Pulling decisions, in turn, into a large-scale, politicized White House staff not only may not resolve a president's desire for greater political control but may exacerbate the need for it. As we have seen, centralization of power, hierarchy, and bureaucratization can breed fragmentation, spe-cialization, and self-interested advocacy that detract from a president's political goals.

Moe is, in part, right when he asserts that "the precise kind of institutional presidency [the president] needs is determined by the kinds of expectations that drive him. . . . He is a politician fundamentally concerned with the dynamics of political leadership." But in their quest for political leadership, presidents must rely on something more than just political control. Respon-siveness surely plays a part, but it must be accompanied, if not tempered, by competence that enables the president to make informed policy decisions and permits him effectively to manage the institutional resources he must draw upon. As Moe himself points out, "Individuals create institutions, but institutions condition individual choices."[7]

Neutral Competence?

"Neutral competence," as defined by Hugh Heclo and others, lies at the other end of the spectrum from responsive competence. As Heclo explains, neutral competence "envisions a continuous, uncommitted facility at the disposal of, and for the support of, political leadership." Unlike responsive competence, it is uncommitted (although not opposed) to the president's ideological program; it is continuous in that it transcends a particular presidency, having "institutional memory" about both policy substance and procedure and drawing upon professional expertise, not just political loyalty and acumen. Neutral competence, Heclo explains, does not involve a "direct line to some overarching, non-partisan sense of the public interest." Nor does it involve opposition to the president's policy goals. Rather, "it consists of giving one's cooperation and best independent judgment of the issues to partisan bosses—and of being sufficiently uncommitted to be able to do so for a succession of partisan leaders." It is not just the capacity to deliver good staff work or meekly follow orders but requires practical knowledge of how the government works and the ability to offer advice worthy of attention. For presidents, its value lies in its ultimate aim of serving partisan leadership, albeit in more complex ways than responsive competence; presidents can draw from its "strange amalgam of loyalty that argues back, partisanship that shifts with changing partisans, independence that depends on others."[8]

Much of the debate about neutral competence has been directed at the Office of Management and Budget and its increasing subservience to political control—to responsive competence—compared with its orientation when it was the old Bureau of the Budget. The BOB/OMB represents a special case in a way because it is a large entity within the EOP composed of professional civil servants, unlike those parts of the White House staff where political appointees make up the bulk of personnel. But the issue of political appointee versus career civil servant aside, the question of neutral competence as an orienting principle among staff members remains important for presidents and staff members. Both political appointees and civil servants within the EOP can follow its norms; indeed many of the directors of the old BOB can be considered "neutral competents," despite their non–civil service status, while their successors in the OMB have by and large tended to view themselves as political advisers, if not in some cases political instruments, of the president.

The issue of the extent to which a president should search for professional as opposed to political advice, and the related question of what degree of each a particular adviser should embrace, open a discussion that cannot be explored here. Suffice it to say that presidents need both perspectives in making policy decisions; neither neutral competence nor responsive competence alone can serve the president's ends.

Because presidents have a natural tendency, by reason of their experience and the nature of their office, to take political advice seriously, it is especially important that professional expertise be evident among those to whom they turn for counsel. Some presidential practices seem to reflect this awareness. The importance of having staff members with an allegiance to the integrity of the policy process and its procedures, for example, is an element that is common to neutral competence and effective staff management of the sort we have explored. So, too, with respect to bureaucratic and court politics: whereas political loyalty tends, as we have seen, to generate a concern for prestige and personal advancement that can prevent the staff system from effectively serving the president's ends, neutral competence establishes norms of professional responsibility and allegiance to the policy-making process that, while not directly linked to the president's policy goals, may more firmly assist in their achievement and that we have identified as important ingredients in effective staff management.

Institutional memory from one administration to the next and even within a particular administration is an especially important facet of neutral competence that presidents could profitably provide. As Stuart Eizenstat has pointed out, Carter's ill-fated decision in 1977 to seek deeper cuts in nuclear arms failed to appreciate the formula the Ford administration had worked out in 1974 with Moscow. So, too, with Carter's 1979 "discovery" of a Soviet brigade in Cuba, which he thought a violation of Kennedy's 1962 agreements; it was in fact part of the limited Soviet military force that Kennedy had sanctioned in Cuba. Ford's suspension of grain sales to the Soviet Union in 1975 failed to recognize Richard Nixon's failed effort to embargo soybeans, just as Carter's embargo on grain in 1980 as a response to the Soviet invasion of Afghanistan failed to consider Ford's difficulties with an embargo.[9] So, too, even within a particular presidency. According to Lloyd Cutler, "There is zero institutional memory in the [Reagan] White House," which went through six national security advisers and five chief of staff arrangements in eight years and systematically excluded high-level civil servants from policy-making groups.[10]

Although our discussion has been confined to the managerial practices of particular presidents and has not considered broader structural reforms in the staff system that might transcend individual administrations, its conclusions about the positive role of informal channels of advice and moving outside a centralized staff system for counsel point to means through which institutional memory might be brought to bear. Most presidents who have called in outside advisers, for example, have generally included within their number persons whose experiences in past administrations replicate in a way the institutional memory that is normally associated with neutral competence; many as well possess the professional expertise that is also associated with it.[11]

Heclo has identified other aspects of neutral competence that resonate with the successful patterns of management discussed in chapters 3 and 4: "smooth communication . . . [that] improves the capacity of elected leadership to get what it wants out of the governmental machine"; a concern with sustained implementation that tempers "boldness with the recognition that [leaders] will have to live with the consequences of misplaced boldness"; and, finally, "a quality of impartiality [that] is less concerned with the short-term political ramifications of who believes what how strongly, and more concerned with the substance of the policy issues themselves."[12]

Cary Covington also notes that certain organizational practices enhance institutional memory. Several of them replicate patterns of White House management that we have examined and that seem successful. An ability to create a positive ethos among staff members, for example, is likely to decrease staff turnover and therefore, as Covington argues, to increase transmission of memory. Formal staff systems, such as Eisenhower's, that are adept at record keeping and make information accessible to members also enhance institutional memory. Effective delegation enhances task variety and discretion, which encourage staff members to use sources of institutional memory. Also, team building (for example, Eisenhower's sensitivity to human relations, his "interactionist" conception of leadership, and his use of deliberative forums to convey his policy views) enhances what Covington terms "goal compatibility" and bringing new members of the staff on board and up to speed.[13]

Thus, patterns of staff management that have effectively coped with the institutional presidency seem to contain elements associated with neutral competence. But effective management is not confined to the practices underlying neutral competence; it has access to a broader menu. Oliver North, for example, provided the Reagan White House with institutional memory and a certain sort of professional expertise. North served under four national security advisers in five years and was able to use his continuity in service to pursue policies he favored. According to one account, "former and current members of the [National Security] Council's staff say he served as the institutional memory of the NSC, providing a continuity that made him almost indispensable."[14] Dealing with the Oliver Norths of the world requires a deeper understanding of the workings of the White House staff system and a broader array of managerial strategies and tactics than simple reliance on neutral competence.

Professional expertise of the sort that neutral competence embraces also has its pitfalls.[15] Luther Gulick, a member of the Brownlow committee, cautions that professionals often misrepresent the boundaries of their fields of knowledge. For example, Gulick observes, economists have limited the parameters of their discipline in order to arrive at a body of knowledge that is translatable in mathematical terms. But although

> they have restricted their field of study [they have] not hesitated to give answers to those who are managing the governments of the world. It's a great temptation. No man can be an expert in every field. Therefore he "specializes," restricts his input and his intellectual analysis, yet doesn't hesitate to turn around and present comprehensive policy recommendations based on conclusions which have been reached without the understanding of their moral and political aspects.[16]

Again, a more encompassing theory of staff management—beyond the bounds of neutral competence—is required to understand the strengths and weaknesses of those to whom a president may turn in seeking information and counsel and performing other staff functions.

Organizational Variation?

Implicit in the debate between neutral and responsive competence is a concern about differences in organizational purpose that may have bearing on how the president organizes and deals with his staff system. The alarm that advocates of neutral competence raise, for example, has by and large focused on the effects of politicization on one unit within the EOP, the Office of Management and Budget, which before its reorganization was viewed as a relatively independent, nonpartisan, and professional resource for the president. Presidential management of the Bureau of the Budget changed when it became the OMB, and its role in the budgetary process shifted accordingly and for the worse, or so the argument goes.

Whether politicization of the OMB has indeed been for the worse I will not discuss further here. But the various purposes that units of the staff system fulfill—whether the OMB, the NSC, the Council of Economic Advisers, or others—and the different ways these units are organized and function are factors that may affect a president's strategy of management.

I have tended to treat the various units of the White House staff as roughly similar in the challenge they present to presidents. There is, I would argue, merit in doing so because most of the characteristics of the institutional presidency and most of its effects transcend particular staff entities, whether one is talking about the more political White House Office or the parts of the encompassing EOP, which tend to be organized around discrete policy areas. Bureaucratic and court politics, for example, are likely to affect whatever part of the staff system one examines. Hierarchy is perhaps less pervasive, especially in the smaller units such as the Council on Environmental Quality or deliberately collegial bodies like the CEA. But even then, their advice to the president is likely to be filtered through the broader domestic policy staff system or presented in collegial settings at which other parts of the staff system are represented and in which some agenda-setting and coordinating mechanism is likely to be in place. Thus presidents face a common institutional challenge in dealing with any part of the staff system. In those areas we have examined in some detail, such as national security and domestic policy, management styles and practices tend to be similar within a particular presidency, for example Nixon's preference for isolation or Lyndon Johnson's ad hoc style. Some particulars differ: Eisenhower's cabinet secretariat system and Adams's role as chief of staff were in contrast to the NSC "policy hill" and the role of the NSC special assistant, but Eisenhower's informal consultations as well as his attention to team building were present in both his domestic and foreign policy-making processes.

But that said, presidents would probably be well advised to organize the parts of their staff systems and devise strategies of management with the organizational and functional differences that can exist in mind. Fine tuning may be required or even broader thinking about the appropriateness of formal or collegial procedures. Although it is not possible for us to examine each of the units of the Executive Office of President, comparison of particular units across time, both within a particular administration and from administration to administration, is likely to yield useful lessons.[17]

Can Presidents Manage?

A more fundamental question than the matter of how presidents may need to fine-tune their managerial strategies to organizational differences within their staff system is the issue of whether the organization and procedures of the White House are so tightly bound to the personal predilections of the incumbent that little change can be expected and speculations about alternative patterns of presidential staff management are pointless. In effect, this question raises the challenge: Can presidents manage the institutional presidency?

The simplicity of that question would seem to yield a ready, affirmative answer. Just as we all deal, for better or worse, with the social environment, so too do presidents deal with their more complex and challenging environments.

But to resolve the question this way may be too easy. How we as individuals deal with our environments and how presidents devise strategic responses to the institutional presidency may both be linked to elements of individual personality that make much change or even adjustment unlikely. The issue of whether presidents can adopt or otherwise emulate successful patterns of staff management is especially complicated by what the preceding chapters have revealed about the nature of that success. As chapter 3 rather clearly shows, effective staff organization and management involves more than the adoption of a certain institutional structure: if that alone were sufficient, few differences could be discerned among the formal systems of Eisenhower, Nixon, and Reagan or between the collegial arrangements of Kennedy and Johnson. As we saw, the sources of success or failure of a particular staff system lie much deeper: the extent to which presidents (and those around them who are concerned with management issues) are aware of and compensate for the weaknesses to which their system is prone and—the argument of chapter 4—the extent to which the more encompassing effects of the institutional presidency are submitted to presidential attention and managerial control. These facets of the institutional presidency involve something more than simple adoption of a particular pattern of staff organization and appear to be intimately linked to organizational skills and individual ways of dealing with others that only certain presidents seem to possess.

Perhaps this is why managerial style has been so important in the literature on the presidency: it neatly links the general recognition of the great differences in presidential personalities—an important theme in presidential scholarship, which has often been biographical and centered on particular presidencies—with the perception of differences in the nature of the White House staff from one presidency to another. But it does so in such a way as to emphasize the psychological and idiosyncratic determinants of these differences: organizational differences (between, say, an Eisenhower and a Kennedy, or a Nixon and a Johnson, or a Carter and a Reagan) are taken into account, but they become reflections of differences in individual personality.

The term managerial *style* is itself revealing on this score: it seems to connote a behavioral manifestation of a dimension of individual personality. This is misleading. Many of the aspects of staff management that have concerned us in the preceding chapters—for example, how the White House staff is structured, what channels of information and advice exist beyond those provided by the staff, and how the roles and responsibilities of those who serve the president are defined, to take merely a few—involve something beyond individual "style." They seem more products of deliberate choice and less intimately connected to individual personality than the term "style" seems to convey.

The problem is not in connecting managerial practices in some way to individual personality. They surely are connected to it in some degree. As Alexander George notes, a leader's impact on high-level policy making reflects a number of elements of personality: a president's cognitive beliefs and style (his ideology and world view and his ways of processing information and advice), his sense of personal efficacy (his skills for meeting the demands of his executive and political roles), and his method of coping with conflicting and complex political values and with uncertainty.[18]

The problem is, rather, in regarding managerial practices (whether defined as managerial style or more broadly) as so *intimately* connected to individual personality that their change or alteration is impossible. To use a rather hackneyed metaphor, the president's mode of organizing and dealing with his staff is like a suit of clothes that must fit the person who wears it.[19] Thus, presidents who cannot deal with personal conflict, who prefer delegating tasks to others, whose cognitive skills are developed in a way that makes them more comfortable making decisions after they have been sifted through a formal staff machinery, and who do not like to get enmeshed in policy details will favor formalistic systems. Conversely, presidents who enjoy give-and-take among their advisers, like to keep a tight rein on the activities of their staff, and prefer exposure to policy details will hew to more collegial arrangements. Putting one president in another's staff system would seem to generate personal stress and organizational dysfunction. The matter would seem to be closed.

Yet this matter cannot be so easily dismissed: there is too much evidence of significant variation in staff structure and management within some presidencies (where the president's personality is presumably constant). And there is too much evidence of variation among presidents that seems linked to factors other than personality. One plausible explanation for these differences is that style is less determined by personality than is usually thought. As George explains,

> performance in executive positions such as the presidency is sensitive to a variety of constraints. A given behavior may be no more than a response to the logic of the situation—i.e., a requirement of the situation rather than a requirement of personality. Or it may be a response to the expectations of others as to how an incumbent president should behave in a particular situation or in situations of a given type. Executive behavior, in other words, is sensitive to *situational* and *role* variables as well as to character-rooted needs or to psychodynamic patterns for adapting to stressful situations.[20]

The study of management in general, not just the president's management of his staff, is replete with different management strategies and practices that managers with varying personalities have adopted. Even among presidents, there is some evidence that general modes of leadership, including staff management, may be adopted for an array of reasons. George Bush's seeming preference in domestic policy for a process of advising that is relatively open to a range of diverse views and amenable to compromise differs from his foreign policy making, which seems to be more isolated, secretive, and, perhaps, rigid. These differences may reflect Bush's personality in some way, but they also may reflect his assessment of his political weaknesses and strengths in each area: he is open on the domestic front, where he is politically more vulnerable, and he wields a freer hand in foreign policy, where he is on politically stronger ground and possesses more expertise. Similarly, Fred Greenstein's characterization of Eisenhower's hidden-hand leadership may be linked to Eisenhower's personal development and makeup, as Greenstein at times argues, but it may also reflect an assessment of how a president might best perform two different roles—those of chief of state and head of government—which Greenstein also points out nicely meshed with Eisenhower's conception and practices of presidential leadership. More generally, as Hargrove notes in his study of Jimmy Carter's leadership,

> the mode of policy making a president favors will not only be a manifestation of cognitive style but of presidential purposes. One who wishes to deal primarily with the politics of policy will favor a loose, disjointed mode of decision making which involves competition among diverse interests. A president who seeks to find substantive approaches to problems will favor a decision process of homework and discussion by knowledgeable officials. Purpose shapes process as much as, or more than, it is shaped in return.[21]

The connection between personality and managerial practices may also be more tenuous if presidents who are able to understand the limitations of their own cognitive skills, sense of efficacy and competence, and toleration of conflict consciously or unconsciously build compensating mechanisms into their selection of staffing arrangements. Indeed one might plausibly imagine a president prone to formalistic modes of decision making deliberately selecting a more collegial pattern (or vice versa) to offset his own personal weaknesses and those of the system he might otherwise favor, even at the price of personal stress and strain.

Of course there is no evidence among recent presidents of an extreme case of this sort. But there does seem to be evidence that presidents whose staff systems closely reflect their personal predilections fare less well than presidents who are open to change or modification. This seems especially true for presidents who bear the costs of the particular system but reap few benefits. Nixon and Johnson, for example, might represent, respectively, a formalistic and a collegial manager who would have fared better if their staffs had been less reflective of some of the idiosyncracies in their personalities. Nixon's predilection for isolation might have been remedied by more collegial personal contacts with his advisers, while Johnson's tendency to overemphasize political considerations to the detriment of hard policy analysis might have been offset by more formalistic procedures.

Furthermore, changes in managerial practices might have occurred in each case. In his Vietnam decision making, for example, Johnson's attentiveness to the opinions of advisers that deviated from those he expected from them might have been piqued had a more formal mechanism for the presentation of policy views been in place and had his advisers been encouraged to express their policy views more openly and fully. As it was, the group dynamics of Johnson's collegial system and Johnson's own mode of interacting with his advisers tended to stifle dissent and the sustained presentation of opposing policy views.

Even if it is conceded for purposes of argument that presidents by and large fall into formal or collegial camps and that these are connected in *some* way to dimensions of their personalities, presidents of either sort who are attentive to the strengths and weaknesses of their staff organization and who engage in a kind of social learning that encourages them to tailor their management practices to the institutional presidency generally have had more effective staff systems. And, as we have seen, this has occurred in administrations with presidents who are very different in their belief systems, cognitive traits, and operating styles.

Furthermore, the argument that presidents of very different personal stripe can cope with the institutional presidency is strengthened not only by the fact that some very different presidents have indeed done so, but also by the different ways and means that have been available to them. There is no one best way to manage the institutional presidency, as the widely divergent Eisenhower and Kennedy cases attest. Presidents may choose or reject an array of possibilities, depending on their preferences.

Aspects of personality, for example self-reflection and openness to change, are likely to facilitate a general awareness of the importance of the organizational environment and the need to develop effective ways and means of staff management. But so too does a president's experience: awareness of the managerial responsibilities of the office may develop in pre-presidential experiences with organizations and collective modes of decision making (for example, Eisenhower), or it may develop on the job (for example, Kennedy). Whatever the source, however, awareness of the organizational context in which a president operates and the relation of that context to staff organization and management is likely to be an important factor in managing, for better or worse, the institutional presidency.

Does Staff Organization and Management Ultimately Matter?

It may seem obvious, after all of this effort, that it is impossible to answer this question in any way but that managing the White House staff effectively does matter. Too many recent presidencies seem largely to turn on precisely this issue.

Yet if we examine the question as phrased—does management of the institutional presidency *ultimately* matter?—the answer is less clear. Success requires that presidents not only develop sound and appropriate public policies—a goal that effective management advances—but that they gain the cooperation of other political elites necessary for the adoption of those policies and that they are able to communicate their ideas to the public and gain its acceptance.[22] A failure at the latter tasks can render even the most effective staff management moot.

But that said, making sound and appropriate decisions is one of the first in the sequence of leadership abilities that can lead to presidential achievement. So in that sense, effective staff management, which can contribute to sound and appropriate decisions—is needed early on the road to presidential success. In its absence, even the best relations with Congress or high levels of public approval are unlikely to yield, over the long run, a record of positive presidential performance.

But although effective staff management can contribute to sound and appropriate decisions, it does not constitute those decisions themselves. Even if we take aiding the president's decision making as the most important function of the White House staff, it is toward the *process* of presidential decision making—broadly defined—that effective management practices are directed. The president's staff members can assist him in determining what should be subject to his attention or what should be delegated, they can provide whatever information and counsel the president requests, they can provide emotional support, they can contribute to the legitimacy of what he decides, and they can aid him in any other way that he deems fit, even on occasion becoming decision makers themselves or the channels through which his decisions are carried out. But while well-crafted staff structures and procedures and astute informal staff relations are likely to contribute to the president's thoughtful and informed choices, they cannot guarantee wise policy choices. Even the best-intentioned and -informed advisors, operating within an optimally designed staff structure, might be wrong, and a president yielding to his own instincts against their advice might prove right.

The historical record of the modern presidency, however, suggests that sound policy advice and an effective staff system provide useful resources for a president and markedly improve the odds for success. And ultimately, of course, a president who is unable to manage the White House staff will probably be unable to manage much else.

APPENDIX
Units of the Executive Office of the President

■ ■ ■

White House Office   1939–present

Bureau of the Budget/**Office of Management and Budget**[1]   1939–present

National Resources Planning Board   1939–43

Office of Government Reports   1939–48

Liaison Office for Personnel Management   1939–53

Office of Emergency Management   1940–43

Office of War Mobilization   1943–44

Office of War Mobilization and Reconversion   1944–46

Council of Economic Advisers   1946–present

National Security Council[2]   1947–present

National Security Resources Board   1949–53

Sources: U.S. Government Manuals, 1939–1991; *U.S. Government Budget Appendices,* 1939–1990; John Hart, *The Presidential Branch* (New York: Pergamon Books, 1987); George C. Edwards III and Stephen J. Wayne, *Presidential Leadership: Politics and Policy Making* (New York: St. Martin's Press, 1985), 176–77; John Helmer, "The Presidential Office," in Hugh Heclo and Lester Salamon, eds., *The Illusion of Presidential Government* (Boulder, Colo.: Westview Press, 1981), 58–59.

Existing offices are set in **boldface** type.

1. The Bureau of the Budget was created in 1921 as part of the Department of the Treasury. In 1939 it was incorporated within the newly created Executive Office of the President. In 1970 it was reorganized and renamed the Office of Management and the Budget.

2. The NSC was created in 1947 and formally became part of the EOP in 1949.

Office of Defense Mobilization   1950–58

Office of the Director for Mutual Security   1951–53

Telecommunications Advisor to the President   1951–53

President's Advisory Committee on Government Organization   1953–61

National Aeronautics and Space Council   1958–73

Office of Civil and Defense Mobilization   1958–61

Office of Emergency Planning[3]/Office of Emergency Preparedness   1961–73

Office of Science and Technology   1962–73

Office of Economic Opportunity   1964–75

National Council on Marine Resources and Engineering Development   1966–71

Council for Urban Affairs   1969–70

President's Foreign Intelligence Advisory Board   1969–77

Council on Environmental Quality   1969–present

Office of Telecommunications Policy   1970–78

Domestic Council/Domestic Policy Staff/**Office of Policy Development**   1970–present

Council on International Economic Policy   1971–77

Office of Consumer Affairs   1971–73

Special Action Office for Drug Abuse Prevention   1971–75

Federal Property Council   1973–77

Energy Policy Office   1973–74

Council on Wage and Price Stability   1974–81

Presidential Clemency Board   1974–75

Energy Resources Council   1974–77

Office of the U.S. Trade Representative[4]   1974–present

Office of Drug Abuse Policy   1977–78

3. Redesignated the Office of Emergency Preparedness in 1968.
4. Name changed in 1981 from Office of Special Representative for Trade Negotiations.

Office of Science and Technology Policy   1976–present

Office of Administration   1977–present

National Critical Materials Council   1984–present

Office of National Drug Control Policy   1989–present

NOTES

■ ■ ■

Introduction

1. James D. Barber, *Presidential Character: Predicting Performance in the White House*, 3d ed. (Englewood Cliffs, N.J.: Prentice-Hall, 1985), 504.

2. Richard E. Neustadt, *Presidential Power: The Politics of Leadership* (New York: Wiley, 1960), 122–23 (emphasis in original).

3. Kenneth W. Thompson, ed., *The Kennedy Presidency: Seventeen Intimate Perspectives* (Lanham, Md.: University Press of America, 1985), 162.

4. Kenneth W. Thompson, ed., *The Nixon Presidency: Twenty-two Intimate Perspectives* (Lanham, Md.: University Press of America, 1987), 84.

5. Hugh Heclo, "The Changing Presidential Office," in *Politics and the Oval Office*, edited by Arnold Meltsner (San Francisco: Institute for Contemporary Studies, 1981), 165.

6. Thompson, *Nixon Presidency*, 168.

7. Robert T. Hartmann, *Palace Politics: An Inside Account of the Ford Years* (New York: McGraw-Hill, 1980), 4.

Chapter One. From President to Presidency: FDR's Legacy

1. Louis Brownlow, *The President and the Presidency* (Chicago: Public Administration Service, 1949), 62.

2. William E. Leuchtenburg, *In the Shadow of FDR: From Harry Truman to Ronald Reagan* (Ithaca, N.Y.: Cornell University Press, 1983).

3. Fred I. Greenstein, "Change and Continuity in the Modern Presidency," in *The New American Political System*, edited by Anthony King (Washington, D.C.: American Enterprise Institute, 1978), 45–86.

4. Stephen Skowronek, "Presidential Leadership in Political Time," in *The Presidency and the Political System*, 3d ed., edited by Michael Nelson (Washington,

D.C.: CQ Press, 1990), 117–62; Bert A. Rockman, *The Leadership Question: The Presidency and the American System* (New York: Praeger, 1984); Richard Ellis and Aaron Wildavsky, *Dilemmas of Presidential Leadership: From Washington through Lincoln* (New Brunswick, N.J.: Transaction Books, 1989); and Erwin C. Hargrove and Michael Nelson, *Presidents, Politics, and Policy* (Baltimore: Johns Hopkins University Press, 1984).

5. Jeffrey K. Tulis, *The Rhetorical Presidency* (Princeton, N.J.: Princeton University Press, 1987).

6. John Hart, *The Presidential Branch* (New York: Pergamon Books, 1987), 10.

7. Figures on the size of the president's staff are taken from ibid., 16, 21. By the end of Hoover's administration, the president was entitled to three secretaries, an administrative assistant, two military aides, and some forty clerks, typists, and messengers (Alfred D. Sander, *A Staff for the President: The Executive Office, 1921–1952* [Westport, Conn.: Greenwood, 1989], 52).

8. As John Hart notes, however, the general recognition that it was not until 1857 that Congress recognized the need for a presidential staff may be misleading. In that year Congress explicitly appropriated money for the first time, but as early as 1789 it had made lump sum appropriations to the president that covered both salary and expenses, presumably including those for secretaries and clerks. For further discussion of the president's staff before FDR, see Hart, *Presidential Branch*, 10–24.

9. Stephen J. Wayne, *The Legislative Presidency* (New York: Harper and Row, 1978), 30.

10. The practice of hiring relatives did not disappear with Grant: Franklin Roosevelt appointed his son James secretary to the president. James Roosevelt was the last person to hold that position before the White House staff resources were expanded in 1939.

11. Hart, *Presidential Branch*, 10.

12. T. Harry Williams, ed., *Hayes: the Diary of a President* (New York: David McKay, 1964), 68.

13. Ibid., 81.

14. Some scholars (see Charles Walcott and Karen Hult, "Management Science and the Great Engineer: Governing the White House during the Hoover Administration," *Presidential Studies Quarterly* 20 [1990]: 557–79) have argued that Hoover's presidency differs from this pattern to such an extent that it, not FDR's, marks the distinctive break with the traditional presidency. The argument for Hoover as the father of a presidential staff system is particularly interesting in view of his interests in organizational reform and his role, after leaving office, in strengthening the institutional capacities of the presidency. Hoover was the first president to be formally authorized three administrative assistants, and they appear to have been more deeply involved in policy formulation and analysis than their more legislatively minded predecessors under Harding and Coolidge. Walcott and Hult also argue that Hoover was the first president to make extensive use of the Bureau of the Budget.

At best, however, Hoover can be considered a precursor to the institutional presidency that was to emerge under his successor. As Walcott and Hult note, Hoover preferred to use his own ideas or those of numerous conferences, committees, and commissions to generate policy proposals. The White House staff remained small, playing at best a coordinating role.

The emergence of the Bureau of the Budget as a managerial resource for the president presents a more compelling argument for dating the institutional presidency before FDR (see Sander, *Staff for the President*, 12–13). Presidents as far back as William Howard Taft had recognized the need to coordinate the annual budget requests of agencies and departments and bring them in line with their programs.

That creation of the BOB in 1921 marked the emergence of the institutional presidency, however, is less clear. Most studies of the bureau credit its emergence as a key player in presidential policy making to its incorporation as part of the Executive Office of the President in 1939, not its creation in 1921. Furthermore, although perhaps a managerial resource, the BOB was not technically part of the institutional presidency (if we mean by that the Executive Office of the President) until 1939. From 1921 until then, the BOB was located within the Treasury Department, although the secretary of the treasury was denied any formal authority over the budget process. There is also some evidence that the BOB was underused as a resource until 1939 (Larry Berman, *The Office of Management and Budget and the Presidency, 1921–1979* [Princeton, N.J.: Princeton University Press, 1979], 8). The characterization of the years 1921–39 as the "green eye shade" era of the BOB is apt: the BOB confined its role to the narrow duty of preparing the president's annual budget and did not even begin to fill the broad organizational and managerial mandate Congress had set for it.

15. Patrick Anderson, *The President's Men* (New York: Doubleday, 1969), 29.

16. Rosenman did return to Washington full time in 1943 in the newly created position of special counsel to the president; his duties, however, were not simply those of legal adviser to the president—which that position largely entails today—but to serve as speech writer, troubleshooter, political confidante, and jack-of-all-trades. See Samuel B. Hand, *Counsel and Advice: A Political Biography of Samuel I. Rosenman*. (New York: Garland Press, 1979).

17. Arthur M. Schlesinger, Jr., *The Coming of the New Deal* (Boston: Houghton Mifflin, 1959), 528.

18. Peri Arnold, *Making the Managerial Presidency: Comprehensive Reorganization Planning, 1905–1980* (Princeton: N.J.: Princeton University Press, 1986), 89–91.

19. Louis Brownlow, *A Passion for Anonymity* (Chicago: University of Chicago Press, 1958), 323–24. Brownlow notes that, despite its administrative disorganization, "the thing worked!"

20. Frederick Mosher, ed., *"The President Needs Help"* (Lanham, Md.: University Press of America, 1988), ix–x.

21. Schlesinger, *Coming of the New Deal*, 535.

22. Brownlow, *Passion for Anonymity*, 314.

23. Both Merriam and Brownlow lobbied extensively for a management study from 1933 until 1936. Roosevelt initially favored turning the matter over to the Committee on Public Administration of the Social Science Research Council. However, during November and December 1935, "he decided that the matter was of such magnitude and importance that it should be undertaken by a governmental,

not a private, body" (Herbert Emmerich, *Federal Organization and Administrative Management* [Tuscaloosa: University of Alabama Press, 1971], 48).

24. The staff of the Brownlow committee included such future lights of public administration and political science as Joseph Harris, James Fesler, Laverne Burchfield, Herbert Emmerich, Arthur Macmahon, John Millett, Schuyler Wallace, Harvey Mansfield, Merle Fainsod, Arthur Holcombe, Robert Cushman, and Paul David. Six participants later served as presidents of the American Political Science Association: Merriam, Gulick, Cushman, Fainsod, Macmahon, and Charles McKinley.

25. Brownlow, *Passion for Anonymity*, 329–38.

26. The one exception is the Joint Committee on the Reorganization of Government Departments, which Congress established during the Harding administration. One committee recommendation, which was not implemented, touched directly on the presidency: it suggested that the number of people reporting directly to the president be reduced.

27. President's Committee on Administrative Management, *Report* (Washington, D.C.: Government Printing Office, 1937), 5.

28. Mosher, *"The President Needs Help,"* vii.

29. Ibid. See also Emmerich, *Federal Reorganization*, 55–56.

30. James MacGregor Burns, *Roosevelt: The Lion and the Fox* (New York: Harcourt Brace, 1956), 345.

31. This famous characterization of the ideal staff assistant was borrowed from Thomas Jones's description of the British War Cabinet. Jones had been private secretary to Prime Minister Lloyd George. Brownlow had met Jones in 1910 and renewed his acquaintance on a 1936 trip to England (Brownlow, *Passion for Anonymity*, 357).

32. Allen Schick, "The Problem of Presidential Budgeting," in *The Illusion of Presidential Government*, edited by Hugh Heclo and Lester Salamon (Boulder, Colo.: Westview, 1981), 89.

33. The other four parts of the executive order expanded and altered both the responsibilities of the president's staff and its structure, but they proved to be less enduring. One provision gave the president the power to create the Office of Emergency Management (OEM), which proved significant during World War II. The OEM, however, did not become a lasting part of the White House staff.

Another provision of the executive order established the Office of Government Reports (OGR), which was designed as a clearing house and information-gathering service for all levels of government. In reality the OGR served to build public support for FDR's policies. It prepared information favorable to the administration for dissemination to the news media, and it distributed such films as *The River* and *The Plow That Broke the Plains*, which extolled FDR's public works projects. Not surprisingly, such activities were controversial for Congress; many members viewed them as bordering on a ministry of propaganda. The OGR became part of the Office of War Information in 1943, then part of the Office of War Mobilization and Reconversion. After the war, some of its functions were also transferred to the Bureau of the Budget. Truman attempted to revive the OGR in 1946, but congressional hostility led to its abolishment in 1948.

The demise of two other key components of the executive order arose from their controversial nature rather than from lack of need once the war was over. The National Resources Planning Board was ambitious in scope and designed to provide data and advice to the president on human and natural resources, to coordinate public works programs at all levels of government, to analyze economic trends and conditions and recommend appropriate legislation, and to provide a central locus for governmental planning efforts (Roosevelt appointed his uncle Frederick Delano as its first chairman). The board's broad mandate provoked significant congressional opposition when it was first proposed as part of Brownlow. Roosevelt succeeded in creating the board through his reorganizational powers, but it was controversial and short lived. Congressional suspicion and mistrust of its broad planning powers and its substantive involvement in economic planning and the development of public works projects led to its abolition in June 1943.

The Liaison Office for Personnel Management had a similarly checkered and controversial history. The Brownlow committee's recommendation that personnel procedures be centralized under a single, presidentially appointed head met stiff opposition. Congress viewed the proposal as a threat to the neutrality of the civil service merit system and preferred the multiheaded authority of the existing Civil Service Commission. Roosevelt resurrected the proposal in modified form as part of his reorganization plan. A White House staff entity, while not having direct control over personnel matters, would serve as liaison between the president and the Civil Service Commission. Stripped of authority, the Liaison Office failed to gain effective control over personnel management for the president and was eventually abolished by President Eisenhower.

34. Mosher (*"The President Needs Help"*) notes that other recommendations of the Brownlow committee, while not specifically implemented, were instrumental in drawing attention to other administrative needs, thereby setting an agenda for future reforms. Brownlow's recommendation to extend the merit system "upward, outward, and downward was recent enough to make probable a connection to two events: the Hatch Act of 1939, prohibiting executive employees' active political management; and the Ramspeck Act of 1940, under which presidents significantly extended the merit system from the 61 percent coverage in 1936 to 73 percent in 1941 and to the 80–90-some percentages from 1947 into the 1980s" (12). As well, Brownlow's concerns about the independent regulatory commissions as a "headless 'fourth branch' of the Government, a haphazard deposit of irresponsible agencies and uncoordinated powers" may have encouraged subsequent changes such as increased power of commission chairs and greater responsiveness to presidential policy concerns (13).

35. For the best, most recent account of the history of executive reorganization, see Arnold, *Making the Managerial Presidency*.

36. For an account of the development of the institutional presidency that stresses presidents' efforts at politicization and centralization—the search for "responsive competence"—see Terry M. Moe, "The Politicized Presidency," in *The New Direction in American Politics*, edited by John E. Chubb and Paul E. Peterson (Washington, D.C.: Brookings Institution, 1985), 235–71.

37. Other units, as of 1989, listed in the U.S. Government Budget Appendix were: the Council on Wage and Price Stability (1989 budget, $2,000; no full-time, permanent positions listed); the newly created National Critical Materials Council

(1989 budget, $350,000; no full-time, permanent positions listed); and the Office of Federal Procurement Policy (1989 budget, $2.3 million; thirty-two full-time, permanent positions).

38. This part of the White House Office was foreshadowed in the Truman administration, when aides were specifically designated to act as the president's lobbyists on Capitol Hill but lacked the specific titles, ongoing responsibilities, and large staffs that Eisenhower would create. Truman also relied on the Bureau of the Budget as part of his liaison operations with Congress. Starting in 1947, through a process called "direct referrals," Congress would inquire through the bureau what legislation the administration intended to propose.

39. Liaison with the president's party also occurred on an informal basis in the Truman White House when Matthew Connelly, the president's appointments secretary, was assigned the task of keeping tabs on the Democratic party.

40. During both presidencies, aides such as Theodore Sorensen (under Kennedy) and Bill Moyers and Harry McPherson (under Johnson) performed duties that might be considered those of a chief of staff.

41. An intergovernmental affairs staff was foreshadowed in the Eisenhower administration with the appointment of Arizona Governor Howard Pyle to act as the president's contact point with state and local governments.

42. Again, there is some evidence that this unit of the staff was foreshadowed in the Truman era. Truman designated David Niles to work with Jewish groups and Philleo Nash to act as his liaison with the black community.

43. On Nixon's "administrative presidency" strategy, see Richard P. Nathan, *The Plot That Failed: Nixon and the Administrative Presidency* (New York: Wiley, 1975).

44. I. M. Destler, "National Security Management: What Presidents Have Wrought," *Political Science Quarterly* 95 (1980–81): 573–88.

45. The figures are taken from ibid., 576.

46. "President's Reorganization Project: Decision Analysis Report," 28 June 1977, Hamilton Jordan Collection, President's Reorganization Project, Carter Library, 20.

47. Arnold, *Making the Managerial Presidency*, 298.

48. "Other EOP Offices," *National Journal*, 25 April 1981, 694.

49. Jonathan Rauch, "Getting the President's Ear," *National Journal*, 10 June 1989, 1439.

50. Another twenty detailees also might be added to this figure, for a total of over seventy-five staff positions.

Chapter Two. The White House Staff as an Institution?

1. See, for example, Stephen Hess, "Advice for a President-Elect, 1976–1977," in *Organizing the Presidency*, 2d ed. (Washington, D.C.: Brookings Institution, 1988), 241–61; Benjamin W. Heineman and Curtis Hessler, *Memorandum for the President: A Strategic Approach to Domestic Affairs in the 1980s* (New York: Random House, 1980); *A Presidency for the 1980s* (Washington, D.C.: National Academy of Public Administration, 1980). Richard Neustadt's memoranda to Kennedy before and after taking office provide especially interesting reading; see, for example, "Memorandum on Staffing the President-Elect," 30 October 1959

(Kennedy Prepresidential Papers, Kennedy Library); "Transition Memos—1960" (President's Office Files, Neustadt Transition Memos, 1960, Kennedy Library), which includes specific papers on "Organizing the Transition," "Staffing the President-Elect," "Cabinet Departments: Some Things to Keep in Mind," "Next Steps in Staffing the White House and Executive Office," "NSC: First Steps," and "CEA: First Steps." After Kennedy became president, Neustadt continued to offer advice on the organization of the staff system, including such papers as "Memo on USIA," "The Science Adviser: First Steps," "Possibilities for Reorganization," and "Organizing the Space Council" (President's Office Files, Neustadt Memos, 1961–62, Kennedy Library).

2. Fred I. Greenstein, "A President Is Forced to Resign: Watergate, White House Organization, and Nixon's Personality," in *America in the Seventies*, edited by Allen Sindler (Boston: Little, Brown, 1977), 94. According to Bruce Buchanan ("Constrained Diversity: The Organizational Demands of the Presidency," *Presidential Studies Quarterly* 20 [1990]: 791–822), "the traditions of the office mean that each new president literally starts over, a tabula rasa, imposing new procedures, new assumptions, and a new atmosphere, or culture. In this sense, each president is a founder. The White House Office is surely the most flexible organization in the executive branch of government."

3. Joseph A. Pika, "Moving beyond the Oval Office: Problems in Studying the Presidency," *Congress and the Presidency* 9 (1981–82): 22.

4. See especially Neustadt, *Presidential Power* (see intro., n. 2); Richard Neustadt, "Staffing the Presidency: Premature Notes on a New Administration," *Political Science Quarterly* 93 (1978): 1–9; Richard Tanner Johnson, *Managing the White House: An Intimate Study of the Presidency* (New York: Harper and Row, 1974); Alexander L. George, *Presidential Decisionmaking in Foreign Policy: The Effective Use of Information and Advice* (Boulder, Colo.: Westview, 1980); Alexander L. George, "The Case for Multiple Advocacy in Making Foreign Policy," *American Political Science Review* 66 (1972): 751–85; Roger Porter, *Presidential Decision Making: The Economic Policy Board* (Cambridge: Cambridge University Press, 1980); and Roger Porter, "Gerald R. Ford: A Healing Presidency," in *Leadership in the Modern Presidency*, edited by Fred I. Greenstein (Cambridge, Mass.: Harvard University Press, 1988), 149–227.

5. Heclo, "The Changing Presidential Office" (see intro., n. 5), 165.

6. Pika, "Moving beyond the Oval Office," 29.

7. The reader should note that this use of *institutional* differs from the way others have used the term. Colin Campbell (*Managing the Presidency: Carter, Reagan, and the Search for Executive Harmony* [Pittsburgh: University of Pittsburgh Press, 1986]) applies the term to the professional and civil service components of the staff system in units such as the BOB/OMB. For former Kennedy aide Theodore Sorensen, *institutional* refers to what he took to be the overly formalized and structured staff organization of the Eisenhower presidency, which his boss rejected: "From the outset he [Kennedy] abandoned the notion of a collective, institutionalized presidency. He abandoned the practice of the Cabinet and the National Security Council making group decisions like corporate boards of directors" (Sorensen, *Kennedy* [New York: Harper and Row, 1965], 281).

8. The characteristics of institutionalization are adapted, in part, from Nelson Polsby, "The Institutionalization of the U.S. House of Representatives," *American*

Political Science Review 62 (1968): 144–68. On the notion of the presidency as an institution also see Lester Seligman, "Presidential Leadership: The Inner Circle and Institutionalization," *Journal of Politics* 18 (1956): 410–26; Norman Thomas and Hans Baade, eds., *The Institutionalized Presidency* (Dobbs Ferry, N.Y.: Oceana Press, 1972); Robert S. Gilmour, "The Institutionalized Presidency: A Conceptual Clarification," in *The Presidency in Contemporary Context*, edited by Norman Thomas (New York: Dodd, Mead, 1985), 147–59; John Kessel, *The Domestic Presidency: Decision-Making in the White House* (North Scituate, Mass.: Duxbury Press, 1975); Lester Seligman, "The Presidency and Political Change," *Annals* 446 (1983): 179–92; John Kessel, "The Structures of the Carter White House," *American Journal of Political Science* 27 (1983): 431–63; John Kessel, "The Structures of the Reagan White House," *American Journal of Political Science* 28 (1984): 231–58; and Campbell, *Managing the Presidency*.

9. Joseph A. Pika, "Management Style and the Organizational Matrix: Studying White House Operations," *Administration and Society* 20 (1988): 11.

10. It is interesting to note that both Sorensen and McPherson were participants in a 1986 conference held at the University of California, San Diego, on presidential chiefs of staff, each representing their respective administrations. See Samuel Kernell and Samuel Popkins, eds., *Chief of Staff: Twenty-five Years of Managing the Presidency* (Berkeley and Los Angeles: University of California Press, 1986).

11. Neustadt, "Staffing the Presidency," 7.

12. Reagan data is from "Policy Development Office," *National Journal*, 25 April, 1981, 684–87.

13. See David Gergen, "George Bush's Balky Start," *U.S. News and World Report*, 20 January 1989, 34.

14. On White House–press relations, see Michael Grossman and Martha J. Kumar, *Portraying the Presidency* (Baltimore: Johns Hopkins University Press, 1981).

15. For further discussion, see Joseph A. Pika, "Interest Groups and the Executive: Federal Intervention," in *Interest Group Politics*, edited by Allan J. Cigler and Burdette A. Loomis (Washington, D.C.: CQ Press, 1983), 298–323.

16. Quoted in Lyndon B. Johnson, *Vantage Point: Perspectives of the Presidency, 1963–1969* (New York: Holt, Rinehart, and Winston, 1971), p. 76. As vice-president, Johnson had made much the same argument about the organizational location of the new Peace Corps. In this case, the decision was whether to make it subordinate to the Agency for International Development, like other foreign aid programs, or house it as a separate unit in the State Department. Johnson argued strongly for the latter: "There's just no question about this. The Peace Corps has got to be a fresh independent group here, part of State but not buried under anything else. There's just no question at all" (quoted in Bradley H. Patterson, Jr., Oral History, Kennedy Library, p. 23).

17. Bradley H. Patterson, Jr., *The Ring of Power: The White House Staff and Its Expanded Role in Government* (New York: Basic Books, 1988), 225.

18. Mosher, *"The President Needs Help"* (see chap. 1, n. 20), 17.

19. Quoted in Theodore Sorensen, "The President and the Secretary of State," *Foreign Affairs* 66 (1987–88): 232.

20. Henry Kissinger, *The White House Years* (Boston: Little, Brown, 1979), 26, 31, 589, 887.

21. Cyrus Vance, *Hard Choices: Critical Years in America's Foreign Policy* (New York: Simon and Schuster, 1983), 409–10.

22. Alexander Haig, *Caveat: Realism, Reagan, and Foreign Policy* (New York: Macmillan, 1984), 84, 91, 141–42, 299–300, 302.

23. Ibid., 306–7.

24. Sorensen, "President and the Secretary of State," 232.

25. Dan Rather and Gary Paul Gates, *The Palace Guard* (New York: Harper and Row, 1974), 240.

26. Mosher, *"The President Needs Help,"* 17.

27. H. R. Haldeman, *The Ends of Power* (New York: New York Times Books, 1978), 58–59.

28. Kernell and Popkin, *Chief of Staff*, 22–23. Reagan also was vexed with leaks by his staff and ordered all top-level members of his administration to undergo polygraph tests. CIA Director William Casey had pushed the plan on Reagan and was supported by Ed Meese and Defense Secretary Weinberger. In this instance it was Secretary of State Schultz who objected, telling the press he would submit to the polygraph once and then resign. Reagan dropped the plan. See Jane Mayer and Doyle McManus, *Landslide: The Unmaking of the President, 1984–1988* (Boston: Houghton Mifflin, 1988): 186–87.

29. Fred I. Greenstein, *The Hidden-Hand Presidency: Eisenhower as Leader* (New York: Basic Books, 1982), 147.

30. Joseph A. Califano, Jr., *Governing America: An Insider's Report from the White House and the Cabinet* (New York: Simon and Schuster, 1981), 148.

31. Ronald Brownstein and Richard Kirschten, "Cabinet Power," *National Journal*, 28 June 1986, 1589.

32. Paul C. Light, *The President's Agenda: Domestic Policy Choice from Kennedy to Carter* (Baltimore: Johns Hopkins University Press, 1982), 55.

33. Greg Schneiders, "My Turn: Goodbye to All That," *Newsweek*, 24 September 1979, 23.

34. Peggy Noonan, *What I Saw at the Revolution: A Political Life in the Reagan Era* (New York: Random House, 1990), 65, 67.

35. George Reedy, *The Twilight of the Presidency* (New York: New American Library, 1970), xii.

36. Kissinger, *White House Years*, 887, 1127–28.

37. Larry Berman, "The Office of Management and Budget That Almost Wasn't," *Political Science Quarterly* 92 (1977): 281–303.

38. Ibid., 294, 295.

39. Ibid., 299.

40. Ibid., 300.

41. Ibid., 299.

42. Kenneth W. Thompson, ed., *The Ford Presidency: Twenty-two Intimate Perspectives of Gerald R. Ford* (Lanham, Md.: University Press of America, 1980), 96–97.

43. Hartmann observes that the changes weren't noted in the press because the story was lost in the news of Nelson Rockefeller's appointment as vice-president: "There was no appreciative murmur from birthright Democrats as there had been from Republicans when Mr. Truman welcomed Hoover back to the White House" (ibid., 97).

44. Ibid., 41

45. Elmer Staats, Oral History, Kennedy Library, 5.

46. Ken Hechler, *Working with Truman: A Personal Memoir of the White House Years* (New York: G. P. Putnam's Sons, 1982), 46–47.

47. Thomas P. Murphy, Donald E. Neuchterlein, and Ronald J. Stupak, *Inside the Bureaucracy: The View from the Assistant Secretary's Desk* (Boulder, Colo.: Westview, 1978), 181.

48. Margaret Jane Wyszomirski, "The Roles of a Presidential Office for Domestic Policy: Three Models and Four Cases," in *The Presidency and Public Policy Making*, edited by George C. Edwards III et al. (Pittsburgh: University of Pittsburgh Press, 1985), 130–50.

49. Kessel, "Structures of the Reagan White House," 232.

50. John Kessel, *Presidential Parties* (Homewood, Ill.: Dorsey Press, 1984), 107.

51. Margaret Jane Wyszomirski, "The De-Institutionalization of Presidential Staff Agencies," *Public Administration Review* 42 (1982): 456.

Chapter Three. The Institutional Presidency: Through a Managerial Lens

1. Mosher, *"The President Needs Help"* (see chap. 1, n. 20), 58.

2. Reedy, *Twilight of the Presidency* (see chap. 2, n. 35), 40.

3. Neustadt, *Presidential Power* (see intro., n. 2), 157; and Schlesinger, *The Coming of the New Deal* (see chap. 1, n. 17), 528.

4. Neustadt, *Presidential Power*, 116.

5. Ibid., 117.

6. Johnson, *Managing the White House* (see chap. 2, n. 4), 238.

7. Ibid., 7.

8. Ibid., 235.

9. See Emmette S. Redford and Richard T. McCulley, *White House Operations: The Johnson Presidency* (Austin: University of Texas Press, 1986), chap. 3. See also Anderson, *President's Men* (see chap. 1, n. 15), chap. 6 on the Johnson staff, esp. "Caligula's Court," 360–72.

10. Porter's typology is set out in *Presidential Decision Making* (see chap. 2, n. 4), 229–52, and "Gerald R. Ford" (see chap. 2, n. 4).

11. Johnson, *Managing the White House*, 233.

12. Pika, "Management Style and Organizational Matrix" (see chap. 2, n. 9), 18.

13. Johnson, *Managing the White House*, 96, 81, 92.

14. Neustadt, *Presidential Power*, 229.

15. Dean Acheson, "Thoughts about Thought in High Places," *New York Times Magazine*, 11 Oct. 1959, 86.

16. See Paul Y. Hammond, "The National Security Council as a Device for Interdepartmental Coordination: An Interpretation and Appraisal." *American Political Science Review* 54 (1960): 895–910, esp. 904–6; and Stanley L. Falk, "The National Security Council under Truman, Eisenhower, and Kennedy," *Political Science Quarterly* 79 (1964): 403–34, 424–28.

17. On the Jackson subcommittee and its report, see Henry Jackson, ed., *The*

National Security Council: The Jackson Subcommittee Papers on Policy Making at the Presidential Level (New York: Praeger, 1965).

18. Eisenhower's other NSC special assistants were Dillon Anderson and Gordon Grey.

19. Robert Cutler, *No Time for Rest* (Boston: Little, Brown, 1965), 313.

20. Quoted in Phillip G. Henderson, *Managing the Presidency: The Eisenhower Legacy—From Kennedy to Reagan* (Boulder, Colo.: Westview, 1988), 75, 76.

21. Ibid., 79.

22. Cutler, *No Time for Rest*, 305.

23. Ibid., 311.

24. Eisenhower diary entry, 6 Dec. 1960, Ann Whitman File, DDE Diary Series, Eisenhower Library.

25. Dwight D. Eisenhower, *The White House Years: Waging Peace, 1956–1961* (New York: Doubleday, 1965), 632. Eisenhower is, of course, referring to members of his cabinet in this passage, but his concerns might just as easily apply to members of the NSC, some of whom, such as Dulles, Humphrey, Stassen, and Jackson, he mentions by name.

26. Joseph A. Pika, "Managing the Presidency: Lessons from the Eisenhower Experience" (Paper prepared for delivery at the Eisenhower Centennial Symposium, 12 Oct. 1990, Gettysburg College, Gettysburg, Pa.), 4, 12, 13.

27. Dwight D. Eisenhower, *The White House Years: Mandate for Change, 1953–1956* (New York: Doubleday, 1963), 114.

28. Dwight D. Eisenhower, Columbia University Oral History, 104.

29. Kernell and Popkin, *Chief of Staff* (see chap. 2, n. 10), 127.

30. Henderson, *Managing the Presidency*, 116, 118.

31. Robert Bowie, Columbia University Oral History, 8.

32. Andrew Goodpaster, Columbia University Oral History, 89.

33. John P. Burke and Fred I. Greenstein (with Larry Berman and Richard Immerman), *How Presidents Test Reality: Decisions on Vietnam, 1954 and 1965.* (New York: Russell Sage Foundation, 1989), esp. 60–63.

34. Thompson, *The Nixon Presidency* (see intro., n. 4), 126.

35. Robert Semple, "Nixon Rules out Control by Staff Aides," *New York Times*, 14 Nov. 1968, 1.

36. Thompson, *The Nixon Presidency*, 130; 127.

37. Ibid., 124.

38. Ibid., 127.

39. Ibid., 8.

40. Nixon to John Ehrlichman, 16 June 1969, White House Special Files, President's Personal File, Nixon Presidential Materials Project, National Archives. All memoranda to or from Nixon cited here are in the Nixon Presidential Materials Project, National Archives.

41. Nixon to Haldeman, 2 Mar. 1970, White House Special Files, Staff Members' Office Files—Haldeman.

42. Nixon to Henry Kissinger, 24 Nov. 1969, White House Special Files, President's Personal File.

43. Nixon to Haldeman, 30 Nov. 1970, White House Special Files, Staff Members' Office Files—Haldeman.

44. Nixon to Haldeman, 30 Nov. 1970, White House Special Files, Staff Members' Office Files—Haldeman.

45. Thompson, *The Nixon Presidency*, 127.

46. Ken Cole to Nixon, 6 Oct. 1969, White House Special Files, President's Handwriting File.

47. Nixon to John Ehrlichman and Ken Cole, 28 Dec. 1972, White House Special Files, President's Personal Files.

48. Thompson, *The Nixon Presidency*, 114.

49. *Ibid.*, 132, 87.

50. *Ibid.*, 234, 124.

51. *Ibid.*, 128, 141.

52. Nixon to Haldeman, Ehrlichman, and Kissinger, 2 Mar. 1970, White House Special Files, Staff Members' Office Files—Haldeman.

53. Johnson, *Managing the White House*, 96, 81, 92.

54. Neustadt, *Presidential Power*, 229.

55. Nixon to Ehrlichman, 23 Sept. 1969, White House Special Files, President's Personal Files.

56. Nixon to Ehrlichman, 17 June 1969, White House Special Files, President's Office Files (emphasis in original).

57. Tom Charles Huston to Nixon, June 1969, White House Special Files, President's Office Files (emphasis in original).

58. Nixon to Haldeman, 16 June 1969, White House Special Files, President's Personal Files (emphasis in original).

59. Kernell and Popkin, *Chief of Staff* (see chap. 2, n. 8), 22–23.

60. Nixon to Haldeman, 10 Mar. 1970, White House Special Files, Staff Members' Office Files—Haldeman.

61. Many of the memoranda contain egregious spellings of names Nixon would readily know and other spelling errors. In a 12 Nov. 1971 memorandum Nixon instructed his staff assistant Alexander Butterfield, "I would like to make another purchase for long-range plans of the 1966 French Bourdeaux, Chateau Margot [sic], Lafite, [sic] Rothschild and Hoitbrian [sic]" (Nixon to Butterfield, 12 Nov. 1971, White House Special Files, President's Personal Files).

62. Frederick Dutton Oral History, Kennedy Library, 52, 51. Similarly, Sorensen notes that "not one staff meeting was ever held, with or without the President. Nor was one ever desirable. Each of us was busy with our separate responsibilities, and each of us met when necessary with whatever staff members had jurisdictions touching our own" (Sorensen, *Kennedy* [see chap. 2, n.7], 262).

63. Frederick Dutton Oral History, Kennedy Library, 54.

64. Lists and summaries of Kennedy's weekend reading are available at the Kennedy Library (National Security Files, Meetings and Memoranda). The following, prepared for Kennedy by McGeorge Bundy for the weekend of 11 May 1963 is just one example:

1. *A number of odds and ends about the European situation*
A. A sharp message from McNamara to Thorneycroft on the Gruson-Lewis stories about NATO planning.
B. Two interesting cables about the situation in Italy. One describes the probable interim government with which you will be dealing, and the other

indicates how the pro-NATO Italians would like us to proceed on the MLF. Ambassador Fenoaltea indicated at lunch yesterday that the 20 percent contribution is quite realistic if the case is well made.

C. The final chapter on the Jupiter withdrawal, which has been a very tidy job.

D. A cable from Bonn on the QUICK article which seems to me to pose questions about our handling of German reporters in advance of your visit. You may wish to talk about this on Monday.

E. A report from Finletter in response to a question which you put to him about fall-back from MLF. I fear it is not very imaginative—but we wrote it in a mood of pessimism which I believe has passed.

F. Henry Owen goes after Henry Kissinger. We are also generating a possible article, probably for publication in *New Republic*.

2. *Indonesia*

A. An interesting report of a recent conversation with Sukarno. Sukarno's impertinent insistence upon string-less aid led me to ask Mike Forrestal for the memo—attached at B, and at C he has also included a statement of the AID position. If you look at the clearances on this outgoing message, you can see how complicated the administration of AID policy is—Sukarno may even have a point.

3. A memorandum reporting actions taken with the Poles on Laos. Averell [Harriman] is watching this himself.

4. Galbraith admires your press conference statement on Bokaro.

5. Thompson reports that low level flights over Cuba would be exceedingly untimely.

6. Bill Foster reports on the Neutrals and the 8-Nation Memorandum in response to questions which Adlai Stevenson put to you. This seems to be in good order, and I doubt if you need to read it unless you are particularly interested.

7. A memorandum you requested on ships engaging in Cuban trade transitting the Panama Canal.

65. Frederick Dutton Oral History, Kennedy Library, 49.

66. McGeorge Bundy to Theodore Sorensen, 8 Mar. 1963, National Security Files, Meetings and Memoranda, Kennedy Library. All memoranda to or from Kennedy cited here are from the Kennedy Library.

67. McGeorge Bundy to Kennedy, 4 Apr. 1961, President's Office Files, Staff Memoranda—Bundy.

68. Sorensen, *Kennedy*, 305, 304.

69. Maxwell Taylor Oral History, Kennedy Library, 9.

70. Sorensen, *Kennedy*, 304.

71. Maxwell Taylor Oral History, 10.

72. McGeorge Bundy interview with the Taylor committee, 4 May 1961, National Security Files, Paramilitary Study Group, 4.

73. For further discussion of the Bay of Pigs fiasco, see Irving Janis, *Groupthink* (Boston: Houghton Mifflin, 1982), 14–47.

74. Maxwell Taylor Oral History, 6.

75. Dictation notes by Mrs. Lincoln, President's Office File, Staff Memoranda.

76. This is not to suggest that such evidence cannot be obtained. But to do so

would require an in-depth analysis of a particular policy problem and its handling by Kennedy and his staff, which is beyond the scope of this study. For an example of such a study, see Burke and Greenstein, *How Presidents Test Reality*, esp. chapters on Lyndon Johnson.

77. Kennedy to Bundy, 7 Aug. 1961, President's Office Files, Staff Memoranda—Bundy.

78. Kennedy to Bundy, 21 Aug. 1961, President's Office Files, Staff Memoranda—Bundy.

79. Kennedy to Bundy, 4 Feb. 1961, President's Office Files, Staff Memoranda—Bundy.

80. Kennedy to Bundy, 5 Feb. 1961, President's Office Files, Staff Memoranda—Bundy.

81. Kennedy to Bundy, 14 Apr. 1961, President's Office Files, Staff Memoranda—Bundy.

82. Kennedy to Bundy, 10 July 1961, President's Office Files, Staff Memoranda—Bundy.

83. Bundy to Kennedy, 16 May 1961, National Security Files, Departments and Agencies.

84. In a 22 June 1961 memorandum to Kennedy, Bundy lists the participants as himself, Walt Rostow, Ralph Dungan, Arthur Schlesinger, Jr., Chester Clifton, Bromley Smith, Carl Kaysen, Robert Komer, C. Johnson, Roger Johnson, Samuel Belk, and Tazewell Shepard (National Security Files, Department and Agencies).

85. See "Memorandum of Meeting in the President's Office—Discussion of Role of General Taylor," 29 June 1961, National Security Files, Meetings and Memoranda.

86. Bundy to Kennedy, 22 June 1961, National Security Files, Department and Agencies.

87. In a 10 Oct. 1961 memorandum to the president, Bundy stated, "You mention[ed] on the way to Dallas that you would like to have regular meetings of the National Security Council. I very strongly agree with this plan. There are lots of kinds of business which ought to be transacted relatively formally, and which we can dispose of more efficiently if meetings are regularly scheduled, and their times set in advance. Calling such meetings on short notice, in the past, has produced incomplete staff work and given unreasonable difficulty to members of the Council and their staffs." Bundy added, "Fred Dutton feels the same way about the Cabinet, and would like to have its meetings scheduled on alternate Thursday mornings. If you will approve this general plan . . . it probably will not bore you more than one time in four." At the bottom of the memo, Bundy left a line for Kennedy's approval. NSC record of action #2438 shows Kennedy's approval of the proposal. National Security Files, Meetings and Memoranda.

88. NSC meetings 496–507, National Security Files, Meetings and Memoranda.

89. NSC meetings 515–519, National Security Files, Meetings and Memoranda.

90. The latter were apparently terminated once Bundy's proposal for a standing group came to fruition.

91. "National Security Council, Record of Actions, Standing Group Meeting," 5 Jan. 1962. National Security Files, Meetings and Memoranda. In attendance were Under Secretary of State for Political Affairs George McGhee, Deputy Under

Secretary of Defense Roswell Gilpatric, CIA Director John McCone, NSC Executive Secretary Bromley Smith, and McGeorge Bundy.

92. Evidence indicates that Bundy's hope here was not fully realized; his own staff began increasingly to provide the background papers, including discussion of options and recommended courses of action, for the group's deliberations. See, for example, the memorandum from David Klein to McGeorge Bundy, "Subject: NSC Standing Group Meeting—Discussions of East-West Trade Policy," 7 Sept. 1963, National Security Files, Meetings and Memoranda. Records for each of the standing group meetings are available from the National Security Files at the Kennedy Library.

93. Bundy to Kennedy, 2 Apr. 1963, National Security Files, Meetings and Memoranda.

94. On the records of the first meeting of the standing committee, see "National Security Council Standing Group, Record of Actions," 16 Apr. 1963, National Security Files, Meetings and Memoranda.

95. The president's news conference, 28 July 1965, in Lyndon B. Johnson, *Public Papers of the Presidents: Lyndon Johnson, 1965* (Washington, D.C.: U.S. Government Printing Office, 1966), 795.

96. Johnson, *Vantage Point* (see chap. 2, n. 16), 125.

97. George Ball, *The Past Has Another Pattern* (New York: Norton, 1982), 389–90.

98. Burke and Greenstein, *How Presidents Test Reality*, 132–33, emphasis added.

99. Maxwell Taylor, *Swords and Plowshares* (New York: Norton, 1972), 338.

100. Burke and Greenstein, *How Presidents Test Reality*, 175.

101. Bundy to Johnson, 24 July 1965, National Security File, Johnson Library.

102. On Humphrey's exclusion from Johnson's decision making, see Burke and Greenstein, *How Presidents Test Reality*, 154, 168, 184.

103. Ball, *The Past Has Another Pattern*, 390.

104. Burke and Greenstein, *How Presidents Test Reality*, 183.

105. Redford and McCulley, *White House Operations*, 73.

106. Burke and Greenstein, *How Presidents Test Reality*, 168, 169.

107. For further discussion of the internal dynamics of Johnson's meetings, see ibid., 232–38.

108. Herbert Y. Schandler, *The Unmaking of a President: Lyndon Johnson and Vietnam* (Princeton, N.J.: Princeton University Press, 1977), 338.

Chapter 4. The Institutional Presidency: Through an Organizational Lens

1. Thompson, *The Kennedy Presidency* (see intro., n. 3), 23.

2. Ibid., 140.

3. For a more comprehensive discussion of Eisenhower's "binocular" use of informal and formal patterns of advice, see Greenstein, *Hidden-Hand Presidency* (see chap. 2, n. 29), 100–51.

4. Dwight D. Eisenhower, Columbia University Oral History, 103.

5. Eisenhower, *Mandate for Change* (see chap. 3, n.27), 134.

6. Transcript of Hotel Commodore meeting, 12–13 Jan. 1953, Ann Whitman File, Cabinet Series, Eisenhower Library.

7. Henderson's calculations suggest a slightly different figure: a total of 227 cabinet meetings during Eisenhower's presidency, at which Eisenhower presided over 205, for an average of 28.4 per year or 25.6 per year (Eisenhower presiding); Henderson, *Managing the Presidency* (see chap. 3, n. 20), 52.

8. Greenstein, *Hidden-Hand Presidency*, 108.

9. Ibid., 115, 116.

10. Dwight D. Eisenhower Oral History, Eisenhower Library, 18.

11. Transcript of Hotel Commodore meeting, 12–13 Jan. 1953.

12. Kenneth W. Thompson, ed., *The Eisenhower Presidency: Eleven Intimate Perspectives of Dwight D. Eisenhower* (Lanham, Md.: University Press of America, 1984), 236–37.

13. Greenstein, *Hidden-Hand Presidency*, 115.

14. Kenneth W. Thompson, ed., *The Johnson Presidency: Twenty Intimate Perspectives* (Lanham, Md.: University Press of America, 1986), 10.

15. Johnson, *Managing the White House* (see chap. 12, n. 4), xx.

16. Joan Hoff-Wilson, "Richard M. Nixon: The Corporate Presidency," in *Leadership in the Modern Presidency*, edited by Fred I. Greenstein (Cambridge, Mass.: Harvard University Press, 1988), 177.

17. Moe, "Politicized Presidency" (see chap. 1, n. 36), 239.

18. George, *Presidential Decisionmaking in Foreign Policy* (see chap. 2, n. 4), 193.

19. See George, "Multiple Advocacy in Making Foreign Policy" (see chap. 2, n. 4), 771–72, 775–76.

20. Ibid., 759.

21. George, *Presidential Decisionmaking in Foreign Policy*, 195–96.

22. Richard Rovere, *Affairs of State: The Eisenhower Years* (New York: Farrar, Strauss, and Cudahy, 1956), 82–83.

23. Emmet J. Hughes, *The Ordeal of Power* (New York: Dell, 1964), 57.

24. Eisenhower diary entry, 18 Jan. 1954, Ann Whitman File, DDE Diary Series, Eisenhower Library.

25. Kernell and Popkin, *Chief of Staff* (see chap. 2, n. 10), 207.

26. Ibid., 220.

27. Kernell and Popkin, *Chief of Staff*, 207–8.

28. Thompson, *The Eisenhower Presidency*, 103.

29. See Kernell and Popkin, *Chief of Staff*, 195.

30. Ibid., 196.

31. In one story, while at a Washington bar, Jordan reportedly spit out his drink at a young lady. In another, Jordan reportedly leeringly told the wife of an Egyptian diplomat, who was wearing a particularly revealing dress, that he had just seen the pyramids. In a third, Jordan was reported to have used cocaine at the New York nightclub Studio 54. The reports have not been authoritatively documented, but appeared in various media sources.

32. Thompson, *The Eisenhower Presidency*, 103.

33. Kenneth W. Thompson, ed., *The Roosevelt Presidency: Four Intimate Perspectives of FDR* (Lanham, Md.: University Press of America, 1982), 10.

34. Thompson, *The Ford Presidency* (see chap. 2, n. 42), 54.

35. Harry McPherson, *A Political Education* (Boston: Little, Brown, 1972), 122.

36. Ibid., 309–10.

37. Ibid., 253.

38. Hoff-Wilson, "Richard M. Nixon," 179–80.

39. Ibid., 181.

40. A. James Reichley, *Conservatives in an Age of Change* (Washington, D.C.: Brookings Institution, 1981), 257.

41. Eisenhower to Henry Luce, 8 Aug. 1960, Ann Whitman File, DDE Diary Series, Eisenhower Library.

42. Greenstein, *Hidden-Hand Presidency*, 81.

43. For further discussion of Wilson's difficulties, see ibid., 83–84.

44. John Gardner, *On Leadership*, (New York: Free Press, 1990), 150.

45. Thompson, *The Eisenhower Presidency,* 5.

46. Fred I. Greenstein, "Dwight D. Eisenhower: Leadership Theorist in the White House," in *Leadership in the Modern Presidency*, edited by Fred I. Greenstein (Cambridge: Harvard University Press, 1988), 86, 85.

47. Walter Bedell Smith to General Maxwell Taylor, 1 Feb. 1956, Smith Papers, Eisenhower Library (cited in John W. Sloan, "The Management and Decision-Making Style of President Eisenhower," *Presidential Studies Quarterly* 20 [1990]: 305).

48. Thompson, *The Kennedy Presidency*, 165.

49. Thompson, *The Nixon Presidency*, (see intro., n. 4), 139.

50. Ibid., 31.

51. Ray S. Cline, "Policy without Intelligence," *Foreign Policy* 31 (1974): 126.

52. Nixon to Haldeman, 2 Mar. 1970, White House Special Files, President's Personal Files (emphasis added).

53. Nixon to Haldeman and Ehrlichman, 16 June 1970, White House Special Files, President's Personal Files.

54. Nixon to Haldeman, 21 Apr. 1970, White House Special Files, President's Personal File.

55. Evidently Nixon's preoccupation with leaks had stirred up the Oval Office. That same day, Haldeman received the following memorandum from Rose Mary Woods, Nixon's private secretary: "Quite a few of the attached memoranda might well be classified 'BURN AFTER—if not BEFORE—READING.' Until we are able to stop the leaks of our confidential memoranda it seems rather dangerous to have some of these floating around. I think conversation in person or on the telephone would be safer on the attached" (21 Apr. 1970, President's Personal Files).

56. Nixon to Haldeman, 12 Nov. 1971, White House Special Files, President's Personal Files.

57. Nixon to Haldeman, 14 Jan. 1971, White House Special Files, President's Personal Files.

58. Frederick Dutton Oral History, Kennedy Library, 60.

59. Ibid., 63.

60. Thompson, *The Eisenhower Presidency*, 80.

61. Letter of 14 Nov. 1951 in *Ike's Letters to a Friend,* edited by Robert Griffith (Lawrence: University of Kansas Press, 1984), 93.

62. Eisenhower to Forrestal, 8 Feb. 1948, *Papers of Dwight D. Eisenhower,*

vol. 9, *The Chief of Staff*, edited by Louis Galambos (Baltimore: Johns Hopkins University Press, 1978), 2243–44.

63. Letter of 21 July 1953, in *Ike's Letters to a Friend*, 109.

64. Bradley H. Patterson, Jr., Columbia University Oral History, 26 (emphasis in original).

65. Hughes, *Ordeal of Power*, 135.

66. Bradley H. Patterson, Jr., Columbia University Oral History, 11.

67. Bradley H. Patterson, Jr., *The President's Cabinet: Issues and Answers* (Washington, D.C.: American Society for Public Administration, 1976), 108.

68. Cutler, *No Time for Rest* (see chap. 3, n. 19), 297.

69. R. C. Cutler, "The Use of the NSC Mechanism," Mar. 1968, Gordon Gray Papers, Eisenhower Library, 2–3.

Chapter 5. Jimmy Carter: The Travails of Centralized Collegiality

1. Leuchtenburg, *In the Shadow of FDR* (see chap. 1, n. 2), 208.

2. Kenneth W. Thompson, ed., *The Carter Presidency: Fourteen Intimate Perspectives* (Lanham, Md.: University Press of America, 1990), 121.

3. Erwin C. Hargrove, *Jimmy Carter as President: Leadership and the Politics of the Public Good* (Baton Rouge: Louisiana State University Press, 1988), 14, 16.

4. William Lee Miller, *Yankee from Georgia: The Emergence of Jimmy Carter* (New York: Quadrangle, 1978), 144–45.

5. Hargrove, *Carter as President*, 16.

6. Charles O. Jones, *The Trusteeship Presidency: Jimmy Carter and the United States Congress* (Baton Rouge: Louisiana State University Press, 1988).

7. See, for example, the comments of Secretary of Education Shirley Hufstedler in Thompson, *The Carter Presidency*, 30.

8. Zbigniew Brzezinski, *Power and Principle* (New York: Farrar, Straus, and Giroux, 1983), 67.

9. Thompson, *The Carter Presidency*, 121.

10. Hargrove, *Carter as President*, 28–29.

11. Campbell, *Managing the Presidency* (see chap. 2, n. 7), 61–62.

12. James Fallows, "The Passionless Presidency," *Atlantic Monthly*, May 1979, 42.

13. Betty Glad, *Jimmy Carter: In Search of the Great White House* (New York: Norton, 1980), 476.

14. Brzezinski, *Power and Principle*, 71.

15. Fallows, "Passionless Presidency," 35.

16. Hargrove, *Carter as President*, 26.

17. Ibid.

18. Jimmy Carter, *Keeping Faith: Memoirs of a President* (New York: Bantam, 1983), 89.

19. Alexander Moens, *Foreign Policy under Carter: Testing Multiple Advocacy Decision Making* (Boulder, Colo.: Westview, 1990), 35.

20. Hargrove, *Carter as President*, 27.

21. Thompson, *The Carter Presidency*, 122.

22. Hargrove, *Carter as President*, 17.

23. Campbell, *Managing the Presidency*, 87.

24. Brzezinski reports that Secretary of State Vance usually chaired PRC meetings, occasionally the secretary of defense, and on two or three occasions, the secretary of the treasury. *Power and Principle*, 59.

25. Moens, *Foreign Policy under Carter*, 39, 40.

26. Hargrove, *Carter as President*, 26.

27. Brzezinski, *Power and Principle*, 70.

28. Ibid., 68.

29. Moens, *Foreign Policy under Carter*, 48, 84.

30. Ibid., 48, 84.

31. Ibid., 172.

32. Brzezinski, *Power and Principle*, 66.

33. Campbell, *Managing the Presidency*, 66.

34. Moens, *Foreign Policy under Carter*, 38.

35. Brzezinski, *Power and Principle*, 66, 65.

36. Ibid., 61.

37. Moens, *Foreign Policy under Carter*, 54, 62.

38. Campbell, *Managing the Presidency*, 138.

39. The eight decisions studied were: requirements for purchasing food stamps, increase in the minimum wage, refinancing of Social Security, the footwear import agreement, wiretap legislation, the decision to build breeder reactors, transfer of conventional arms, and rural telecommunications policy.

40. "President's Reorganization Project: Decision Analysis Report," 28 June 1977, Hamilton Jordan Collection, President's Reorganization Project, Carter Library, 3. All memoranda to or from Carter cited here are from the Carter Library.

41. Ibid., 2.

42. Ibid., 11–12, 16.

43. Ibid., 10, 16.

44. Ibid., 11.

45. Ibid., 17–18.

46. Campbell, *Managing the Presidency*, 59.

47. Light, *The President's Agenda* (see chap. 2, n. 32).

48. Campbell, *Managing the Presidency*, 59–60.

49. Hargrove, *Carter as President*, xix.

50. "President's Reorganization Project: Decision Analysis Report," 28 June 1977, Hamilton Jordan Collection, President's Reorganization Project, 13.

51. Ibid., 13–14, 17.

52. Ibid., 13, 14.

53. Ibid., 16, 10.

54. Ibid., 15, 2.

55. Hargrove, *Carter as President*, 45.

56. Ibid.

57. Ibid., 46.

58. Ibid.

59. Ibid., 19–20, 18.

60. Hamilton Jordan to Carter, Jordan Collection, White House Staff Coordination/Changes 1978 File. Although the memo is undated, it can be inferred from Carter's subsequent actions in late January that it was forwarded to the president some time that month.

61. In a subsequent memo to Carter, Jordan noted the need for greater staff communication and coordination, outlining a proposal, which was subsequently implemented, for more frequent staff meetings, especially of the senior staff, which Jordan would chair. In his discussion of the senior staff meeting Jordan especially requested that Carter not attend, unless "you have a special gripe or request" (Jordan to Carter, no date, Jordan Collection, White House Staff Coordination/Changes 1978 File).

62. Jordan to Carter, 26 July 1979, Jordan Collection, Staff Changes/Chief of Staff 1979 File.

63. Jordan to Carter, no date, Jordan Collection, White House Staff Coordination/Changes 1978 File.

64. Campbell, *Managing the Presidency*, 89–90.

65. Hargrove, *Carter as President*, 45.

66. Campbell, *Managing the Presidency*, 93.

67. Thompson, *The Carter Presidency*, 149.

68. Cecil V. Crabb and Kevin W. Mulcahy, *American National Security: A Presidential Perspective* (Pacific Grove, Calif.: Brooks/Cole, 1991), 158, 161.

69. Hargrove, *Carter as President*, xx.

70. Ibid., 30–31.

71. Hargrove, *Carter as President*, 31, 182 (emphasis added).

Chapter 6. Ronald Reagan: The Travails of Collegial Formalism

1. Martin Anderson, *Revolution* (San Diego: Harcourt Brace Jovanovich, 1988), 219.

2. Michael Deaver, *Behind the Scenes* (New York: William Morrow, 1987), 174. According to Campbell, the breakfast meetings ended in late 1982 (*Managing the Presidency* [see chap. 2, n. 7], 102).

3. Anderson, *Revolution*, 220.

4. On Nixon's administrative presidency strategy, see Nathan, *The Plot That Failed* (see chap. 1, n. 43).

5. The chairs pro tem of the five original councils were: Treasury Secretary Donald Regan—CCEA: Commerce Secretary Malcolm Baldridge—CCCT; Health and Human Services Secretary Richard Schweiker—CCHR; Interior Secretary James Watt—CCNRE; and Agriculture Secretary John Block—CCFA.

6. Chester Newland, "Executive Office Policy Apparatus: Enforcing the Reagan Agenda." In *The Reagan Presidency and the Governing of America*, edited by Lester Salamon and Michael Lund (Washington, D.C.: Urban Institute Press, 1984), 156, 160.

7. Campbell, *Managing the Presidency*, 74.

8. Ibid., 74, 77, 79.

9. Similar difficulties may also have occurred on the national security side. As one of Campbell's interviewees told him, "at least in the national security area, the president himself doesn't have the background and the middle-level grasp of the machinery that he does in the domestic area. So we really operate a bottom-up system. The president has a good overall idea of where he wants to go. . . . But, there's not really much push coming from him in the form of initiatives or unifying

policies at an early stage. It's more waiting for issues to come up when they get critical" (*Managing the Presidency*, 71).

10. Anderson, *Revolution*, 226.

11. Newland, "Executive Office Policy Apparatus," 167–68.

12. Benjamin W. Heineman, Jr., "Comment: Executive Office Policy Apparatus," in *The Reagan Presidency and the Governing of America*, edited by Lester Salamon and Michael Lund (Washington, D.C.: Urban Institute Press, 1984), 170.

13. James Ceaser, "The Theory of Governance of the Reagan Administration," in *The Reagan Presidency and the Governing of America*, edited by Lester Salamon and Michael Lund (Washington, D.C.: Urban Institute Press, 1984), 63–64.

14. I. M. Destler, "The Evolution of Reagan Foreign Policy," in *The Reagan Presidency: An Early Assessment*, edited by Fred I. Greenstein (Baltimore: Johns Hopkins University Press, 1983), 117–58.

15. Newland, "Executive Office Policy Apparatus," 168.

16. Donald Regan, *For the Record: From Wall Street to Washington* (San Diego: Harcourt Brace Jovanovich, 1988), 188, 142.

17. Campbell, *Managing the Presidency*, 58.

18. Ronald Reagan, *An American Life* (New York: Simon and Schuster, 1990), 296, 253, 511.

19. Regan, *For the Record*, 188. At other points in his memoirs reflecting on his service as chief of staff, Regan makes similar observations about Reagan's style in group settings. In cabinet meetings or in dealing with his close aides, persons he had come to know well, "Reagan was generally animated; he loved the give and take of policy discussion in the Cabinet councils, when he had a chance to pronounce on the broad general principles that primarily interested him." In other contexts, he would behave differently. He "was habitually shy and withdrawn in personal meetings with people he did not know well, especially if the visitor happened to be present as an expert. . . . When the subject was esoteric, Reagan would be particularly passive, and as we grew to know each other better I would occasionally ask him why after the meeting was over. It would usually turn out that he had hesitated to ask questions because he did not wish to seem uninformed in the presence of people he did not know well" (273).

20. Deaver, *Behind the Scenes*, 104.

21. Regan, *For the Record*, 143–44.

22. For further discussion of this memorandum, see ibid., 265–68.

23. Ibid., 266–67.

24. Campbell, *Managing the Presidency*, 43.

25. John Tower, Edmund Muskie, and Brent Scowcroft, *The Tower Commission Report: The Full Text of the President's Special Review Board* (New York: Random House, 1987), 62–63.

26. Regan, *For the Record*, 234.

27. Reagan, *An American Life*, 488.

28. Regan, *For the Record*, 267.

29. Ibid., 266.

30. Reagan, *An American Life*, 516, 537 (emphasis in original).

31. Campbell, *Managing the Presidency*, 110.

32. For further details on Reagan's testimony at the Poindexter trial, see *New York Times*, 23 Feb. 1990, 18–19.

33. Kessel, *Presidential Parties*, 107 (see chap. 2, n. 50); and see also Kessel, "Structures of the Reagan White House" (see chap. 2, n. 8).

34. Newland, "Executive Policy Apparatus," 143, 144.

35. Ibid., 135, 137.

36. Campbell, *Managing the Presidency*, 106, 107.

37. See Porter, *Presidential Decision Making* (see chap. 2, n. 4).

38. Campbell, *Managing the Presidency*, 108.

39. Ibid.

40. Discussion of the Darman case is based on a journalistic source: Dick Kirschten, "Under Reagan, Power Resides with Those Who Station Themselves at His Door," *National Journal*, 25 Feb. 1984, 362–63. I have no reason to doubt its veracity, but the usual problems of relying on such sources should be borne in mind.

41. Deaver, *Behind the Scenes*, 170.

42. Regan, *For the Record*, 268.

43. Dick Kirschten, "Inner Circle Speaks with Many Voices, but Maybe That's How Reagan Wants It," *National Journal*, 28 May 1983, 1100, 1103.

Chapter 7. George Bush in Midstream

1. James Pfiffner, "Establishing the Bush Presidency," *Public Administration Review* 50 (1990): 66.

2. See David Hoffman and Ann Devroy, "The Open Oval Office Door," *Washington Post*, National Weekly Edition, 14–20 Aug. 1989, 6–7.

3. Burt Solomon, "A Gathering of Friends," *National Journal*, 10 June 1989, 1402.

4. Burt Solomon, "When the Bush Cabinet Convenes," *National Journal*, 1 July 1989, 1704–5.

5. Michael Duffy, "Mr. Consensus," *Time*, 21 Aug. 1989, 19.

6. Solomon, "When the Bush Cabinet Convenes," 1705.

7. Burt Solomon, "In Bush's Image," *National Journal*, 7 July 1990, 1642.

8. On Quayle's role, see Burt Solomon, "War Bolsters Quayle's Visibility," *National Journal*, 2 Mar. 1991, 522–23.

9. Duffy, "Mr. Consensus," 19. Also see Burt Solomon, "Bush Works the Phones Incessantly to Stave off Isolation," *National Journal*, 1 Apr. 1989, 810–11.

10. Gerald Seib, "Personal Touch," *Wall Street Journal*, 30 Nov. 1989. See also Burt Solomon, "Bush's Passion for Friendship," *National Journal*, 8 Dec. 1990, 2986–87.

11. Hoffman and Devroy, "Open Oval Office Door," 6.

12. Burt Solomon, "In Atwater's Absence, Sununu Is Bush's Top Political Adviser," *National Journal*, 23 June 1990, 1554–55. See also Andrew Rosenthal, "Clearer Signs of Broader Role for Sununu," *New York Times*, 11 May 1990, 1.

13. Burt Solomon, "No Nonsense Sununu," *National Journal*, 16 Sept. 1989, 2251.

14. Solomon, "In Bush's Image," 1644.

15. Stephen Engelberg, "Sununu Says He Revised Speech," *New York Times*, 5 Feb. 1990, 15.

16. Solomon, "No Nonsense Sununu," 2252.

17. Maureen Dowd, "Sununu Sayonara," *New York Times*, 5 Dec. 1991, 8

18. See, for example, David Hoffman and Ann Devroy, "The White House Tough Guy," *Washington Post*, National Weekly Edition, 5–11. Feb. 1990, 6–7; and Maureen Dowd, "Bush's Woes Stir Grumbling over Sununu," *New York Times*, 29 Oct. 1990, 18. According to a *Time* magazine cover story (Dan Goodgame, "Big Bad John Sununu," *Time*, 21 May 1990, 29),

> Sununu has made plenty of enemies through sheer insolence. He slammed down the phone during a foreign policy argument with Republican Congressman Mickey Edwards of Oklahoma. He shouted obscenities at Senate Republican leader Bob Dole's press secretary over a routine news release. He berated House Republican leader Bob Michel for not supporting the president with sufficient enthusiasm, moving Michel to note that "sometimes we have to remind Governor Sununu that this is not the New Hampshire legislature." Democratic Senator Tim Wirth of Colorado says what many Washington insiders feel: Sununu "thinks he's the only smart guy in town. He shows little respect for anyone else's intelligence or point of view."

19. On Darman's role in the Bush White House, see Paul Blustein, "A Suddenly Charmin' Richard Darman," *Washington Post*, National Weekly Edition, 22–28 May 1989, 31; Lawrence Haas, "Budget Guru," *National Journal*, 20 Jan. 1990, 110–16; and Marjorie Williams, "What Makes Richard Run?" *Washington Post*, National Weekly Edition, 1–7 Oct. 1990, 6–8.

20. Burt Solomon, "It's Not Been a Pleasant Time As Reputations Falter on Deficit," *National Journal*, 20 Oct. 1990, 2254.

21. See W. John Moore, "A Consumer Adviser with a New Agenda," *National Journal*, 4 Aug. 1990, 1903.

22. See Paul Starobin, "In the Loop," *National Journal*, 24 March 1990, 715–18; and Robert Hershey, "Happy Days for Economic Advisers," *New York Times*, 5 Sept. 1989, 16.

23. Bush's decision to hold a December 1989 summit with Gorbachev in Malta, his planning for the overthrow of Noriega and for Scowcroft's secret visits to China in the aftermath of the Tienanmen Square crackdown are the most notable examples. The stormy weather Bush encountered at Malta might have been anticipated if Bush had had his staff check with experts on normal weather patterns there; Bush also did not inform Defense Secretary Cheney or CIA Director William Webster that a summit was in the offing. Bush kept Chief of Staff Sununu and Press Secretary Marlin Fitzwater in the dark about Scowcroft's first secret visit to China. See David Hoffman, "Zip My Lips: George Bush's Penchant for Secret Decisions," *Washington Post*, National Weekly Edition, 15–21 Jan. 1990, 23; and Maureen Dowd, "Basking in Power's Glow," *New York Times*, 31 Dec. 1989, 1.

24. Kevin V. Mulcahy, "The Bush Administration and National Security Policy Making: A Preliminary Assessment" (Paper prepared for delivery at the 1990 Annual Meeting of the American Political Science Association, San Francisco), 5.

25. David Hoffman, "The Politics of Timidity," *Washington Post*, National Weekly Edition, 23–29 Oct. 1989, 6.

26. Andrew Rosenthal, "National Security Adviser Redefines Role," *New York Times*, 3 Nov. 1989, 16.

27. Tower, Muskie, and Scowcroft, *Tower Commission Report* (see chap. 6, n. 25), 91.

28. See Christopher Madison, "No Sharp Elbows," *National Journal*, 26 May 1990, 1277–81.

29. Mulcahy, "The Bush Administration and National Security Policy Making," 17, 16.

30. This description of the Bush NSC apparatus is taken from Mulcahy, "The Bush Administration and National Security Policy Making," and David Morrison, "Retooling the Security Machine," *National Journal*, 10 June 1989, 1425.

31. Elizabeth Drew, "Letter from Washington," *New Yorker*, 30 Oct. 1989, 100.

32. Hoffman, "Politics of Timidity," 6.

33. For example, on some of the problems in the Panama invasion of 1989, see John Broder and Melissa Healy, "Panama Operation Hurt by Critical Intelligence Gaps," *Los Angeles Times*, 24 Dec. 1989, 1.

34. This analysis of the administration's decision making in the early stages of the Persian Gulf crisis is drawn from Bob Woodward and Rick Atkinson, "Launching Operation Desert Shield," *Washington Post*, National Weekly Edition, 3–9 Sept. 1990, 8–10, and Elizabeth Drew, "Letter from Washington," *New Yorker*, 24 Sept. 1990, 103–12.

35. According to Elizabeth Drew, "A final argument [at the first NSC meeting held in the wake of the invasion] that was persuasive to policymakers—but one that, for obvious reasons, they don't talk much about publicly—was that if Hussein succeeded in his recent action his ultimate target would be Israel, in which event we couldn't stand by" (*New Yorker*, 24 Sept. 1990, 106).

36. Quoted in Woodward and Atkinson, "Launching Operation Desert Shield," 9.

37. Thomas Friedman, "Baker Seen as Balance to Bush," *New York Times*, 3 Nov. 1990, 1.

38. This figure comes from the *New York Times*/CBS News Poll, reported in the *New York Times*, 2 Mar. 1991, 1. *USA Today*, according to the *Times*, reported Bush's popularity at an unprecedented 91 percent.

39. Maureen Dowd, "A Different Bush Conforms to Nation's Mood," *New York Times*, 2 Mar. 1991, 1.

40. On the possibility of a negotiated settlement among Arab states, see Drew, *New Yorker*, 24 Sept. 1990, 102–12, and John Newhouse, "The Diplomatic Round: Misreadings," *New Yorker*, 18 Feb. 1991, 72–78.

41. On the change in American military strategy, see Thomas Friedman and Patrick Tyler, "From the First, U.S. Resolve to Fight," *New York Times*, 3 Mar. 1991, 1.

42. Burt Solomon, "A Tangle of Old Relationships," *National Journal*, 30 Sept. 1989, 2418–19.

43. Solomon, "No Nonsense Sununu," 2250.

44. Solomon, "In Bush's Image," 1642.

45. Hershey, "Happy Days for Economic Advisers," 16.

46. Elizabeth Drew, "Letter from Washington," *New Yorker*, 11 Mar. 1991, 85.

47. Quoted in Burt Solomon, "For Now, at Least, Collegiality," National Journal, 2 Mar. 1989, 298.

48. Quoted in Solomon, "In Bush's Image," 1644. In the wake of the budget debacle of fall 1990 and the prolonged tension over the crisis in the Gulf, some fractures in collegiality apparently developed among White House staffers. According to one report in the *New York Times* (Maureen Dowd, "The Sniping Begins and All Is Normal," 17 Nov. 1990, 18),

> everything was cozy as long as President Bush's approval ratings were high. But when he hit wind shear with the budget fiasco and his clash with Congress about sending more troops to the Persian Gulf, the inevitable sniping began. Once the bipartisan budget deal fell apart, John Sununu . . . blamed House Republicans for deserting the President. Mr. Sununu's aides blamed Richard Darman, the budget director, for cozying up too much to the Democrats. Mr. Darman blamed Mr. Sununu for being too abrasive. . . . And Mr. Darman and Mr. Sununu privately blamed the President for his inability to understand the nuance of the position they had developed for him. . . . With the Persian Gulf policy mired in mixed messages, Secretary of State James A. Baker 3d blamed the White House speechwriters for their inability to present the President's policy in a compelling fashion. The speechwriters were furious at Mr. Baker. . . . Many top Bush advisers blame Mr. Sununu for surrounding himself with a second-rate staff and for creating a vacuum where a communications strategy used to be.

49. The one exception to this pattern might be Lauro Cavazos, Bush's secretary of education, who was forced to resign over the minority scholarship fiasco and his apparent inability to further Bush's goal of being the "education president."

Conclusion

1. Karen Hult and Charles Walcott, *Governing Public Organizations: Politics, Structures, and Institutional Design.* (Pacific Grove, Calif.: Brooks/Cole, 1990), esp. chap. 4.

2. James D. Thompson and Arthur Tuden, "Strategies, Structures, and Processes of Organizational Design," in *Comparative Studies in Administration*, edited by James D. Thompson (Pittsburgh: University of Pittsburgh Press, 1959), 195–216.

3. Since there are nine possibilities in Hult and Walcott's schema (two dimensions with three possibilities in each dimension), this is not an exhaustive list. The other combinations are: uncertain causation/uncertain outcomes (inspiration or market processes), uncertain causation/controversial outcomes ("collegial-competitive" or "collegial mediative" structures involving representation of stakeholders and experts); certain causation/controversial outcomes (collegial-competitive or collegial mediative structures); controversial causation/certain outcomes (adjudicative structures involving formal rules of argumentation and disinterested judgment); and controversial causation/controversial outcomes ("legitimation" structures involving fair representation).

4. George, *Presidential Decisionmaking in Foreign Policy* (see chap. 2, n. 4), 81.

5. Moe, "The Politicized Presidency" (see chap. 1, n. 36), 239.

6. Kenneth W. Thompson, ed., *The Truman Presidency: Intimate Perspectives* (Lanham, Md.: University Press of America, 1984), 92.

7. Moe, "The Politicized Presidency," 239, 238.

8. Hugh Heclo, "OMB and the Presidency: The Problem of 'Neutral Competence'," *Public Interest* 38 (1975): 81, 82.

9. Stuart Eizenstat, "A 'Historical Memory' for Presidents," *New York Times*, 14 Jan. 1987, 27.

10. Mosher, *"The President Needs Help"* (see chap. 1, n. 20), 20. I have counted the troika arrangement of Reagan's first year and James Baker's emergence as Reagan's chief domestic policy adviser as two staff arrangements.

11. But, as Eizenstat cautions, "while presidents in crisis should seek counsel of outsiders who have gone through similar experiences, such ad hoc use of historical memory is no substitute for an institutionalized memory in the White House involved in day-to-day policy making" (Eizenstat, "Historical Memory," 27).

12. Heclo, "OMB and the Presidency," 82.

13. Cary R. Covington, "Development of Organizational Memory in Presidential Agencies," *Administration and Society* 17 (1984): 174–75.

14. Keith Schneider, "North's Record," *New York Times*, 3 Jan. 1987, 1.

15. On problems with professional expertise, see John P. Burke, *Bureaucratic Responsibility* (Baltimore: Johns Hopkins University Press, 1986), 24–31, 142–60.

16. Mosher, *"The President Needs Help,"* 53.

17. The same might be said about particular problems within each policy area. An earlier study I undertook comparing Eisenhower's and Johnson's decision making on American military intervention in Southeast Asia revealed differences in their respective decision-making systems and procedures, as well as strengths and weaknesses of each. See Burke and Greenstein, *How Presidents Test Reality* (see chap. 3, n. 33).

18. George, *Presidential Decisionmaking in Foreign Policy*, 5–7.

19. Luther Gulick, one of the last surviving authors of the Brownlow report, suggested in 1987 that the Brownlow committee may have gone "too far in assuming that a structure and system we designed for one character, FDR, would meet every man's requirements in the years ahead. After all, the harness must fit the horse" (Mosher, *"The President Needs Help,"* xi).

20. George, *Presidential Decisionmaking in Foreign Policy*, 6.

21. Hargrove, *Carter as President* (see chap. 5, n. 3), 29.

22. For further analysis of these and other components of presidential success, see Rockman, *The Leadership Question* (see chap. 1, n. 4), 194–97.

INDEX

■ ■ ■

The Institutional Presidency

Composed by WorldComp
in Times Roman with Helvetica Condensed display

Printed by R. R. Donnelley and Sons
on 50-lb. Sebago Cream